Also by Lucy Jones

Losing Eden: Our Fundamental Need for the Natural World and Its Ability to Heal Body and Soul

Matrescence

Matrescence

On Pregnancy, Childbirth, and Motherhood

LUCY JONES

PANTHEON BOOKS · NEW YORK

Published in the United States by Pantheon Books,
a division of Penguin Random House LLC, New York.
Originally published in hardcover in Great Britain by Allen Lane, an imprint of Penguin Press,
a division of Penguin Random House Ltd., London, in 2023.

Pantheon Books and colophon
are registered trademarks of Penguin Random House LLC.

Library of Congress Cataloging-in-Publication Data
Name: Jones, Lucy, author.
Title: Matrescence : on pregnancy, childbirth, and motherhood / by Lucy Jones.
Description: First United States edition. New York : Pantheon Books, 2023.
Includes bibliographical references and index.
Identifiers: LCCN 2023033894 (print) | LCCN 2023033895 (ebook) |
ISBN 9780593317310 (hardcover) | ISBN 9780593317327 (ebook)
Subjects: LCSH: Motherhood.
Classification: LCC HQ759 .J687 2023 (print) | LCC HQ759 (ebook) |
DDC 306.874/3—dc23/eng/20231013
LC record available at https://lccn.loc.gov/2023033894
LC ebook record available at https://lccn.loc.gov/2023033895

www.pantheonbooks.com

Jacket image: *Pregnant Woman,* 2008 by Louise Bourgeois © The Easton Foundation /
VAGA at Artists Rights Society (ARS), NY; photograph: Cristopher Burke
Jacket design by Jenny Carrow

Printed in the United States of America
First United States Edition

2 4 6 8 9 7 5 3 1

For Naomi E
May C-B, Lottie A
Chloe S-M
With gratitude.

Contents

Matrescence

M*M*M*M

Z<*O*>ZZ <O>

W*WqW*W qqq

qqqqqq qqq

q q q q qqqq qqq

q q q q q q q q

q qqqqqq

qqqqqqqqqqqq q qqqqqq q q q q q q q q qq Qqqqqqqqqqq

qqqqqqqqqqqqq q qqqqqqqqqqqqq q q q q q q q q q qqqqqqqqqq

q

q

q

q

q

q

q

q

*When a human egg melds with sperm enzyme, zinc fireworks spark.[1]

Prologue

It's early autumn and the forest is a rainbow. The tops of the broad-leaved beech trees are copper, swelling to yellow. Green chlorophyll holds on underneath. Above, a great tit chitters. A dog barks nearby. Cars swoosh in the distance.

I'm here to find slime molds.

I am looking for slime molds for a few reasons. First, they are beautiful and peculiar. Second, though abundant, most of their forms require unearthing, and I am interested in hidden things. Third, I don't know very much about them—no one does—but I know that they undergo radical, irreversible metamorphosis, and I think that this is what has been happening to me.

Myxomycetes—the scientific name for slime molds—are fungus-like organisms. For a long time, scientists thought they were fungi (hence *Myceto*) but now they are classified in the kingdom *Protista*, a ragtag group of beings that aren't animals, plants or fungi. Part of their life cycle is spent as fruiting bodies that can look a little like minuscule mushrooms, and they live anywhere there is organic matter: decaying logs, sticks, leaf litter, dung. I search the bark and stumps around me for the tiny, bodacious flashes of color I have seen online or in my field guide: iridescent ingots of petroleum, corn dogs made of peach glass, balloons of lip gloss on black stilts, pink foam dissolving into sherbet, licorice buttons with a hundred spider legs.[1] I know what shapes to look out for with my hand lens: eggs, cones, nets, plumes, goblets; in clutches, or alone; no more than a millimeter or so high.

Although I have read that they are everywhere, I have never seen a slime mold at this fleeting stage of its life.

Myxomycetes actually spend most of their existence in a state more characteristic of an animal. This is the slime mold as plasmodium: a thin, slick mass. It moves around, scoffing fungal hyphae, algae, spores and other organic matter, squeezing through tiny holes and crevices in wood, advancing and growing. Commonly, it is bright yellow. In this state, it can grow significantly, spreading over bark and mulch, in the shade where it is moist and dark. Occasionally there are sightings of plasmodium meters wide. Although they are single-celled, with no brain or nervous system, biologists have found they can solve problems, such as mazes, learn, anticipate and "teach" younger slime molds pieces of knowledge.[2,3] Astronomers have relied on their networking behavior to help map the dark matter holding the universe together.[4]

I think I have seen a plasmodium here before. It was about the size of a child's hand and looked like an acid yellow gob vomited across a fallen log, dripping over the bark, but so vital it might have reared up, smeared its way towards us, and chased us through the forest.

Sometimes, a plasmodium will be enclosed by a slime sheath and leave behind a glossy trail as it wanders. Then, after a number of days or weeks, when it runs out of food—or for other reasons unknown—it moves into a drier, more exposed habitat and transforms into a colony of completely different beings, with a new existence and purpose: sessile and spore-releasing. It, you could say, becomes they. The woodlands of the world glisten and crawl with myxomycetes, invisible to the human eye unless you're looking.

I get down on my knees, combing old logs and sticks, stroking and parting filigrees of lichen and moss.

Over the past couple of years I have found myself increasingly drawn to the fluidity of the woods, and the abstruse fluidity of slime molds—an organism with 720 sexes.[5] To the complex relationships between lichen and moss and bacteria and spores and fungi and mycelium and trees and decaying matter and dead wood and frass. The complex life-processes and "intelligence" of these organisms expand my perception of life and help me see our wider ecologies more clearly.

Half an hour or so passes, and I don't find what I'm looking for, exactly. A daddy longlegs walks past, ghostly gentleman sprite.

Spindly mushrooms stand on stalks. Purple gills, white gills. The mossy knolls are filled with tardigrades and rotifers and springtails. Dead-man's-fingers leer erect. Epiphytes and moss nestle. Puffballs puff. Worms metabolize compounds. Underneath me, the mycorrhizal network resides: pulsing, combining, attending, underpinning the whole forest.

The forest will turn from autumn bright to brittle snooze, from germination to new growth, from life to death to life, and I will keep searching for rafts to climb on to, powered by the urge to comprehend what the world is like, and what my little ecosystem could be.

Introduction

Women and love are underpinnings.
Examine them and you threaten the very structure of culture.

Shulamith Firestone, *The Dialectic of Sex:*
The Case for Feminist Revolution

Sorry this Write up sucks I'm still mentally totally a wreck
after baby for some reason. Like my iq is down about 50 points
and words seem weirdly difficult lol.

Grimes, Instagram, 2020

When a human animal grew inside my body, I started to realize that some hoodwinking had been going on. When she left my body, I noticed more.

Pregnancy, then birth, and then—big-time—early motherhood simply did not match up with the cultural, social and philosophical narratives I had grown up with. What I felt and saw did not accord with what I had been taught about women and men, fathers and mothers; I could not connect my present experience with what I had so far absorbed about the body, the mind, the individual and relational self, and our collective structures of living.

At first, I thought that I must be going mad. I searched desperately for ways of understanding what was happening to me. I started to realize that my mind had been colonized by inadequate ideas about womanhood, about motherhood, about value, even love: there was canker in the roots of my habitat.

A sense that I had been fundamentally misinformed about the female body and maternal experience set in fast. The first day that I felt nauseous, five weeks or so pregnant, I was excited. "Morning sickness" was a sign of a healthy pregnancy, I had read, and it confirmed to me what had seemed so mysterious and diffuse: that inside me was the child I had always dreamed of, finally. When it came, the nausea was immediately severe, but I figured, Well, let's see, the morning is around four hours of the day—not even a quarter of my waking hours—I can deal with that. I nibbled ginger biscuits and took sips of water.

Then noon came around. Severe nausea persisted.

3 p.m. Still there.

6 p.m. What?

8 p.m. How?

10 p.m. It remained.

Then, like this, the next day, and the next and the next and the next. All day, every day. For five months.

Meanwhile, a parallel, more disquieting change seemed to be happening in my mind. I was overjoyed to be pregnant, attached to the growing creature within, but I found myself becoming subdued, more introverted, increasingly disrupted as the weeks passed. I had no language with which to understand or describe this change, but my consciousness felt different: restructured or rewired. This freaked me out. It was as if someone else had moved in, making a home in both my uterus *and* my brain. I thought I must be imagining it; I had understood pregnancy to be a relatively straightforward physical process with a few "hormonal" days here and there. I thought the baby would grow inside my body, as in a flowerpot, that I would still be the same person. But that didn't seem to be the case.

As I came close to term I realized that something else had been accreting within me, too: a strange admixture of unexamined moral assumptions about motherhood.

At the time, I couldn't fathom exactly where I'd picked up these ideas, but it became clear, once the baby was born, that I felt that self-sacrifice was an essential component of being a good mother. My past independence had to end, and I would now need to live to serve others in an intensive and ultimately self-sacrificing way.

Really, I knew next to nothing about the maternal experience or the work of raising and caring for other human beings. I had never seen a painting of a woman giving birth. I had never heard a song about pregnancy. I had never read a book about the loss of self in early motherhood. I had never watched a play about maternal mental illness. I had never changed a diaper or spent time with young children. And still, I had a curiously adamantine conception of what it required.

As the baby grew, I found that if I tried to do anything for myself, I would be agonized by guilt and a diffuse sense of discomfort. I became increasingly driven to try and untangle these punishing feelings—to separate them from my desire to protect, love and care for my baby. I needed to locate the origins of this dissonance, so as to work out how to nurture her, while living some kind of life of my own. I began to look everywhere for clues.

O

Eventually, I encountered the concept of the "institution of motherhood," developed by the feminist poet and essayist Adrienne Rich in her book *Of Woman Born.*[1] Writing in 1976, she showed how wider societal conditions—in a word, patriarchy—had turned motherhood into a "modern institution," with its own rules, strictures and social expectations, all of which were designed to control women's behavior and thought. Rich made clear that it was the sociocultural *institution* of motherhood, not the children themselves, that oppressed women and could even mutilate the relationship between mother and child. The institution fostered the idea that women are born with a "natural" maternal "instinct" rather than needing to develop knowledge and skills as caregivers. The uneven power relations between mother and child were, she argued, a reflection of power dynamics in society. It was a setup, in which mothers were destined to fail. The institution found "all mothers more or less guilty for having failed their children."[2] Perhaps I wasn't going mad.

I was amazed by how relevant *Of Woman Born* was, forty-something years after it was first published. Rich's was the first voice that described the dilemma that had engulfed me. She had her children in the 1950s. Almost seventy years later, the taboos she described were still strong. It shocked me to realize that the leading assumption I held about motherhood was identical to Rich's:

> That a "natural" mother is a person without further identity, one who can find her chief gratification in being all day with small children, living at a pace tuned to theirs; that the isolation of mothers and children together in the home must be taken for granted; that maternal love is, and should be, quite literally selfless.[3]

How could this be? I had grown up reading Greer, Beauvoir, Firestone. How could I have reached my thirties with this archetype still deeply sewn into me?

While I had always wanted children, I realized, with a jolt, that I didn't hold mothers or the work that mothers do in high esteem. I had felt the need to hide certain aspects of my pregnancy and early motherhood from colleagues and employers. I had internalized the message that I had to keep motherhood separate, cloistered; I expected to be judged and found wanting by the working world for having children. I saw how the work of motherhood was valued neither economically nor socially: it was not regarded as a site of power or esteem. In fact, it was the opposite. While society still judges women without children, to be associated with "the maternal" was to be silenced, limited and diminished. I was frightened of being defined by my reproductive labor—and being written off for it.

As I began to interrogate my attitude towards motherhood, I was shocked. I saw that I had perceived it as mindless and unintellectual, of low worth and of low value, dull, nothing to write home about. It wasn't *productive* in the real sense. Looking "mumsy" was not something I aspired to. I didn't want to carry the "stank of uncool motherhood," as the writer Rufi Thorpe puts it.[4] Being a caregiver wasn't challenging, wasn't high status. I thought it was *easy* work. Ha!

I would soon learn that caregiving was much, much harder, more confronting, exciting, creative, beautiful, stressful, alarming, rewarding, tedious, transformative, enlivening and (occasionally) deadening than I imagined, and much more essential to a working society than we give it credit for. I felt increasingly compelled to figure out the reasons for the continuing lack of authentic respect and support for the invisible work of pregnancy, birthing children and caregiving. Not least because I was finding out firsthand how harmful it could be.

O

The experience of giving birth had been bamboozling. I was attracted by the idea of a "natural" birth, and I believed what I'd heard and read: that, if I was relaxed and used my mantras and positive affirmations, I wouldn't feel too much pain, and everything would be fine. This was not the case.

In the hours, weeks and months that followed, I grew more and more alienated, frustrated by the lack of language to articulate the reality of childbirth. I had always believed in the power of words but, here, they failed me. No one was talking about pain; about birth as an emotional process; about how it felt to have grown another human, to be two people at the same time, and then to be vacated, to push a person into being.

I knew nothing about the emotional and psychological transition that follows birth. I had no idea that something was happening to my brain—that it was literally changing shape. I had no idea what was coming: the anxiety, the life-exploding romance, the guilt, the transcendence, the terror, the psychedelia, the loss of control, the rupture of self.

So instead, for a while, I acquiesced. I used the language I had been given: the official lexicon for talking about motherhood. I fell in line, finding that you could sometimes admit it was a bit tiring as long as you mostly assured the person you were talking to that you loved the child and oh, yes, it was definitely the best thing that had ever happened to you.

Blindsided and increasingly isolated, I fell down a rabbit hole. I had gone, but I didn't know where, or if I would return. I found I was confronted with my selves anew: my childhood self, the bare, naked roots of early psychic disturbances. This, I did not expect. I thought early motherhood would be gentle, beatific, pacific, tranquil: bathed in a soft light. But actually it was hard-core, edgy, gnarly. It wasn't pale pink; it was brown of shit and red of blood. And it was the most political experience of my life, rife with conflict, domination, drama, struggle and power.

O

Questions swirled around me. What was happening to my brain, my mind and my body? Why did it feel so wrong to be alone at home, mothering my young child? Why did it also feel so wrong to be away from her? Why did it seem as if my nervous system hadn't evolved for this?

I set about trying to solve the puzzle. Since I had a background in science, health and ecology journalism, I turned first to research papers and journals, and read about neurobiology, endocrinology, the study of maternal mental illness. I soon realized that cultural apathy towards this most dramatic of transitions in a person's life went hand in hand with the failure of science—biological and social—to address it. In 2011, researchers from Scotland wrote in the *Journal of Psychiatric and Mental Health Nursing* that there was a "vacuum in the evidence base" in research on postnatal depression, the primary mental illness associated with motherhood.[5] But a growing field of research had begun to focus on the maternal experience. Through the second half of the 2010s, the first landmark neuroscience studies had been published, showing just how drastically pregnancy and early motherhood alters the brain, as well as how looking after infants can change the brains of nonpregnant caregivers.

As I read, I realized that there was a lot more "nature" happening to me than I had been led to believe, but also a lot more "nurture." I studied the history of "the modern institution of motherhood," learning how and why expectations of maternal servitude and self-sacrifice were first constructed, and how capitalism and patriarchal systems had combined to create our current ideas about womanhood and motherhood—producing what I will call the modern institution of *intensive* motherhood. I interviewed experts in the fields of evolutionary biology, social science, psychoanalysis, philosophy, neuroscience, healthcare and psychiatry, and saw how new parents were being failed by inaccurate assumptions about the benefits of the "traditional" nuclear family structure—assumptions which routinely forgot or ignored how babies are raised by networks of people in the majority of the world.

When our baby was about nine months old, I had had a breakthrough. I happened upon a word I'd never read before, in an article in *The New York Times* written by a reproductive psychiatrist called Alexandra Sacks.[6] It was a word which brought together everything I was feeling, seeing and reading about.

Matrescence.

"The process of becoming a mother, which anthropologists call 'matrescence,' has been largely unexplored in the medical community," Sacks writes. "Instead of focusing on the woman's identity transition, more research is focused on how the baby turns out. But a woman's story, in addition to how her psychology impacts her parenting, is important to examine, too."

I breathed.

The article mentions the mixture of emotions that mothers experience. Joy, yes, "at least some of the time." "But most mothers also experience worry, disappointment, guilt, competition, frustration, and even anger and fear."

The idea that this was normal made my shoulders drop in relief for the first time in months. I kept reading.

"Too many women are ashamed to speak openly about their complicated experiences for fear of being judged. This type of social isolation may even trigger postpartum depression."

I looked for "matrescence" in my dictionary. Matins. Matisse. Matricide. No matrescence.

I checked my *Dictionary of English Etymology.* Matriarch. Matriculate. Matrimony. No matrescence.

I wondered if I could at least find any words that associated motherhood with an emotional journey.

I turned to the word *mother.*

A. female parent.
B. womb, from the fourteenth century, preceded by a cross, meaning obsolete. And ah, here was something. *Hysteria* (also with a cross). I looked up hysteria. "Functional disturbance of the nervous system, which was thought to be due to disturbing of the uterine functions."

I looked to the next entry for mother. "Dregs, scum," from the sixteenth century. A "mucilaginous substance produced in vinegar by fermentation," from the seventeenth century. And "original crude substance." I wondered if these uses had been influenced by the biblical story of Eve—eating the apple, disobeying God, the original sinner.

I checked other dictionaries. No entries for "matrescence." As I typed it on my computer the word processor insisted on underlining it with a dotted red line. It's still there now, years later, blotting the page with red. This isn't a word, it says. This isn't a thing.

Only, it is. After childhood and adolescence, there is no other time in an adult human's life course which entails such dramatic psychological, social and physical change.

I ordered a book published in 1973 called *Being Female: Reproduction, Power and Change*. It was edited by Dana Raphael, the late American medical anthropologist. Her essay "Matrescence, Becoming a Mother, A 'New / Old Rite de Passage'" is cited as the first mention of the word. The book cover is typically 1970s: brown, orange and cream. Under the title, there is an artist's rendering of a woman sitting on the floor, her naked body partly concealed by her limbs.

In the essay Raphael compares Western cultures with that of the Tikopia, who live on a remote, volcanic island in the southwest of the Solomon Islands. In the West, when a child is born, the announcement would be "a child is born." The Tikopia would say, instead, "a woman has given birth." The Tikopia have a sense of the *newborn mother*.[7]

Raphael laments the historical lack of interest ethnographers have had in motherhood rites because, in the West, she explains, motherhood is considered "dull and unchanging."

I looked up rites of passage—celebrations or rituals that mark important transitions in a person's life. I couldn't think of any for matrescence. The list on Wikipedia for "Coming of Age" includes Bar and Bat Mitzvah, Sweet Sixteen, Debutante Ball, Scarification, First Menstruation, Walkabout. Then, there is a section on religious rituals. I have had the Christian ones. Baptism. Confirmation. I wondered if "Baby Shower" might be included, the closest to a matrescence ritual I could think of. It wasn't. There was nothing about becoming a parent.

"The critical transition period which has been missed is MATRESCENCE, the time of mother-becoming," writes Raphael. "During this process, this rite of passage, changes occur in a woman's physical state, in her status within the group, in her emotional life, in her focus of daily activity, in her own identity, and in her relationships with all those around her."[8]

The book was published ten years or so before I was born. Almost half a century later, we still barely acknowledge the psychological and physiological significance of becoming a mother: how it affects the brain, the endocrine system, cognition, immunity, the psyche, the microbiome, the sense of self. This is a problem. Everyone knows adolescents are uncomfortable and awkward because they are going through extreme mental and bodily changes, but, when they have a baby, women are expected to transition with ease—to breeze into a completely new self, a new role, at one of the most perilous and sensitive times in the life course.

O

Learning about matrescence eventually gave me the confidence to talk openly to other new mothers, and I soon realized that many were similarly startled by what they were experiencing. Many were feeling that they were to blame for the extent of their struggles. We joked obliquely about the stress we were under, about the "maternal hospital fantasy"—the idea that breaking a minor limb would be a good way to get a rest and be looked after for a night. Here, I realized, were the results of twenty-first-century parenting norms, which had become much more intensive, child-centered and demanding than they ever had been before. These norms, combined with neoliberal economic policy, the erosion of community and the requirement for most families to have two incomes to live because of the ever-higher cost of living, were leading to staggering levels of tension, guilt and ill health among mothers.

Pregnancy and early motherhood is a vulnerable time for a woman's health and well-being. Across the globe, a woman dies every two minutes due to pregnancy and childbirth, with the majority of deaths happening in low-income countries.[9]

Even with advances in modern medicine, and in high-income countries with skilled medical care, new mothers are highly susceptible to illness and disease. It is difficult to know exactly how many women become unwell in the period before and after becoming a mother. In the UK, where I live, it was previously thought that 10–15 percent of women develop a mental health problem in pregnancy or the first year of new motherhood—including mild and moderate to severe depression, anxiety, PTSD, psychosis—but more recent figures suggest it could be as many as 20 percent of women.[10] This means over 100,000 women a year in the UK become mentally unwell in matrescence. Globally, the prevalence of postnatal depression is 17 percent. With two billion mothers in the world, this means over 350 million women experience perinatal mental health problems. The likelihood of depressive episodes doubles during this period, compared with other times in a woman's life.[11] This figure rises for women of color, those in disadvantaged socioeconomic groups who face systemic health inequalities, and women who have experienced loss (miscarriage, stillbirth, neonatal death or a child taken into care).[12,13,14] Suicide is the leading cause of death in women in the perinatal period between six weeks and one year after giving birth in the UK.[15] Clearly, this is a grave situation.

But these figures are likely too low: the National Childbirth Trust (NCT), the most influential parenting institution in the UK, estimates that in fact half of new mothers experience mental health problems but only half of those will seek help.[16] Many women, for various intersecting reasons—many of which are to do with the threat of stigma and discrimination and, ultimately, the fear of their babies being taken away from them—are reluctant to seek treatment. As the writer and activist Sandra Igwe has written, this is a serious problem facing Black women in England, for whom a lack of trust in services, fear and shame represent major obstacles to seeking the medical care they need.[17]

"Generally in society we don't pay the attention we should to mental well-being," Dr. Alain Gregoire, a consultant perinatal psychiatrist, told me.[18] "Or value mothers or take an interest in parents and young children." The lack of adequate investment in maternity services and poor postnatal care attests to this. In 2014, a report from the Chief Medical Officer for England concluded that postnatal care was "not fit for purpose."[19]

A 2019 survey commissioned by *Motherdom* magazine showed just how many women were feeling low (45 percent), anxious (54 percent) and depressed (35 percent) since having a child.[20] One in five hadn't told anyone about their feelings, and over half (59 percent) said they did not feel supported by their family. Almost half the new mothers surveyed (45 percent) said they had to deal with everything alone. Why would this be? Perhaps the fact that just over one in five

(22 percent) thought they would appear "weak" has something to do with it. Earlier research suggests half of mothers with children under five experience "intense emotional distress" on a regular or continual basis.[21]

Fathers, too, are suffering. In 2022, a study by researchers at Ohio State University found that 66 percent of parents met the criteria for burnout, where stress and exhaustion overwhelm the ability to cope and function.[22]

As my matrescence continued, with the births of my sons in 2019 and 2021, I found that the overwhelming majority of the mothers I met and listened to over the course of those years were bewildered and disoriented. I felt compelled to continue my investigation into what the transition to motherhood entailed, and why. I wanted to find out how much maternal mental illness was inevitable and how much might be avoided through improved treatment and care—through a fairer society. To what extent was postnatal mental illness intrinsic and biological, and how much of it was an understandable response to the design of modern parenthood? Why was motherhood in my society so dangerous for women's mental health and well-being? I suspected that the rise in perinatal mood "disorders" must be telling us something important about the way we live. Unlike other cultures, which treat becoming a mother as a major, traumatic life crisis, with special social rites and rituals, Western societies had been failing to recognize matrescence as a major transition: a transition that involves a whole spectrum of emotional and existential ruptures, a transition that can make women ill, a transition in which the mother, as well as the baby, could be celebrated. We had been failing to care for mothers, or for one another, very well at all.

O

Soon after reading about matrescence for the first time, I interviewed Alexandra Sacks. She told me that we should start by simply talking about matrescence: in some cases, this would be enough to prevent women from getting ill. "Women would know that this ambivalence is normal and nothing to be ashamed of; they would feel less stigmatized and more normal and it would reduce rates of PND [postnatal depression]," she said.[23]

I have written this book in the spirit of Sacks's instruction: as an invitation to start talking about matrescence. It is a personal story—a record of what happened to me mostly during my first experience of pregnancy, childbirth and new motherhood—and I offer it here as a case study. I have shared the most compelling and rigorous scientific research that I encountered as I tried to make sense of what was happening to me at each stage.

This is a story of my matrescence as a woman who has carried biological children within a heterosexual relationship. But, of course, not all mothers are pregnant, or give birth, or are biologically related to their children. Nor is the work of mothering an exclusively female activity. Men mother. Grandparents mother. People without their own children mother. However, women still do most of the caregiving in the society I live in, especially in the early years, and I am interested in the particular cultural and social gendered expectations and pressures on female parents, and women socialized as female, so I use the word "mother" more frequently than "parent."

The new research into the maternal brain and maternal mental health—much of which has only been published in the last few years—ought to change the way we think about new families and the support they need, the structure of the working world, the sorry state of investment in perinatal care. Recent evolutionary and anthropological research underlines how extraordinary and oppressive our modern-day maternal ideals are. Science tells us that the neurobiological process of parent–infant bonding and the shift into new motherhood is more diverse and interesting and wild than the bland fantasies on Mother's Day cards. Matrescence troubles the idea that we are self-contained individuals, separated from the rest of the living world.

With this book I hope to begin new conversations about how becoming a mother changes a person, about what it means to metamorphose, about what we can do to recognize new mothers in their matrescence and how we can reimagine the institution of motherhood. My hope is that this book might be a thread of mycelium that leads to other ways of thinking. Alongside my own story, I have drawn in ecological case studies: stories of change, process and metamorphosis in the rest of the living world that helped me place my experience into our wider ecological context. I have done so partly to show that natural change is not always beautiful, and that our ideas of the "natural" are largely invented. Matrescence has been the most ecological, biological experience of my life, and these stories were my wayfinders. Engaging with the earth—thinking with the earth—enabled me to see and think more clearly.

My children have brought me joy, contentment, fulfillment, wonder and delight in staggering abundance. But that's just part of the story. This is the rest.

PART I

Tadpoles

Frog spawn mass together in a jellied gloop, each globe squidgy and hard like an eyeball. The black round dot in the middle is the size of a peppercorn. It doesn't seem possible that it will change but one morning, well, there it is and the peppercorn is no longer a peppercorn but an elongated comma. The next day a few start to wriggle—hectic—like small charcoal ribbons. Feathery gills emerge overnight from their necks, like ruffs. They wiggle out of their jellied beds, free. Now, they alternately pause and float at the top of the water, or silk-twitch around, looking for food. A few days later, their tails suddenly thicken and lengthen, becoming one long black arrow encased in 30-denier tights. For much of this time, they fall throuuuugh the water, and let their bodies carry them down,

down,

down.

Some are bigger than others. Some are quicker than others. Some move less. Over the next few days, their heads grow until they look like cartoon sperm, propelled through the water. Small nubs appear, the beginnings of legs. Their bodies turn from opaque to translucent, speckled with gold. Next, feet appear on each side, webbed and splayed. At the end are threadlike tree-branch toes. They suck the sides of the tank where we are raising them with their black ring mouth. Their hearts? Red. A waste tube trails beneath. *Flick!* Their tails can ripple the surface of the water. They dive up and down, then become still and rest. Now, the bodies are dark green-black with bronze lacquer spots. Beady, crocodilian eyes emerge on top of their heads. Then, their arms emerge, with four-fingered hands. The head becomes more pointed and the skin becomes less translucent. Then, it is a froglet with a tadpole tail! It is! Then—and you can barely believe it—it is a frog. It is!

A week later, one is lying at the bottom of the pond, pale and lifeless. Ten or so tiny, bright-pink bloodworms are going at it furiously, taking its body into their bodies, bit by bit.

I.

All-day sickness

The ego is first and foremost a bodily ego.

Sigmund Freud, *The Ego and the Id*

What I expected in pregnancy
Sickness in the morning
Glowing skin
Shiny hair
Bigger boobs
Weird cravings

What I did not expect in pregnancy
Restless leg syndrome
Acne
Hair loss
Kiss curls
Eczema
Sciatica
Constant and severe nausea
To feel stoned
Mysteriously high white blood cell count
Mysterious infections
Numb hands

Pins and needles
Hotter (in body temperature)
Incredible sense of smell
Color changes (darkened nipples; vulva; hair color)
Linea nigra
A digestive roller coaster
Heightened sense of threat
Shame
Flatter nose
Increased vascularity leading to increased intensity of orgasm
Dry eyes
Pinguecula
Wider jaw
Needing to wee six times a night
A mouth full of blood after toothbrushing
Ecstasy
Insomnia
A preoccupying obsessive urge for the baby to live
Brain fog
Di
s. s
ol
u t. i. o.

n. of the self

And then

To become

Something

Else

O

It happened around the time I grew a heart.

I could smell everything. The armpits and groins of those who passed by on a wide road. Specks of food on a train seat. A cigarette around the corner. The town—population: thousands—and what kind of soap people used that morning. Coconut or tea tree oil or Pears or if they missed a shower, all chundering around in a horrible soup. At night I could smell leftover cooking fumes as if they were particulate matter in a pillow spray. Rotting seaweed from the other end of the beach. The breakfast breath of a shop assistant. Chip fat across a highway. Postmix syrup and pub carpet seeping into the street.

Pregnancy gave me the one superpower no one has ever wanted: an extremely good sense of smell.

I was a dog now. Sniffing for danger.

Cars on the road sounded louder and appeared more aggressive; I lay awake at 4 o'clock in the morning worrying about the state of the world. My hair came loose. My forehead speckled with zits: bulbous, greasy.

I had an urge to eat most of the time. I wanted salty, fatty or sweet food on my tongue. It gave the slightest relief from the nausea.

Soft boiled potatoes. Fizzy cola. Heavy croissants. Crispy bacon and cream cheese. Melted cheese. Salt and vinegar–drenched chips. Salt and vinegar crisps. Salty tuna covered in mayonnaise. Fizzy orange. Rice and soy sauce and grated mature cheddar. Extra-mature cheddar. Pickled-onion-flavored crisps.

On the bus to the British Library in London where I was working on the final edits of my first book, I would nibble oatcakes to suppress the bile climbing up my throat. Visitors are not allowed to bring food into the Reading Rooms so I'd sneak them in under my sleeves and bite secretively as I checked my sources on vulpine biology.

As soon as it turned 11 o'clock, I would make my way over the road to the greasiest spoon I could find. Order a baked potato with tuna, sweet corn, extra cheese—melted on top, please. Yes, and butter. Yes, mayonnaise on the side. Scatter salt on top. Ring pull click.

Fizz. Cold brown cola. I would sit and gorge, ignoring my humiliation at being an early morning gobbler in public. In return I'd receive twenty minutes of milder nausea.

The first trimester wasn't the healthy time I had aimed for. Fresh salad and vegetables turned my stomach most of all, and I couldn't swim more than a few lengths in the pool without tiring. One day, I watched a video on the NHS website.[1] "The exercise and the healthy eating will push you in the right direction for a nice, quick labor and a lovely healthy baby at the end of it." A nice, quick labor? That sounded ideal. I'll get back to healthy eating and exercise soon, I thought.

But as I looked on forums and read other women's accounts, it started to become clear that many were feeling sick round the clock, some throughout pregnancy, and no one knew what caused it, how to treat it properly, or why on earth it was called morning sickness.

O

In the late 1980s Margie Profet, a biologist from the United States, developed the hypothesis that pregnancy sickness is an adaptation to protect the growing embryo, particularly at the time of organogenesis. This stage in the development of the fetus is the most vulnerable and susceptible to disruption. Profet's research suggested that nausea protected the embryo from toxins because it arrests the appetite.[2]

A small but interesting study found that women carrying male fetuses have higher levels of disgust and food aversions, because male fetuses are more vulnerable than female.

Samuel Flaxman, an evolutionary biologist at the University of Colorado, built on Profet's work with a review published in 2000 that supported her hypothesis.[3] Flaxman found that the most common aversions were towards alcohol, meat, eggs, fish and strong-tasting vegetables: foods which would've been habitats for microorganisms and toxins in our fridge-less evolutionary history.

Strangely, despite the fact that almost 70 percent of women experience pregnancy nausea and vomiting, and severe pregnancy sickness can be fatal for both baby and mother, we still don't know much more than this.[4]

At least the medical establishment no longer believes that pregnancy sickness is the manifestation of immorality. In the surprisingly recent past, it was blamed on "neurosis, an unconscious desire for abortion, a rejection of motherhood, a scheme to avoid housework, and sexual dysfunction," explains the ecologist Sandra Steingraber in her 2001 book *Having Faith: An Ecologist's Journey to Motherhood.*[5] A Scottish physician writing in the 1940s believed that morning sickness could be caused by "excessive mother attachment."[6] Even Simone de Beauvoir wrote in *The Second Sex* that vomiting in pregnancy was a manifestation of fright at the alienating experience of growing a child within, of being the "prey of the species, which imposes its mysterious laws upon her" and the "conflict between species and individual in the human female."[7]

These bizarre ideas were the legacy of the theory of "maternal imagination," which was prevalent between the sixteenth and eighteenth centuries.[8] Physicians believed that pregnant women could change the growing fetus *with their minds* and thus congenital disorders were the fault of the mother. If she was startled by a frog, for example, the child might end up with webbed feet. Or if she spent too long gazing at a picture of Jesus, the baby might come out with a beard.

Perhaps there is a residue of the "it's all in her head" school of thought today. The long-held idea that women's bodies and minds are in some way untrustworthy, threatening and subject to whims of irrationality—such as the Ancient Greek belief of the pesky "wandering womb" roving the body causing problems—might explain in part why pregnancy sickness is still not accurately described.[9]

But almost every story we've been told about the reproductive process is entangled with ideology, with prevailing ideas about gender. I was taught in science lessons at school that sperm are released and race each other until the fittest and fastest sperm wins and penetrates the egg; a retelling of the hero myth, essentially, with the egg as the passive vessel. In fact, we know now that this isn't what happens at all. Sperm cells are immature when they arrive in the vagina. Then women's oviduct cells secrete chemicals which mature the sperm and allow it to swim. Instead of the sperm poking the egg like a needle, the egg actually enfolds the sperm and the two cells melt into one.

In 2020, a paper was published in the *British Journal of General Practice* by a group of clinicians who recognized that the condition of nausea and sickness in pregnancy hadn't been clearly described by medicine or statistically modeled in any way that would enable the term "morning sickness" to be accurately analyzed.[10] The women they studied experienced it, yes, all day, with a peak in the morning.

The study concluded that "referring to nausea and vomiting in pregnancy as simply 'morning sickness' is inaccurate, simplistic, and therefore unhelpful."

In 2023, the NHS still refers to pregnancy sickness as "morning sickness."[11]

This terminology serves to minimize the problem. It helps explain why medical care, treatment, research and wider social support is still inadequate, especially for women who suffer most severely.

Hyperemesis gravidarum, the most extreme form of pregnancy sickness, suffered by one to three women in a hundred, can lead to hospitalization, dehydration, starvation, brain atrophy, blood clotting and death if untreated. In the largest survey to date of women suffering from the condition, 67.8 percent were bedridden throughout pregnancy and 25.5 percent thought about suicide.[12] Younger age, social deprivation and an ethnic minority background are associated with more severe illness. Women report not feeling taken seriously, having their symptoms brushed off and being told they are exaggerating.

O

The list of foodstuffs I needed to avoid was long and peculiar: liver, Gorgonzola, Roquefort, shark, too much coffee, licorice root, more than four cups of herbal tea a day, more than two portions of oily fish per week (although I must have two).[13] I kept hearing how important my diet was for the development of my future child and so I tried to eat healthily, but I couldn't help but be struck by how the conversation around prenatal health was focused solely on the individual woman's lifestyle choices (her alcohol intake, her weight, her physical activity, as well as her diet), without any meaningful consideration of the wider environment she inhabits.

One of the foods I was instructed to avoid was fish with too much mercury, such as tuna, as it can harm the unborn baby. The NHS also advises limiting the intake of oily fish because of the pollutants—dioxins and polychlorinated biphenyls—within.

Although some mercury occurs naturally, the reason fish—one of the foods that contains the fatty acids needed to promote healthy development of the fetal brain—is now considered harmful is down to human industrial activity, particularly the operation of coal-fired power plants which emit mercury.[14] Since 1882, when the world's first coal-fired power station, the Edison Electric Light Station, was built in London, industrial nations have been poisoning sea creatures and those that eat them, including pregnant women.

It's easy to avoid eating fish if you live, as I do, in a place where other foods are plentiful, but harder in countries where it is a major food group. Pregnant Inuit women from Nunavik, for example, are exposed to high levels of contaminants.[15] In 2017, 22 percent of women in that group exceeded guidance levels for mercury and polychlorinated biphenyls. Exposure to mercury has been associated with ADHD symptoms in Inuit children.[16]

"When it comes to environmental hazards, not only do we dispense with the principle of 'In ignorance, abstain,' we fail to inform pregnant women that the hazards even exist," writes Steingraber.[17] She studied how various industry groups downplayed the dangers of mercury, lead and other toxins. And, over two decades later, Steingraber's questions remain relevant: "Why does abstinence in the face of uncertainty apply only to individual behaviour? Why doesn't it apply equally to industry or agriculture?"[18]

What does it mean to be pregnant at the most ecologically destructive time in human history?

In 2020, a study found that microplastics cross over to the placenta, joining such dubious record locations as the top of Mount Everest and the deepest ocean.[19] "It is like having a cyborg baby: no longer composed only of human cells, but a mixture of biological and inorganic entities," said Antonio Ragusa, director of obstetrics and gynecology at the San Giovanni Calibita Fatebenefratelli hospital in Rome, who led the study. "The mothers were shocked." The health impacts are still being studied, but scientists say microplastics could cause long-term damage and affect the developing immune system.

How on earth does a pregnant woman protect her baby from microplastics? Or from the black carbon emitted by vehicles, which, we now know, can penetrate the placenta?

How does she protect herself from the nitrogen dioxide emitted by diesel vehicles, which increases the risk of mental illness?[20]

How does she avoid high levels of air pollution, which seem to be linked to miscarriages?

"Pregnant women, or those who want to become pregnant, must protect themselves from air pollution exposure not only for their own health but also for the health of their foetuses," says Liqiang Zhang at Beijing Normal University, who found a link between exposure to air pollution and miscarriage.[21] But how? By not going outside?

I avoided heavily trafficked roads when I could but there was nothing, really, I could do to stop the baby being born pre-polluted. My carbon monoxide levels were read by a midwife via a pump—in case I was lying about not being a smoker, I presume—and were slightly higher than normal because I lived near a railway station. I walked to places through the local park, avoiding the locus of trains.

But it stuck in the craw. I saw no sign of genuine urgency or action from governments to reduce air pollution and protect future generations at the most vulnerable period of their lives. I, though, had to avoid soft cheese and too much tea.

The Canadian philosopher Quill Kukla (writing as Rebecca Kukla) looked at the results when searching for "pregnancy" in an academic library, and found that 80 percent of the material related to toxins (such as alcohol and caffeine) that women had to avoid in pregnancy.[22] This skew has wider consequences. It leaves "corporations, fathers, insurers, legislators and others" off the hook, they write.

O

The impact of environmental destruction is minimized or ignored, and so are the social ills that affect our health: economic inequality, structural racism, sexism, classism, ideology, misogyny.

A study of a million births in England between 2015 and 2017 published in the *Lancet* found that racial and social inequalities account for adverse pregnancy outcomes including preterm births, stillbirths and reduced fetal growth.[23] The largest inequalities were seen in South Asian and Black women living in deprived areas. The outcomes were preventable. The research group estimate that 24 percent of stillbirths, 19 percent of live, preterm births and 31 percent of live births with fetal growth reduction would not have occurred if all women had the same risk of adverse pregnancy outcomes as those in the least deprived group.

In the US, the risk of pregnancy-related death is three times higher for Black women and American Indian and Alaska Native women than white women. The majority of these deaths are preventable and caused by structural racism and implicit bias. Despite being the richest country in the world, the US is the most dangerous place in the developed world to be pregnant and give birth, with a disgracefully high maternal mortality rate (238 per every 100,000 live births).

In an article titled "Black Mothers Matter: The Social, Political and Legal Determinants of Black Maternal Health Across the Lifespan," published in the *Journal of Health Care Law and Policy,* Elizabeth Tobin-Tyler of Brown University wrote that the structures driving the extreme disparities include the "social status of Black mothers in American history and society, the political disempowerment and scapegoating of Black mothers that has shaped harmful public policies and poorly designed and enforced laws and systems that not only fail to protect Black mothers from discrimination but, at times, exacerbate it."

In 2020, *The New York Times* published a guide for Black mothers to protect their health, and lives, in childbirth and the perinatal period. Written by health educator and doula Erica Chidi and Dr. Erica P. Cahill, it aimed to give Black women agency in their care and thus feel safer. It also offered medical providers a framework and specific strategies to acknowledge and work against how racism affects the care of women in their matrescence.

In 2023, there is a critical chance for structural change in the US which would save the lives of mothers and their babies. The Black Maternal Health Momnibus Act—a package of thirteen bills to improve maternal health and eliminate racial disparities—was first introduced to the House in 2021. In May 2023, it was reintroduced by Cory Booker, Lauren Underwood and Alma Adams.

Yet, the focus in mainstream healthcare in the postindustrial Global North remains overwhelmingly on individual responsibility, maintaining the illusion or ideology that we are impermeable, impenetrable machines, disconnected from the social world around us—and, furthermore, separate and immune from those in power who orchestrate the world.

O

Never has this power and the myth of individualism been unmasked so shockingly in my lifetime than with the US Supreme Court's decision to overturn *Roe v. Wade* and remove women's constitutional right to abortion in 2022. Even though the majority of Americans support legal termination of pregnancy, a small group of Republicans succeeded in turning ideology into law in a move that will kill women, erode healthcare, bodily autonomy and human rights, and cause peril, trauma and suffering. Pregnancy can be a vulnerable and dangerous time—and trigger the most life-threatening conditions, such as sepsis, mental illness, autoimmune disease—and the consequences of forced pregnancy will be myriad and devastating.

The ruling means that doctors across the United States face severe criminal penalties in an uncertain legal landscape and are unable to provide adequate medical care for women with high-risk pregnancies or miscarriages.

"It's like you bring lots of people to the top of a high-rise and push them to the edge and then catch them before they fall," Dr. Alireza A. Shamshirsaz, an obstetrician and fetal surgeon who practiced in Houston, told *The New York Times*. "It's a very dangerous way of practicing. All of us know some of them will die."

Access is fluctuating at the time of this writing, but it is estimated that roughly half of the states will ban abortion. In the summer of 2023, thirteen states had banned abortion. Many states have no exception for rape and incest, including Alabama, Arizona, Arkansas, Florida, Kentucky, Louisiana, Mississippi, Missouri, Ohio, Oklahoma, South Dakota, Tennessee, Texas, West Virginia and Wisconsin. In 2022, a doctor who helped a ten-year-old rape victim obtain an abortion—who had had to travel from Ohio to Indiana—was investigated, harassed and disciplined for discussing the case with a reporter.

Compelling women to motherhood, to pregnancy, to childbirth is only possible in a world where those in power—namely men—are catastrophically ignorant about the health and mortality risks and vulnerability of pregnancy, and the reality of birthing and raising children—and deeply, cruelly indifferent to the health, dignity and survival of women.

Imaginal discs

When a caterpillar is ready for the next stage of its life, it finds a quiet and safe place and spins itself into a cocoon or chrysalis. Then, the caterpillar releases digestive enzymes and dissolves itself. It disintegrates into a goo. If you were to pierce its protective case, a liquid would pour out. Its metamorphosis relies on this period of being broken down and melted.

Almost. The caterpillar holds on to groups of cells called "imaginal discs." These disc-shaped structures grew when the caterpillar was still inside its egg, and there is one for each adult body part. One disc for the legs, another for the wings, one for the thorax, antennae and so on. The caterpillar sheds all that it doesn't need, leaving only these discs, which grow, powered by an amino acid–rich protein broth. It also carries previous memories into butterfly-hood or moth-hood. A research team of biologists from Georgetown University explored the retention of memory through metamorphosis. To do this, they tested whether moths (*Manduca sexta*, the tobacco hornworm) could remember what they had learned when they were a caterpillar. The scientists trained a group of caterpillars to avoid the odor of ethyl acetate—a sweet and fruity smell—by using electric shocks. The caterpillars learned. After the caterpillars transformed into moths, the scientists tested the moths to see whether they would still have an aversion to the smell of ethyl acetate. They did, leading the team to conclude that memory, via intact synaptic connections, survived metamorphosis.[1]

For a while, the essential parts of the caterpillar are hidden within the goo—its neurons, its sensory experiences—but they do remain, and are remodeled to form the next stage of life.

2.

The emotional placenta

Hang the clothes you wore before you were pregnant in a place where they are easy to see as that will motivate you to keep your weight under control and go back to the same weight you were before you gave birth. And buy a hairband so that you don't look disheveled after having the baby.

Seoul city government's advice to pregnant women, 2021

Just like the desire to write: a desire to live self from within, a desire for the swollen belly, for language, for blood. We are not going to refuse, if it should happen to strike our fancy, the unsurpassed pleasures of pregnancy which have actually been always exaggerated or conjured away—or cursed—in the classic texts. For if there's one thing that's been repressed, here's just the place to find it: in the taboo of the pregnant woman.

Hélène Cixous, *The Laugh of the Medusa*

INGREDIENTS FOR FIRST-TRIMESTER HORMONAL SOUP

Estradiol
Estrone

Progesterone
Testosterone
Prolactin
Osteoprotegerin
Allopregnanolone
Human chorionic gonadotropin
Thyroid-stimulating hormone
Relaxin
Cortisol
Oxytocin
FSH (follicle stimulating hormone)
LH (luteinizing hormone)
Probably others that we don't even know about yet[1]

At eight weeks, we went for a scan in a private clinic in London. I was anxious and tense. We hoped we were paying £80 for reassurance. I lay on tissue paper on a cold, plastic bed and the sonographer swept her wand over my stomach. We saw what looked like iron filings, or flakes of ice, clumped into a reptile shape.

A heartbeat flickered.

The sonographer scanned a part of my body I'd never heard of, the adnexa—an appendage to the uterus—to check for fibroids. Everything was normal. Seeing the living fetus on the screen, I could start to process this new plurality. It was 1.5 centimeters long, making itself at home in my womb, which was now the size of a tennis ball—it had doubled over the last few weeks.

During this period, when the baby was constructing herself, stretching my womb to make space for her growing body, severe nausea continued through each waking moment. My squished bladder woke me often in the night, interrupting my dreaming psyche. I would fret for hours in the dark, trying to make sense of what was happening, and what was to come. *A living being inside me, a living being inside me.*

I was being exposed to hormones that my body had never experienced before, some that didn't even have a name. Science had so ignored and overlooked the female body, not to mention the pregnant body, that it was hard to get a handle on what was happening. At the time, I had no idea that a number of hormones had increased in levels by 200 or 300 times. The tiredness was unlike anything I had experienced before. I would get home from work and immediately fall into a thick sleep on the sofa. Turns out it's quite a thing growing another person. Who knew?

All this hormonal churn may be what stirred up the silt of my consciousness. Impressions from the past were unlocked. The look of melted butter on a crumpet reminded me of a long drive at a wedding and of hay on the ground at dawn; a copy of *Antony and Cleopatra* triggered a flash of a black iron grille at my aunt's home in London in the late 1990s; going underwater in the bath transported me to a shopping mall in Helsinki.

Time started to bend. I was carrying the future inside me. I would learn that I was also carrying the eggs, already within my baby's womb, that could go on to partly form my potential grandchildren. My future grandchildren were in some way inside me, just as part of me spent time in the womb of my grandmother. I was carrying inside me a pool of amniotic fluid, which was once rivers, lakes and rain. I was carrying a third more blood, which was once soil and stars and lichen.[2] The baby was formed of the atoms of the earth, of the past and the future. Every atom in her body existed when the earth formed 4.5 billion years ago. She will live for many years, I hope, when I have returned to the ground. She will live on the earth when I am gone. Time bends.

O

By twenty-three or so weeks, I was in no doubt of our plural state. The baby throbbed and I throbbed back with welcoming relief. At first I thought I must be imagining the movements: it seemed fantastic that there should be a creature within me. But soon she moved definitely, regularly. A nail scratching. A foot pressing. A hand exploring. A head turning. As she grew, I wrote down that it felt like she was making Play-Doh figures with my innards. She moved my body independently of me. I was me, but not me. I was two.

I liked to watch my belly dome, and see her limbs move under my skin. I would stroke where her foot or hand might be and press gently while talking to attempt to communicate with her. I tried to remember my mother's womb, to imagine what life must be like in there. The pulse of a heartbeat. The bubbles of stomach and intestines. The water sweet and hay-like. Held, comfortably suspended.

If I couldn't feel her at all I would fly into a teeth-gritted anxiety, terrified that she was ill or had died. I'd drink something sweet or eat chocolate and lie down to feel out for her. Usually she would move. If not, I'd go to the hospital to be monitored on a machine. I'd watch the red LED numbers of my heartbeat and hers, which was much faster than mine. Two hearts under one skin.

It was disconcerting sharing my body with another, a being with her own drive, her own future, her own vulnerable corporeality. I was confronted, for the first time, with my fundamental lack of control.

I didn't learn anything about these emotional or existential aspects of pregnancy in the week-by-week books or the apps, which mostly discussed the size of the baby in comparison to fruit. Kiwi, banana, pineapple. Even though most pregnancies involve a level of stress and emotional disturbance, such as anxiety, depression, worry, insomnia and impaired concentration, the information in pregnancy emails was about baby outfits and how much coffee one could drink. The psychological destabilization that came with being inhabited by another person was left unaddressed.

Overcome by the strangeness of it all, I began to fall silent. Barely any of my peer group had children. I had friends around for a birthday cake and a cup of tea and I barely said a word. At my baby shower, I felt behind a pane of glass. I couldn't convey what was happening to me. "She feels herself vast as this world; but this very opulence annihilates her, she feels that she herself is no longer anything," wrote Simone de Beauvoir of pregnancy, managing to describe the experience with uncanny precision.[3]

It reminded me of early adolescence. That old feeling of teenage awkwardness, of not knowing what was going to happen next, or how to be. Of finding myself in social situations as a fourteen-year-old and being shy, unsure of what to say or how to act and wide open to judgment, criticism and the influence of others. Of being unsettled by the changes in my body, the growing breasts, the blood. Crimson on white tissue paper. A dawning awareness that this meant I was becoming a new being. My parents were emotional that day. I didn't understand it then, but I do now. The end of childhood.

In adolescence, though, there were rituals and rites of passage and songs and films and fashions and slang. We bonded and reinforced who we were becoming through music and booze and phone calls and outfits and gigs and poetry. We watched films about coming of age, read books about coming of age, listened to songs about coming of age. It wasn't easy, but it was expected, and we were together. In pregnancy, in matrescence, I felt alone.

O

I tried to find out anything I could about what was behind the existential rupture and brooding I experienced in pregnancy. But these perspectives took some time to find.

It wasn't just that they were missing from contemporary pregnancy books or health apps: the fields of psychiatry and psychoanalysis have almost entirely ignored how pregnancy affects a woman's mind, body and development. Repression and denial of the pregnant and maternal body and experience is deeply entrenched. Rosemary Balsam, of the Western New England Institute of Psychoanalysis, calls this absence the "vanished pregnant body."[4] Indeed, I would discover that in Freud's twenty-three volumes of work there are only around thirty mentions of pregnancy.

It is almost as if the liminal pregnant state, the state of being two in one, no longer a discrete self, might make people feel uncomfortable. Balsam suggests Freud might've been referring to pregnancy and childbearing when he described how man "fears some danger . . .

[A] dread is based on the fact that woman is different from man, for ever incomprehensible and mysterious, strange and therefore apparently hostile."[5]

Strange. I did feel strange, especially when I went swimming at the local lido. I walked out of the changing room, in my maternity costume, newly self-conscious, especially around men, especially towards the end. The male gaze felt different. Men averted their eyes from my spherical uterus. Was it because pregnancy is a sign of sex? Was I a symbol of bodily fluids—of ejections, seeping, slime, of the occult messy insides of the body? Was I reminding them of their own mothers and their early dependence? Was it, as Adrienne Rich suggests, simply that "he is reminded, somewhere beyond repression, of his existence as a mere speck, a weak, blind, clot of flesh growing inside her body?"[6]

I imagine it could have been, as the French philosopher Julia Kristeva writes, that "I am at the border of my condition as a living being," and this threshold state can be horrifying or sickening, for it reminds us of our corporeal reality, or, in other words, death.[7]

Finally, a couple of years later, when considering trying to have a second child, I found the work of the psychoanalyst and social psychologist Joan Raphael-Leff in a book called *Pregnancy: The Inside Story*, which was published in 1993. She explains pregnancy as a state of being between two worlds: "On a deep unconscious level, the pregnant woman hovers between internal and external worlds, at a crossroads of past, present and future; self and other."

Raphael-Leff offered me a language to describe the "emotional disequilibrium" and the reactivation of "dormant conflicts."[8] She developed the idea of the "emotional placenta," where internal images and unconscious historical facts are the nutrients or poisons that influence the "mental gestation" of pregnancy.[9] She normalized the internal distractions which disrupt the "ordinary illusion of unified identity and indivisibility." Looking back on the anxiety I felt, and the need for reassurance and monitoring, Raphael-Leff's concept of "internal badness"—the mother's fear about her own moral shortcomings and whether the baby would be able to withstand them—was illuminating.[10]

At the time I found the disequilibrium highly disturbing but I can see now that it was an inevitable and necessary part of the process of metamorphosis and a new, emerging concept of self. What was more difficult was the pressure to pretend that pregnancy was a less dramatic and drastic event than I felt it to be. Unlike in societies where ceremonies mark the transition from one stage of life to another, the pregnant woman in this "interim period of strangeness," as Raphael-Leff calls it, is made to feel profoundly alone.[11]

When we found out that our baby was a girl, my inner ferment deepened. I was nervous about bringing a girl into the world, and about how my relationship with her might play out. As I considered the daughter within me, long-forgotten senses, fears and feelings bubbled up. I looked at the predictions of climate breakdown and biodiversity collapse with a new intensity of alarm. She would be my age in 2047. How much of the Earth would still be habitable then?

It was heady. The baby was right there in the middle of it all. There was no hiding. I didn't realize until later that the essential activity of my pregnant body—processing and metabolizing the "good nutrients and bad waste" in order to feed the baby—would continue after she was born, through digesting and interpreting the baby's psychosocial experience of the world until she is able to do it for herself. As Raphael-Leff suggests, the "container" state of pregnancy is ongoing, perhaps indefinite.[12]

O

When I was around seven and a half months pregnant, or thirty-three weeks, London experienced a heat wave. I had a short-term contract editing at a trendy men's magazine near Soho and would take a bus every day to get there. A new leadership team was in place and I hadn't met them yet.

I put on a yellow and green oversized sack dress and left the house. It was early and quiet but the heat from the pavements was rising. Tomatoes in front gardens were punctured and collapsing. I was sweating by the time I heaved myself onto the bus. My feet were swollen with edema so I wore large, ugly sandals. When I pressed my fingers into my feet, the marks would stay for a while. My midwife told me that while sitting I should raise my feet. I would have to find some kind of box.

The new staff were younger and hipper than the ones I knew before. I didn't entirely get their jokes and references. They were all men, and the one woman I used to chat to had moved on. When I walked in I felt acutely aware of my pregnancy. People seemed to look away and avoid eye contact. Maybe they weren't expecting me, or my friend who left hadn't had a chance to tell them I had been booked in. When I approached the new editors' desks at various times of the day, I felt that they were willing me to go back to my chair. Was my massive bump making them feel uncomfortable?

I felt like Alice in the White Rabbit's house. In the 1951 film, she grows suddenly, her white-stockinged legs destroying everything in their way as they push through the ground-floor windows and doors, her arms squeezing through the upper-floor windows as the rabbit screams for "Help! Assistance!" She is stuck: too much, too expansive.

I was asked by the boss to track down a drug dealer for an interview in a way that suggested he didn't think I could. He glanced at my womb and his eyes flicked away. I had, I realized suddenly, become "mumsy."

The heat wave continued. The bus journeys were getting harder with my swollen feet and growing baby. I decided that I couldn't commute any more. I had suffered from nausea for a few days and the heat and my body were not on good terms. I felt no guilt—unusually for me—about bowing out of the contract. I felt exceptionally calm and placid, pleasantly vague, like nothing could touch me. In those final weeks it was as though there was a force field around me and the baby within. It was remarkably different to the low-level hum of anxiety I had lived with during most of the pregnancy. I'd made lots of normal social plans for that time towards the end, but my body seemed to have new ideas. I found that I wanted to be near home and I was happy to be alone.

Later I would discover that there are physiological changes unique to the many discrete stages of pregnancy, including the very end. In the 1990s and early 2000s, researchers in the field of endocrinology—the study of hormones—found that as pregnancy advances the reactivity of the stress response system is dampened. It takes a larger dose, for example, of exogenous CRH (corticotropin-releasing hormone) to trigger an ACTH (adrenocorticotropic hormone) response, which stimulates the production of cortisol. In other words, the hormonal changes the pregnant body undergoes seem to dampen its reaction to stress towards the end of pregnancy, meaning that a woman in the later stages might feel relaxed.

In a study published in the *American Journal of Obstetrics and Gynecology*, the scientist Laura Glynn found that women in late pregnancy rated being in an earthquake less stressful than did those who were in early pregnancy.[13] Women in the postnatal period, however, had similarly high stress responses to those in the first trimester of pregnancy. The data also suggested that the degree of stress experienced earlier on in pregnancy affected gestation length—women who experienced the earthquake sooner in their pregnancies had shorter pregnancies. From this, Glynn and her research group concluded that there may be a down-regulation of physiological and behavioral stress responses in late pregnancy. Why would this be? They theorized that increased immunity to stress may protect the mother and unborn baby from the negative impact of potential threats and raised cortisol levels in the final weeks.

A number of studies have found that women in late pregnancy develop a heightened ability to identify emotions in facial expressions. "Emotion-reading superpowers," as Linda Geddes puts it in *New Scientist.*[14] Late in pregnancy, it seems women can parse emotions associated with threat or harm—fear, anger and disgust—especially well. This enhanced emotional perception is associated with high levels of the hormone progesterone, which can increase by fifteen times during pregnancy (with previous studies also suggesting that this sensitivity in nonpregnant women increases when levels are highest during the menstrual cycle). Rebecca Pearson, a leading researcher in maternal health, suggests this might be an evolutionary adaptation to prepare the mother to protect and nurture a baby and become more vigilant.[15] But higher sensitivity could also make new mothers more vulnerable to anxiety.

Still, most of the information women are given in mainstream health literature relates the hormonal experience of pregnancy to physical characteristics—the body is preparing to make milk, the ligaments are relaxing to make room for the growing baby—or to the simple narrative that pregnant women might cry more at sad films.

Much of my life had been spent eye-rolling at gendered ideas about female hormones, which seemed always to stereotype and tether women. Even so, I had often taken the contraceptive pill throughout my menstrual cycle so as to avoid the business entirely, suppressing my cycle so I wouldn't have to bleed and could have more control of my body. I repressed these parts of myself that I deemed "feminine," which would have me put in a box and labeled, in order to get ahead in a man's world. I had been afraid of being labeled "hormonal" and not taken seriously. But in pregnancy, in matrescence, I had no choice. The neurobiological changes were so dramatic and uncontrollable that I simply had to find a way of integrating my new, female animal body into my sense of myself.

O

I was, on the whole, intrigued by the way my body was changing. While having lunch with a friend at a café, she asked, What are you thinking about feeding? I'm excited, I said. I think it's amazing that my breasts will produce milk. A couple of droplets came out the other day. It tastes sweet. How amazing that I can make milk! And it's free, and I think quite straightforward. You can do it wherever, you don't need any equipment. It will save us money for the first six months or however long.

I was breastfed, every mother I knew breastfed. Of course I would breastfeed. Breast is best.

Later that day, I sat in the hospital waiting room. We pregnant women gave each other shy smiles. Some sat on their own, others next to partners. There was a hum of excitement in the air. A public service reel about breastfeeding played on an old-school TV in the corner of the room. Breast milk is great because mum will never run out, it said. I sat, in awe of my body, in awe of the fact I would be able to make enough food to sustain a baby's growth for six months or more.

We attended a class on feeding at the hospital soon after. A midwife sent a knitted boob down the row and showed us how the baby would latch on. We were instructed to wait until the baby's mouth opened wide and then guide the nipple into the mouth, giving the baby more of the flesh of the breast underneath than on top, and then guide the mouth over and on to the areola to latch on. We were told about the many benefits to mother and baby, and that it would help us lose our baby weight and shrink the uterus. We were told about supply and demand: how the body makes more milk, the more the baby feeds. How we should let the baby feed whenever they wanted to. There was a short section about formula milk, mostly focused on how dangerous it could be if bottles weren't sterilized properly.

A man raised his hand. Can I help with the night feeds by giving the baby some formula?

The room went quiet. People's printed handouts ruffled and a fan whirred.

It's much better for baby to be fed directly from the breast at the beginning, or from breast milk in a bottle, said the midwife, coolly. After about eight weeks or so, once breastfeeding is established, mum can pump milk and then dad can help out.

My mind wandered into a milky reverie about how lovely it would be when my baby was out and I could feed her.

I'd put on quite a bit of weight in my pregnancy, so I was relieved that this simple action would sort that out. As my midwife said, nine months on, nine months off. I would shrink back to my normal state in no time.

○

One evening, I was discussing the concept of "womb envy" with my husband. The theory is that, historically, men's desire to work, to create and to dominate women and control their reproduction arose because they were envious of a woman's biological ability to bear children.[16] It was an idea developed in the early twentieth century by the German psychoanalyst Karen Horney.

I don't think that's right, he frowned. Boys, kids, at school, nursery, are driven to do stuff, and make things, probably without a sense that they can't carry a baby.

He found a thread on Reddit. It was titled: "I'm a guy and I wish I could be pregnant."[17]

In the post, the writer explains how much he wishes he could experience pregnancy. "If it were possible to give me a uterus transplant I'd consider it," he writes.

The post had been voted 96 percent "unpopular." It was one of the most unpopular opinions ever seen on the forum.

The top comment was "Lmao wtf," made by a moderator.

Others commented:

"This is absolutely insane."

"I'd happily shoot my uterus in the face, so I can't say I understand or relate. Out of curiosity, are you looking for the whole bleeding crotch experience too or just the pregnancy?"

"No I will not deform my meats into a living house for another human being who will then claw their monstery way out of a way too small orifice."

Hundreds of comments made by people disgusted by the idea of pregnancy.

Defensively disparaging birth and pregnancy is a consistent feature of Western misogyny, which the writer Siri Hustvedt suggests might be summarized as: "it may look as if pregnancy and birth are all about women, but they're really all about men."[18] Hustvedt quotes the anthropologist Margaret Mead, who wrote that it is men "who spend their ceremonial lives pretending it was they who had borne the children, that they can 'make men.' "[19]

This strange pretense, with its strong whiff of envy and anxiety, is smeared all over the historical sources of wisdom that we cleave to. Here's Aeschylus: "The one who gives birth is the man who impregnates her."[20] Here's Thomas Aquinus: "Woman is defective and misbegotten, for the active force in the male seed tends to the production of a perfect likeness in the masculine sex; while the production of woman comes from defect in the active force or from some material indisposition, or even from some external influence."[21]

The extremity of the outpouring online was interesting to me. Horney and Kristeva might chalk it up to a masculine fear and loathing of the generative power of the mother.

Here's what the commenters didn't know. Despite the challenging symptoms, both physical and emotional, being in the closest possible physical relationship with another being was one of the most enlivening, wild and interesting experiences of my life.

Eels

The eggs of the European eel hatch in the Sargasso Sea.

The eel larvae are transparent, and look like scraps of see-through ribbon or Scotch tape with eyes and teeth. They join the Gulf Stream and travel for 5,000 kilometers through the Atlantic Ocean, and when they reach the edges of Europe, after a year or two of drifting, they change into glass eels. In this stage, the eels are still see-through but thinner, like cellophane noodles. As they enter new habitats—fresh water, brackish waters—they darken, and change into elvers. While living in fresh water, they mature yet again into yellow eels, fattening and growing over six to twenty years. When they are ready to reproduce, they transform into silver eels with a metallic body and larger eyes.

Five life stages, thousands of kilometers and multiple habitats later, they return to the Sargasso Sea to spawn and die. Some European eels live for half a century. Human activity—including habitat destruction and overfishing—has led to a 95 percent decline in forty years.

3.

Zombie cells

This is where it transpires whether subject and object separate in the sense of the classical knowledge relation, or whether the subject enters the object to such an extent that the latter gives up its object character, indeed its presence and capacity for oppositeness as such.

Peter Sloterdijk, *Bubbles*

Twenty-first-century biology is fundamentally different from twentieth-century biology. It is a biology of relationships rather than entities. The biology of anatomic individualism that had been the basis of genetics, anatomy, physiology, evolution, developmental biology, and immunology has been shown to be, at best, a weak first approximation of nature.

Scott Gilbert, "Rethinking Parts and Wholes"

Towards the end of pregnancy, when I felt sick or sore or tired or scared, I looked forward to having my body back: to being just me again, able to eat cheese and unlimited chocolate and drink five coffees a day. I thought, then, pregnancy was transient, a nine-month event, that my body was a box to grow a baby in. Once she was out, I'd return to my normal self.

Not so fast. During pregnancy, cells are exchanged between the mother and fetus via the placenta. When the baby is born, some of those cells remain intact in the mother's body. For decades.[1] Perhaps forever. The phenomenon is called microchimerism. The exchange creates what the leading geneticist Dr. Diana Bianchi calls a "permanent connection which contributes to the survival of both individuals."

Cells have been found in subsequent siblings, too. If you have a younger brother or sister, they may have your cells within them, and, if they are older, their cells may be within you. Maternal cells also remain in the child. Dr. Bianchi and her team also found that a live birth was not required for a woman to "become a chimera," meaning an organism containing cells from two or more individuals. Women who have miscarried will likely carry fetal cells within them.

How does this cell exchange happen? Humans have one of the most invasive placentas among mammals. The human placenta invades around one hundred uterine vessels and arteries and grows thirty-two miles of capillaries. If the capillaries in one placenta were laid out on the River Thames they would stretch across the entirety of London. The tissues formed by the placenta to keep the baby alive would cover the floor of a small room (120 to 150 square feet). The invasiveness of the placenta means more cellular exchange, which would suggest humans have more microchimerism than other species. When I was pregnant with my second child, after learning about this phenomenon, I was in awe of the placenta within me, and a little bit intimidated. It enabled the baby to eat and drink me.

In 2012, a research group in Seattle conducted a postmortem analysis of the brains of fifty-nine women who had carried babies.[2] Almost two-thirds—63 percent—of the women had traces of DNA from fetal cells in their brains. Fetal cells have also been found in the liver, heart, lung, spleen, intestine, uterus, kidney, lymph nodes, salivary glands, heart, blood and skin. The baby's impact on the maternal body extends far beyond the womb, endures long after delivery.

Why are these cells sticking around? What are they doing? How do they influence maternal biology and experience? There is a range of hypotheses.

Dr. Amy Boddy, a biologist at the University of California, Santa Barbara, takes an evolutionary approach to the subject.[3] In the 2010s, while studying breast cancer and reading the literature, she discovered that scientists had found fetal cells in tumors in the breast.

"I thought: that's weird," she told me, over Zoom from her home in California. She dug in a little more and found that fetal cells were also remaining in other tissues in the maternal body, and specifically in "really interesting, reproductively important tissue" that might play a role in maternal health.

She started working in this area while pregnant with her second child. Unlike her easygoing first pregnancy, she found the second demanding and exhausting, which drove her interest in the conflict between fetal and maternal systems. Sometimes the baby *wants more than the mother can give*.

The lingering cells may just be a by-product of the lodger's exit. But, in Boddy's view, they must be there for a reason—possibly to do with the baby's survival.

"Over one hundred million years of evolution, there is definitely time for manipulation of the maternal system," Boddy said, likening it to an insurance policy for after the baby is born, especially in humans, where infants require intensive parental care.

One theory links it to breastfeeding. Fetal cells in breast tissue might help lactation, which is in the baby's interest. They may also trigger the expression of important hormones in the maternal body, such as prolactin or oxytocin, which are respectively associated with feeding and bonding.

The impact of these microchimeric cells is a controversial and contested area of research. The presence of fetal cells in healed Cesarean section wounds suggests they could migrate to the site of damage to help in repair. But they're also found at sites of disease, which could suggest they may have detrimental roles. Pre-eclampsia—a common but serious condition in pregnancy which raises blood pressure—is associated with an over-proliferation of fetal cells. Fetal cells are also strongly implicated in the pathogenesis of autoimmune diseases, such as Graves' and Hashimoto's, as well as thyroid disease and inflammation that might contribute to postnatal psychiatric illness.

Still, we don't know what the cells are doing at the sites of disease. They may have protective and regenerative roles: participating in tissue repair and regeneration, cell replacement or homeostatic maintenance. Women who have had children are more likely to survive lung cancer, which suggests that fetal cells—which establish in the lungs in particular—might suppress tumor development. They may have neutral roles, and be mere by-products.

The picture remains paradoxical. The interests of the mother and child are aligned in some areas but in conflict in others—both in pregnancy and once the baby is born.

Boddy suggested the research into fetal cells was in a similar place to microbiome science at the turn of the century. "People said, there's bacteria and it's important but we don't know much about it. And now we know it's very, *very* important for health. We're at that stage of microchimerism where we know we have this diversity of cells within us but we don't know how important that is yet."

Bianchi's landmark paper on microchimerism describes pregnancy as enacting a "long-term, low-grade chimeric state in the human female."[4] From the moment I was pregnant, I didn't just feel different. I *was* different. I *am* different. On a cellular level. I would never be singular again.

O

Everything was ready for the baby's arrival. We had bought soft new onesies and jumpsuits and friends had passed down clothes and slings. The baby would sleep in a family Moses basket and we had swaddles and a car seat. I learned that I would bleed for a while after giving birth, so I bought a box of sanitary napkins. That was it, I thought. Nothing I had read or heard suggested that what would come next would be a time *I* needed to prepare for.

I would end up needing around twenty boxes of specialist maternity pads for the blood loss following the birth.

In a meta-analysis of pregnancy lay literature and popular childbirth literature, academics Jennifer Benson and Allison Wolf found that the emotional and physical challenges of the postnatal period were "minimally acknowledged or simply ignored."[5] A major pregnancy book called *Your Pregnancy* dedicated just 0.08 percent of the book to maternal care after birth. Sections on maternal recovery focused on hair loss and weight loss.

Benson and Wolf conclude that the erasure of postpartum women in pregnancy and childbirth literature—what they call "the invisible postpartum mother"—is a form of misogynist oppression. They build on Sandra Bartky's theory of psychological oppression, in which the oppressed experience a "lack of a viable identity." "Frequently we are unable to make sense of our own impulses or feelings . . . because we are forced to find our way in a world which presents itself to us in a masked and deceptive fashion."[6]

It is no surprise, then, that a 2018 study by researchers at the University of Louisville, Kentucky, found that women leaving hospital after giving birth did not know about the risk factors for maternal mortality and problems, including mental illness. Over 60 percent had no idea that pregnancy-related complications can occur for up to one year after birth.[7]

O

In the final days of pregnancy I hauled myself out of the house, barreled down the road and into a local park. The boundaries between myself and the rest of life here were thinner, more porous. I felt open to the processes around me, as if the membrane of my consciousness was stretching, like the taut skin across my stomach. I lifted my hand to stroke the bark of a plane tree. I was starting to find more of a mirror, or a sense of kinship, in the natural world than I did in any of the books or leaflets I read, or the stories I heard, which failed to provide a compass for the existential upheaval I was experiencing. I was beginning to understand myself in a new way, as an ecological being. Suddenly, I smelled flesh. I lifted my head. It smelled like meat, blood, burgers, salt. I looked around and saw a shape on the ground. My eyes focused and I walked towards it. It was the wings and remains of a bird. The feathers were striped in light and dark brown and its body had been removed. All that remained were the soft wings and strands of sinew, tissue and blood on its skeleton and cartilage. The smell was so strong I had to walk away. The bird would degrade and disintegrate, as my baby strengthened and fattened.

I imagined how she must feel in my womb, cramped and tight, warm and soft, bound by the elastic walls of abdominal muscles and fascia. A house within a house. She could be touching the blue ribbed scarf of the umbilical cord, waiting for the pattern of food she had become used to. I thought about how life started, for all of us. That experience we all have in common: we began in a body, in loud fluid, within a tight space, a dark, wet, rhythmic nest, in a being also becoming. Our first world.

I felt a great sense of responsibility to bring her safely onto the earth. Tears of tension fell. My patience waxed and waned. The world was beautiful. Colors were vivid. Birdsong was a symphony. Then, I would be fed up. I couldn't sleep. I couldn't talk. I was obsessed with the baby's departure from my body, our first uncoupling. Aquatic to terrestrial, dark to life, occult to revelation, small hot cave to earthly consciousness. Memories of childhood teachings about Ruach from Genesis—the spirit that moves over the face of the waters—lapped over me in the early hours of the morning.

The magma was melting, the mantle would shift, and soon there would be an eruption, though I didn't know exactly when, or what form it would take.

PART II

Volcano

A volcano is an opening. It is a hole, between our bit of the Earth up here and the crust of the Earth down there. Beneath the crust, there is magma, gas and ash. When magma travels above the earth, it is called lava. Lava forms different types of rock when it's extruded: tuff, pumice, obsidian, basalt.

No one can predict when a volcano might erupt. Volcanoes are diverse, as well as capricious. Hawaiian eruptions are associated with lava fountains. The lava is fluid and forms rivers and lakes, moving slowly but steadily. Strombolian eruptions are characterized by gassier lava which spurts into the air up to 10 kilometers as if shot from an enormous water pistol. Vulcanian eruptions are caused by pasty, thick lava which can cause a buildup of pressure and lead to even bigger explosions. Plinian eruptions are the most destructive. One of these wiped out Pompeii and Herculaneum.

Volcanoes erupt when magma—hot liquid rock—rises to the surface. This can be caused by activity in the Earth's crust, such as tectonic plates pulling apart or when one plate is pushed under another. If tectonic plates collide in a particular way, the temperature and pressure cause the plate to melt the mantle. The buoyant magma rises through the throat, or canal, of the volcano and, if the pressure is just so, can erupt through the main opening, the neck or cervix.

Volcanoes are the ultimate agents of change. They can destroy but they can also create. Few beings are more dynamic. Their explosions create new landforms: islands, mountains, coastlines. In 2020, eruptions caused the coast of the volcanic island Nishinoshima to grow by five hundred feet. In 2009, an underwater volcano created a new island off the coast of Tonga.

4.

Birth

When Ina said to me one evening with real anger in her voice, "I don't ever want to see another John Wayne movie again" I knew exactly what she meant. So many of the women in Western movies were simply the background figures standing at stoves or pleading with their husbands not to go out to a gunfight. You hear a lot about the gunfights in Westerns; you don't hear so much about hauling up the water after a perineal tear.

Robert Caro, *Working*

If they are educated or influenced by Western philosophy, they learn to minimize and fear birthing labour, which I believe should stand at the centre of a maternal history of the flesh.

Sara Ruddick, *Maternal Thinking: Toward a Politic of Peace*

The overriding impression I got, from birth classes at the hospital and the books and information I read, was that, as I had a low-risk pregnancy with no complications, I should strive for a "natural" or "normal" birth. This didn't just mean delivering the baby through the vagina, it also meant giving birth without "unnecessary" interventions or analgesics, and also with a particular attitude.

Achieving a "natural" childbirth, as I understood it, meant that I would use hypnobirthing, breathing exercises, active birth positions (rather than lying on my back) and gas and air (if I really, really needed it) to calm my fears and lessen the pain. If I avoided pain relief, such as an epidural or meperidine, I understood, the birth was more likely to go well, and, crucially, my baby would be born alert which would, I heard, help us bond and establish breastfeeding. If I could manage without pain relief, that would be better for everyone. I heard that an epidural—an injection of anesthetic into the spine—could slow labor down and I wouldn't know when to push. On an NCT information page, I read that an epidural could affect the baby, but also that epidurals had little or no effect on the baby.[1] I was confused by the mixed information, so I decided to go with options that would protect the baby from any (supposed) risks. Implicit in all of this was the idea that using pain relief would be putting my needs above the baby's and that the pain wouldn't be too bad.

I kept hearing the phrase "a cascade of interventions" which I understood I needed to avoid at all costs by taking control and letting my body do what it could naturally do, so long as I was active, calm, relaxed and bold enough with my birth plan in the hospital. There was a sense that I should leave things to "nature," and that I must be wary of people trying to meddle. I could overcome any issues if I had the strength of mind to cope with the pain. I was frightened by the idea of our baby being pulled out with forceps or a ventouse and I wanted to do what I could to avoid that.

Before pregnancy, I was wary of any fetishization of the "natural." I was aware that "natural" as a label was a misnomer, frequently used to sell products or to promote nostalgic yearning, rather than to refer to anything real or tangible. I liked evidence, data and research. I was suspicious of ideology, of fantasies that concealed old lies. But I also wanted a birth that I could control in some way. So I was attracted to the idea of a "natural birth" without pain relief. Looking back, now, I realize how potent the ideology is, and how it intersects powerfully with broader ideas about how women should be and behave, and what they should tolerate.

My knowledge of what birth actually entailed was as scant as the details of the first birth I was told about, from the Gospel of Luke: "While they were there, the time came for the baby to be born, and she gave birth to her firstborn, a son. She wrapped him in cloths and placed him in a manger, because there was no guest room available for them."

Birth was, I thought, a non-affair. Painful, yes. But not a big deal. No one talked about it. A couple of friends had babies years before I did, and we would change the subject if they brought up anything to do with childbirth. We didn't know what to say.

O

"Natural childbirth" has had a renaissance over the last twenty years, but suspicion of medical interventions—of technology—has much older roots.

As late as the 1930s, childbirth was still extremely dangerous for women and babies in the UK. One pregnancy in two hundred ended in maternal death—that's nature for you—until 1935.[2] Through the nineteenth century, birth had become increasingly medicalized but the impact on women was complex. Childbirth had previously been the domain of women—overseen by a female birth attendant, or midwife, who would use knowledge and skills passed down through communities and word of mouth, such as the use of herbal medicine and birthing positions. But in the eighteenth century the rise of obstetrics (led by male doctors of medicine, as women were excluded from learning) and the "man-midwife" wrested power, prestige—and the better-paid work—from traditional midwives.[3] Mothers were caught in the middle of this struggle for the control of childbirth.

The problem wasn't just that midwives were annoyed that men were monopolizing their ancient work. There were grave consequences to the shift to a male-led, more mechanical approach to childbirth. One of the primary drivers of high maternal mortality rates in the early twentieth century was the number of unnecessary or misguided medical interventions, particularly the heavy-handed and unskilled use of forceps.[4] Epidemics of puerperal fever, caused by doctors delivering babies without washing their hands after touching cadavers, broke out in modern hospitals, having been far less prevalent in midwife-led spaces.[5] In the 1930s, the development of antibiotics, safer Cesareans and antimicrobials would significantly reduce the rate of mortality.[6]

The historian Jean Donnison records that doctors exaggerated the dangers of childbirth to scare women into believing male attendance was necessary. Men-midwives argued that managing difficult births was beyond the capacities of women; some even called for the abolition of midwifery. The educated male doctor represented the post-Renaissance enlightened age while midwives, whose ranks included illiterate and superstitious women and who had in recent history even been executed as witches, appeared to be relics of a past which scientific knowledge was discrediting.[7]

This isn't to say that medical measures hadn't made birth better for women at all: pain relief techniques had begun to improve the birth experience as early as the mid-nineteenth century. In 1847, the discovery of chemical anesthesia led to the use of chloroform in labor, including by Queen Victoria in 1853.[8] When James Young Simpson, professor of Midwifery in Edinburgh and the creator of the type of forceps used today, gave it to a patient called Mrs. Carstairs, she was so grateful she named her baby girl "Anaesthesia."[9]

In 1914, a group of American feminists set up the Twilight Sleep Association to advocate for the use of "Twilight Sleep," a mixture of morphine and scopolamine administered to women during labor, which meant that they would forget the experience and not feel pain.[10] Scopolamine was extracted from a pretty, mauve-colored, bell-like flower, also called devil's breath. In 1914, an American woman called Francis X. Carmody gave birth with it in Freiburg, Germany, where the method was common, and popularized it on her return to New York, from where it spread.[11] One of these supporters, Constance Todd, wrote in a letter to *The New York Times* in 1936 of the "blessed oblivion" of her own labor.[12] Similar associations sprang up in England, which saw the formation of the National

Birth Trust Fund in 1928.[13] It was led by a group of women who campaigned to improve maternity care and particularly to extend access to pain relief to lower-class women.

Not everyone was pleased by these moves to minimize women's pain in birth. Simpson's early call to employ pain relief "by every principle of true humanity" in 1847 was opposed by clergy and physicians for religious and moral reasons: in Genesis, Eve is cursed by God for eating the apple, her punishment being that childbirth should hurt—"I will make most severe Your pangs in childbearing; In pain shall you bear children."[14] (Adam's punishment was to deal with thistles and wild plants, which seems a little unfair.)

This Bible verse inspired the confused belief that "natural" or "normal" childbirth meant childbirth without pain relief, which was further fueled by a romantic conflation of "natural" with "moral" or "good." The idea took hold among moral arbiters and medical practitioners alike and, in the 1930s, a row broke out in the Letters section of *The New York Times* when a doctor alleged that pain in childbirth was an "essential experience" and that pain relief "may cause great damage to . . . personality."[15]

It wasn't until 1956 that pain relief in childbirth was sanctioned by Pope Pius XII. But, in his address on the matter, he reiterated the same moral arguments wielded by its detractors. First, that childbirth wasn't always painful, or didn't have to be painful. Second, the pains are the fault of the woman's attitude or behavior in labor. "It could be true that incorrect behavior, psychic or physical" in laboring women caused or increased difficulties in childbirth, he said. Third, childbirth pain and suffering may have spiritual value. "Suffering can be a source of good, if she bears it with God, and in obedience to his will."[16] So, essentially, take the drugs, but only if you want to be a terrible Catholic.

This idea that extreme pain is valuable might seem strange, but you can see it stretching into the modern day. In 2008, Belinda Phipps, then chief executive of the NCT, said: "If we just dropped babies like eggs without noticing, what would that say about the responsibilities we're taking on for the next twenty years? Birth marks you out as a mother and a carer for a very long time."[17] In 2009, Dr. Denis Walsh, a leading midwife in the UK, wrote a piece about the overuse of epidurals: "Pain in labour is a purposeful, useful thing, which has quite a number of benefits, such as preparing a mother for the responsibility of nurturing a newborn baby," he said, echoing the pope's statement half a century earlier that "motherhood will give the woman suffering to bear."[18]

Contractions—the source of most pain during childbirth—are obviously useful: the uterus is literally pushing the baby downwards. However, there is no evidence that pain in birth helps prepare mothers for looking after a baby. Perhaps Walsh was making a radical, roundabout point about the masochism required to be a mother in today's unforgiving society. Or a more philosophical point about how suffering can be heroic, a test of strength, and surviving it is therefore empowering for some. In any case, it shows there is more to the idea of giving birth "naturally" than not having a "sleepy baby"—the oft-repeated and emotionally powerful phrase some birth educators give as a reason to avoid proper pain relief—at the end of it.

The notion that the pain of childbirth could be tolerable and even empowering was also central to the work of prominent second-wave-feminist birth activists such as Sheila Kitzinger, Janet Balaskas and Ina May Gaskin, who influenced multiple generations with their call to give women more choice and autonomy in their birthing experience. They advocated woman-centered, midwife-led, female-controlled and non-medicalized birthing environments, and worked to claim power and control back from male-dominated obstetrics. Kitzinger—perhaps the most influential voice in the movement—believed that pain in childbirth could be "constructive": she wanted to give women the choice to experience the "pain of creation, of mountains moving, of energy welling up from your pelvis."[19] She believed that the environment and love shown to women in labor was instrumental in allowing the pain to be experienced in a positive way.

But real choice and autonomy are beyond reach for many women today, as the birth experience is obscured by myths and half-truths. Women are made to feel that they have failed if they haven't achieved an intervention-free, analgesic-free birth. In fact, the failure lies with the decision not to give women all the facts, not to prepare them for the risks and the reality.

O

Who made this decision? As I read, I realized that we owe our contemporary fixation on "natural childbirth" not to feminists or faith leaders who preached the value of pain, but to a midcentury English obstetrician called Grantly Dick-Read, who coined the phrase. Dick-Read proposed the curious idea that "healthy childbirth was never intended by the natural law to be painful." His theories were laid out in a number of popular books, including *Revelation of Childbirth* (1947), in which he writes that "woman herself . . . is adapted primarily for the perfection of womanhood, which is, according to the law of Nature, reproduction."[20] From this patriarchal conception of womanhood, the notion of "natural childbirth" was born.

Dick-Read's influence has been immense. The NCT was founded in 1956 in order to "promote and better understand" his method and teachings.[21] His books were hugely popular and translated into numerous languages. Their teachings traveled to the United States and elsewhere via the increasingly popular "Lamaze technique" and the "Bradley method," both of which offered women practical tips for dealing with pain in labor and achieving a natural birth, and focused largely on breathing techniques. In the 1950s Dick-Read received a silver medal from the pope for his services to "natural childbirth." The BBC filmed him delivering a baby, which was the first birth shown on television. There is a quote on the back of an old edition of *Revelation of Childbirth* from Queen Elizabeth II. "Into a world where pain and fear are rampant, this book brings a message of hope," she wrote.

Dick-Read rightly wanted to protect women from the "sepsis, infection and haemorrhage" that could be brought about by anesthetics and forceps, which had been catastrophically misused in the preceding decades. But his portrayal of birth and motherhood was highly idealized, and wrapped up in sentimental ideas of the maternal. Birth is normally "carried out by *natural* processes from beginning to end, influenced by *natural* emotions and perfected by the harmony of the mechanism [with the woman] conscious throughout the progress of her baby's birth."[22] Motherhood was a "holy estate" of "supreme happiness."[23]

Revelation of Childbirth begins with the story of a birth that Dick-Read attended early in his career in Whitechapel. He offered the laboring woman chloroform, which she declined. Afterwards he asked her why. "It didn't hurt. It wasn't meant to, was it, doctor?" she replied.[24] The line returned to him repeatedly over the next months until he "saw the light" and realized "there was no law and no design in nature that could justify the pain of childbirth."[25] It was not meant to hurt, he decided.

Why, then, does it? He believed that the "more cultured the races of the earth have become, so much the more positive they have become in pronouncing childbirth to be a painful and dangerous ordeal."[26] Civilization and culture had caused "fear and anticipation" to tense up the muscles of the body and create pain. The "modern" woman had lost the art of birth-giving, lost touch with her "natural instincts" and instead was faced with the dangers of "interference" from an obstetric doctor or midwife. He placed her in stark contrast with the "primitive" woman who "isolates herself, and, in a thicket, she quietly, patiently waits."[27]

His objective in persuading women that childbirth didn't hurt was about more than their sensory experiences: he felt there was a moral imperative to his call to breed: "If we are to survive as a people, and as an Empire, we must constantly be alert to improve our stock."[28]

In his correspondence and pamphlets, he comes across more as a spiritual pseudo-guru than a doctor, given to pronouncements such as, "No woman who remembers her child's birth ever ceases to love that child, and no child who has been born in love and learned of its mother's love, ever ceases to love its mother."[29] His obsession with mother-love is fervent, religious. Indeed, he was compared to Liberace and Elvis Presley in his ability to whip up hysteria. His writing is florid and highfalutin, antithetical to his scientific training. At the time, his claims were regularly disputed by other physicians for being unscientific, exaggerated and mystical. His theory that fear was the main cause of painful contractions was criticized for lacking evidence.[30]

But in many ways, Dick-Read's popularity at the time makes sense. After decades of dangerous obstetric heavy-handedness, his commitment to giving power back to individual women must have been highly attractive.

O

"Fear-tension-pain syndrome" is Dick-Read's most long-standing and influential theory. It holds that feeling frightened triggers the mother's fight-or-flight response, which inhibits labor progressing and causes pain. If a labor is uncomplicated, pain will only arise as a result of the sympathetic nervous system being aroused by fear, he said. Physical and mental relaxation is the solution.

At first glance, his fear-tension-pain syndrome does seem plausible. A "fight-or-flight" response may result in increased adrenaline and cortisol, as well as vasoconstriction (which could decrease oxygenated blood to organs including the uterus), all of which may increase pain.[31] And, of course, an environment free of tension or fear would absolutely be a good thing for a birthing woman. Nevertheless, his contention that a "child passes through a relaxed vulva with almost complete absence of sensation to the mother" is stunning in its fantasy and physiological ignorance.[32]

Still, his work is often quoted today in birth and breastfeeding conferences. In 2013, his final book, *Childbirth Without Fear,* was published in a new edition. It's quite remarkable that a man who believed that "woman fails when she ceases to desire the children for which she was primarily made" is still so influential. But traditional ideas about sex and gender emerge sharp-toothed from the shadows when women become mothers.

Do his claims about relaxation hold up to scrutiny? A systematic review of the major studies of relaxation techniques for pain management in labor, published in 2018 by the leading evidence-based review body, *Cochrane Review,* found that relaxation, yoga and music "may have a role in reducing pain" but the quality of the evidence was "low" to "very low." The majority of studies had a high risk of bias and the authors warned that the results should be read with caution.[33]

Another review by *Cochrane,* published in the same year, looked at the effectiveness and acceptability to women of opioid painkillers.[34] The authors were concerned about the effect of opioids on the baby. They analyzed a number of studies with data from over eight thousand women. They concluded that opioids do give some pain relief but that they can also cause nausea, vomiting and drowsiness. No clear evidence for adverse effects on the newborn was found. Again, the quality of the evidence was low, but the results were stronger.

Ideas about childbirth go in and out of fashion. My mother had meperidine—an opioid—when she gave birth to me in the 1980s. When I told women of her generation (born in the 1950s) that I was planning to eschew pain relief, apart from laughing gas, some seemed horrified. Why have today's childbirth norms swung so far back towards the "natural"?

O

In the 1980s, directly inspired by Dick-Read, Marie F. Mongan, a mother of four and erstwhile dean of a women's college in New Hampshire, started running self-hypnosis birthing classes using her own method.[35] Word spread and the classes grew in popularity. Mongan set up the HypnoBirthing Institute in New Hampshire and her ideas spread across the Western world. Speaking to the *Washington Post* in 2000, she said: "In birthing, when the mind accepts the belief that without complication, birthing proceeds naturally, no pain exists and no pain is experienced."

No pain exists and no pain is experienced.

Today, most NHS trusts offer hypnobirthing classes. The Rosie Maternity hospital in Cambridge, England, where I was born, offered hypnobirthing video tutorials for £39 at the time of writing in 2021. Books, DVDs, MP3s and weekend courses are popular. Most of my friends did hypnobirthing. It is mentioned in prenatal appointments as a way of making birth happier, calmer and more relaxed. "We have also found that babies born using hypnobirthing techniques tend to be more alert and feed and sleep better, as they have been brought into the world at their own pace in a more calm and gentle way," is how a consultant midwife at the Rosie described its highly appealing power. There is rarely any acknowledgment that the evidence for whether hypnobirthing works is limited. There are very few studies, and the evidence that exists is of low quality. A review of clinical studies published in the *Cochrane Review* in 2016 concluded that "there is not enough evidence to say whether hypnosis helps women feel more satisfied about their pain relief in labour, nor whether it improves their sense of coping with labour."[36] It found that hypnosis may reduce the overall use of pain relief in childbirth, but not an epidural. Another study, also limited by a small sample size, found that the women had "unexpectedly positive" experiences of self-hypnosis. Much higher-quality data is needed.

When I first gave birth, I believed what the leaflets and classes told me: that hypnobirthing would get me through. I believed what I heard on my hypnobirthing MP3s, especially those authorized by the NHS: *my body was the perfect body to birth my baby, my baby was the perfect size to be birthed by my body, my baby was in the right position to be birthed calmly and gently, I could choose to turn any discomfort into joy, safe in the knowledge that any unusual or new sensations were a natural part of birth.* These were the mantras that I listened to, over and over again, in the weeks and days leading up to the birth and as labor began. They were read by a soothing, relaxed, female voice, often with the sound of waves in the background. I could birth my baby, they suggested, *peacefully*. I just had to think positively.

Hypnobirthing is offered by NHS trusts because some women do find that it helps. Many women *want* to try and experience the power of giving birth without drugs. Epidural use in the UK fell by 6 percent between 2008–2009 and 2018–2019 (though this might not truly reflect mothers' choices: many women have reported being denied their request for an epidural).[37] The idea that birth could be a calm, gentle, even transcendental experience is seductive; it was very seductive to me. Assuming an upright position for labor, rather than being stuck on my back, made sense. Claiming agency in the birthing room, rather than passively awaiting interventions, was attractive.

But there was more to it than that. An uncritical embrace of "natural childbirth" has led birth discourse too far into the realms of myth and misinformation, and birthing women into a place of silence and shame. The understandable aim of giving women and birthing people choice, autonomy and agency has unfortunately been distorted by misogynistic ideas about women and pain. The truth is simply that birth *really* hurts for most women. Studies and figures vary but suggest that a third to 45 percent of women experience traumatic childbirth. It is believed that 4–6 percent of women will develop PTSD after giving birth.[38, 39]

Perhaps the cultural obsession with "natural" birth reflects the extent of our detachment from our bodies and from the Earth. We are so disconnected from the rest of the natural world that we don't know what "nature" is: bodies failing, cuckoos pushing eggs out of nests, a weirdly small human pelvis and a big infant head, illness and disease, shit and blood, ticks and cockroaches. "Natural childbirth" in the "natural world" often ends in infant or maternal death. "Natural" childbirth can end in clitoral tears, sepsis, rectoceles, fistulas and psychosis.

Our contemporary idea of what is "natural" is neutered and vague when it comes to childbirth, and, indeed, the wider world. It is a fantasy. Just as we want to think of nature as bluebells and lambs and rainbows—as, I imagine, a defense against death and mortality—so the mythical image of "natural childbirth" is a quiet woman, surrounded by fairy lights and oils and whale sounds, peacefully and lovingly bringing a child into the world.* If that is the expectation, and it doesn't go to plan, many women feel that they have failed.

Subscribing to this "natural" ideal of the female body and its functions was a volte-face for me. Before entering matrescence, I had learned to hide what was "natural"—body hair, evidence of menstruation, hormonal mood swings, any extra fat that deviated from prevailing ideas of beauty. I painted my nails and my face and dyed my hair, adhering to cultural norms. Now I was expected to reject all that technology, that "optimization," and return to my supposed earth-mother roots. Only this vision of what birth was like, of what my body should do, was a fabrication.

I wonder now whether the fantasy of "natural birth" persists in part because taboos around childbirth are still so potent. We don't have stories or images or songs or films about how humans are born, so ideals about women "breathing" a baby out can freely proliferate.

And perhaps we're sacralizing birth—the "ultimate phenomenon of a series of spiritual experiences," as Dick-Read would have it—in order to meet a growing hunger for the numinous in an increasingly secular world. Most of us lack access to such "spiritual experiences," unless we adhere to a religion. Perhaps the attraction of "natural" childbirth is that it corresponds to our quest for something "more," for feeling our bodies are powerful rather than degenerate, for facing danger and risk head-on. Childbirth has become a site for the sacred and that is understandable. It offers a means of connecting with the ritual events of human history. There is great power in birth, and many women do find it empowering. But there is a point at which the absence of information becomes manipulative.

O

By the time my due date came around, a Saturday, I was very ready for the baby to leave my body. My friend suggested eating a

---

* I'm not dissing whale sounds. I watched David Attenborough's *Blue Planet* in my third labor and watching whales and other sea creatures helped me to manage the pain.

burrito—it worked for her—so we did. The contractions started at about 9:00 p.m. I was happy, and excited.

My mother had gone into labor with me at about 10:00 p.m., and I had arrived at seven the next morning, so this was the template I expected. Some women, I read, had a longer early labor, and if that happened I could rest between contractions, go for a walk, have a bath or even bake brownies.

My mother had always told me the pain of childbirth was fine, that my large feet would make it easy because it supposedly meant my hips were wide. Then, towards the end of my first pregnancy, she broke rank. She told me the pain was really quite bad and questioned my decision to do it without drugs.

A contraction feels nothing like period pain, or an ache, or a cramp. It is not a familiar feeling, but a white-hot searing rumble. It is in the core of me—off, mysterious and frightening. My body, but not my body. A quake disturbs internal tectonic plates that shift and scrape and shake and clank. They last around sixty to ninety seconds, and there is a break of four or so minutes between them.

Within hours, my body was being overpowered. I was buckled by their force, crying out and falling to my knees. I needed to be leaning on the bed or my birth ball. I made a new sound, a deep, guttural moan. I was overwhelmed by how regular the contractions were, but I was also thrilled that we would meet our baby within hours, probably by the morning. I listened to my hypnobirthing tracks and read my positive birth books. I felt calm, but the pain was increasing.

By Sunday morning, the contractions were still at the same frequency. The pressure of a uterus contraction is, according to midwife lore, the same as a tube door closing. We hadn't slept. With *The Office* on in the background, we timed each one and jotted down the minutes in between, anticipating an increased frequency which would require a move to the hospital. Once there were three contractions in ten minutes we could go in.

Another twelve hours passed. It was now Sunday evening and I had been contracting in this way, this regularly, without any sleep, in increasingly intense pain, for twenty-two hours. Was this normal?

How would I have the energy to birth my baby? Over the phone, a midwife told us to come in.

It was dark by the time we got into the taxi. I'd checked that this taxi rank would take women in labor, as some refuse. I was relieved when he allowed us to sit in his car. I kept the TENS machine wrapped around my belly, grappling with the wires, and pressed the button as I tensed up every time we went over a speed bump. When a contraction hit, I felt embarrassed by the seething sounds my body made. I was a banshee, a tornado, I left myself and couldn't keep my mouth closed. I sat forward and breathed, trying to focus on the streetlights and the twenty-four-hour grocery shop where we got our pickles and labneh and bread and coriander and the upmarket kebab joint that had just opened and the jazz club and the laundrette and the pet parlor and the pizza place.

In the waiting room, women were bent over double and moaning. A man in Hasidic garb stood to one side. A woman next to me wearing a hijab was stroked by a companion. We were all waiting for the same process, for our cervix to open and thin, our taut doughnut of innermost pale pink muscle which must efface, ripen and dilate.

A kind midwife examined me. I was praying that my cervix would be 4 centimeters dilated and I could be admitted and get this baby out.

But I was only 2 centimeters dilated.

The size of a fucking Cheerio.

I had been contracting every four or so minutes, in profound pain, for twenty-six hours, and I was not even in established labor. Crestfallen, we were sent home. Home is the best place to be at the moment, said the midwife. We got back in a taxi.

By sunrise on Monday morning, I hadn't slept for two days. The gaps between contractions had only been a few minutes, not enough time to sleep. I felt confused and panicky. No one had said that early labor could last so long, and with such regular contractions. Was there something wrong? I thought about the movies. A woman's waters break in a puddle, she is rushed to hospital and a baby appears soon afterwards. Was that not how it goes? After another few hours of contractions, we went back to the hospital. The contractions were almost at the holy grail of three in ten minutes, and it had taken thirty-five hours. Thankfully, when examined, I was 4 centimeters dilated, meaning we could be admitted. Gas and air took the edge off. I hadn't taken any drugs or alcohol since entering recovery three years earlier, and I was secretly pleased to be able to get a licit high on nitrous oxide.

As my cervix effaced, so too did my previous self, the person I was before. As she was readying to be born, part of me was dying. As she was born, I was divided. I didn't realize this until later.

The birthing suite was windowless, so I lost sense of time. It was a large room, with a bathtub, a double bed and equipment to sit or squat on, or lean over. I contracted for some hours, gripping the lavender-sprayed pillow I'd brought from home. Another examination. Still 4 centimeters, after forty hours. With her fingers still inside me, the midwife offered to break my waters to speed the motion up. I agreed. She pierced the sac with a small crochet hook and a warm amniotic lake soaked the towels on the wipe-clean bed. A dial was turned up, the contractions intensified, juddering through me. I'd planned not to use pain relief, but I decided I wanted the opioid meperidine. I found myself quietly begging. I need it. Please. Let's try the water first, the midwives said, because you can't use the bath after taking opioid pain relief. In the pool, gas and air pipe clamped between my teeth, I started tripping.

A procession of characters I recognized from preverbal childhood danced in front of me. Objects from the depths of my psyche arrived to spur me on. A gunky slice of lava cake, crimson and egg-yolk yellow. With eyes and spindly legs. Three rabbits in woolen shoes, tap-dancing. A frog playing a creaking accordion. A hedgehog waltzing. A hare called Mr. Tibbins. I realized that everything that had happened in my life had led to this perfect, awful moment of giving birth to my child and it was always meant to be.

This is how big it needs to be This is how big it needs to be

This is how big it needs to be

This is how big

it needs
to be
This
is how
big it

needs to be
This is how

big it needs to

be This is how big it needs to be
This is how big it needs to be
This is how big it needs to be

Forty-one hours in, it was time for the final act, but my bladder was blocking the baby's exit. I was too high to wee, so the midwives inserted a catheter. To my dismay, the gas and air was withdrawn, so I had no choice but to push her out without any pain relief.

At one point, it appeared the baby could tear through my perineum, so I was swiftly moved into another stance. Over the next couple of hours, I was placed in various positions to harness the force of gravity: all fours, a sort-of chair pose, kneeling and, finally, lying on my side with one leg on a midwife's shoulder because, by then, I couldn't hold myself up. I was at my most feral and primitive. I wanted to burn the hypnobirthing industry to the ground.

Pushing a person out of my body was an extraordinary feeling. The pain was unrecognizable. I trusted the midwives and my husband, who were encouraging me, but surely I was dying or at least splitting in half. It burned and stung and my eyes rolled back and forward as I sucked in and held the oxygen that allowed my body to push. It took over an hour. Cut her out, cut her out, cut her out. I was birthing a hurricane. A spiked mace. A heap of barbed wire. A bladed melon. An inflated pufferfish. A prickle of hedgehogs. A Christmas tree.

Suddenly she was in jeopardy. Her heart rate had dropped. One of the midwives pressed a big red emergency button above the bed. Doctors multiplied, filling the room in seconds. I was naked and surrounded by people. It was remarkable to feel so vulnerable and watched and attended to after many years of self-reliance. A man asked permission to use a ventouse to suck her into the world. I could barely speak, so nodded. I was an animal now. Dying. I was terrified she could die. My insides and outsides, vagina and cervix, skin, muscle and soul roared. I had never wanted anything more than to get the baby out and for her to be alive and healthy. I pooled my last drops of strength into a final push. She broke through and spurted out. The barrier was breached; the seal broken. Her dark eyes were humongously wide. Her hands splayed open. She was placed on my chest. My heart exploded.

This is the sublime.

And still, it was not finished. Did I want an injection to speed up the placenta's ejection? After forty-three hours, I was over my wish for an intervention-free birth. It flopped out after ten minutes or so. I asked if I could see it before they took it away. It was surprisingly navy; bulbous, slimy, as big as a beret. I felt something for it, but I didn't know what. Where would they take it? A bin? The sea?

I looked around and my cave resembled a crime scene. Quickly and briskly, the blood was cleaned up. I was sewn back together in the middle of the room—I had a second-degree tear (vaginal, not anal, which are the more severe tears)—sucking on gas and air with my eyes resting on my daughter, naked on her father's bare chest.

O

"I'll come to the hospital," my mother had said. I hadn't understood why.

She strode into the birthing room as soon as she was allowed. Burst through the double doors and into my new world. She was familiar, but not.

And after the blood, the psychic splitting, the prospect of death (death lurks behind a veil in childbirth), I knew why she was there, why she had come.

"It was so bad," I said. So. Bad.

As I sat there with my daughter sucking fatty yellow liquid from my breast, I was mindblasted with the thought that this was what it takes for a human life to be.

O

In the days and weeks afterwards, I thought about the birth constantly. I felt the need to talk about it, but to whom? I recalled the ecstasy and the agony. I was in shock and also in awe of my body. I was fascinated by what happened, how overwhelming it was. How close to death I had felt. How close to death it felt like we had been. It was the most dramatic and frightening experience of my life. The pain and loss of control took me to a place that I don't think I've ever returned from. I wanted to talk about it, but there was no one really to talk to and there were only so many times I could subject my husband to reliving it over and over again. It felt isolating and alienating.

I would particularly dwell on the crowning, the moment the baby's head moved through the vaginal opening. It was such a new experience of pain, so awful and so full of power. The words we have for pain don't accurately describe it. People call it the "ring of fire" and there is a searing to it but it also felt like being pulled apart and turned inside out. The euphoria which followed was the highest high I have ever felt. I didn't want sleep deprivation to chew the memory away.

I was gripped by a desire to see pictures of crowning. I struggled to find this anywhere apart from the brief crowning shot in the film *Knocked Up*.

And then I stumbled across a page called Empowered Birth Project on Instagram. It showed the graphic pictures of childbirth I was after, but I noticed that many of the images kept getting taken down. The page mentioned there was a lot of censorship of real images on smaller birth sites, too.

Later in that first year, when I started researching matrescence, I spoke to the Empowered Birth Project's founder, Katie Vigos, a nurse based in Los Angeles. Why, I asked, did the photos keep getting removed by Instagram?

"The female body in the midst of giving birth—blood, pubic hair, buttocks, the image of a baby exiting a woman's vagina—seems to trigger people to report images," she said. "But there is no reason why we shouldn't be able to show photos of physiological birth. It's straight-up censorship."[40]

At the time, in 2017, Instagram categorized any image of genitals as offensive material, alongside pornography, threats of violence and hate speech.

Vigos believes that it comes down to the social belief that the female body is only desirable and acceptable in a certain state, that vaginas are "only OK when they're clean, tight and hairless—a porn pussy."

"It's sending a message to women that your power to give birth is offensive and obscene and should be hidden."

Lauren Archer, whose birth photos were removed, told me about the sense of shame she felt afterwards.

"As a woman, when someone censors you, there is this flicker of shame, this feeling of regret, like 'I must have done something inappropriate' even though I had nothing to be ashamed of."

Both women talked about the importance of seeing images of birth, of enabling women to conceptualize a vagina opening for a baby to pass through.

"As a mother or a mother to be, seeing photos of the raw strength and power of your body is utterly empowering," said Archer. "Birth is scary, but only because our society has shrouded it in mystery and shame. Allowing uncensored photos pulls back that curtain."

I was fortunate. I gave birth in a country with advanced medical practices and technologies that meant that we were at less risk. I was supported by a loving husband and good, smart and caring midwives. My daughter was jaundiced but healthy, and we could spend time together immediately. My second-degree tear was nasty but nothing like a third- or fourth-degree tear or severe birth injury.

And yet. I felt dismayed by the expectations I had held, as I realized how false and ideologically motivated they were. I had been misled. This was, I could see, partly a failure of language. Our vocabulary occludes the maternal: we do not have words for the different kinds of pain that occur in childbirth. "Pain" just doesn't cut it. And partly it was because of the continuing taboo around birth, even within the spaces where talking about tearing vaginas should happen. Remembering the moment when the pain was most severe, I felt furious. Angry that I hadn't been warned. And even though the physical suffering was over, the subsequent silence was a new, lasting violence.

On paper, I was told, the birth was "textbook." It was long, but it was "normal."

Looking back now, I wonder if the hypervigilant, anxious state of mind that followed the birth may have been a symptom of birth trauma or PTSD. I hesitate to use the word "trauma," because we were both fine—I had my beautiful, wonderful daughter in my arms. But for a few awful, life-changing moments, I thought that she might die. That I might die.

What we have come to accept as "normal" birth is, in fact, deeply disturbing for many women.

○

It is too soon to tell, perhaps, but things might be starting to change. In 2017, the year after I first gave birth, the Royal College of Midwives (RCM) ended its Campaign for Normal Birth. "What we don't want to do is in any way contribute to any sense that a woman has failed because she hasn't had a normal birth. Unfortunately that seems to be how some women feel," said Professor Cathy Warwick, the chief executive of the RCM.[41] The campaign had run since 2005.

In 2022, the shocking publication of the Ockenden review, an investigation of the avoidable deaths and injuries of many babies and mothers in Shrewsbury and Telford, found that an obsession with natural birth was partly to blame.[42] Women were denied Cesarean sections when they should have been given them. Staff were subject to targets to keep Cesareans low. They lacked compassion.

Following the report, the head of the RCM, Gill Walton, apologized for its part in promoting "normal" births that had contributed to the deaths of mothers and babies.[43] Walton said some midwives had turned understandable efforts to improve maternity care into a harmful ideology that had gone too far. She admitted that some aspects of the campaign were not evidence-based, such as telling midwives to "wait and see" and "trust your intuition" during labor.

Still, the fantasy persists.

○

I would go on to give birth to my second child, a son, at home, a few years after my daughter was born. I was desperate for a shorter labor, terrified of repeating the sleeplessness and torment of the first time round. I thought that the taxi journeys and being in the hospital with its bright lights might have slowed down the process of my first labor, and hoped that being at home might make it less drawn out. Statistically, I had been told, it was safer to have a second baby at home. And the hospital was five minutes away anyway.

The pain was, again, extraordinary. This labor was a tundra, cold and hostile. The midwives brought one can of nitrous oxide but they had to go back to the hospital to fetch more. Towards the end, the pain became hot and fiery, as if my body was filled with waves of lava. The baby was blocked in some way. He was moving down and back, down and back. A cervical lip was acting as an obstacle. Thankfully I had an experienced and skillful midwife who manually pushed it out of the way, letting his head descend. His body was fished out of me, slippery-quick. He was placed on my naked body as the midwives rubbed his back. And then, what we had been waiting for: a high-pitched meow-like desperate-sounding squeal. A cleaving. The purest Ecstasy pill in the world.

While waiting for the placenta to emerge and the shakes and shock to subside, I turned to my midwife. "How do you do such a scary job, and stay calm, when the outcome could be horrendous?" I garbled at her. "I trust women's bodies," she said.

It was not traumatic. Still, I wrote down afterwards: you must never, ever do this again.

But I did. This time, the third time, I prepared with all my might, using more realistic pain management techniques I learned from a book by the physiotherapist Juju Sundin,[44] along with the occasional positive, but measured, audiobook to calm my mind. The baby was ten days late. Since we were in the middle of the Covid-19 pandemic, I resolved to give birth at home so that my husband could be present. A few weeks before my due date I had freaked out and asked my midwife if I should have a Cesarean because of a historic anal fissure that had reopened painfully but a consultant said not to worry.

I went into labor in the evening, and the breathing exercises and visualizations did help me cope with the deranging contractions. But after eight or so hours, I was told that the labor needed help to progress. My waters were broken manually. What happened next was unexpected.

The baby's head moved rapidly through me and suddenly the pain was much more severe. I felt as if I'd been struck by lightning. His head was out of me, and his body still inside, for nearly five minutes. A person: half in, half out of me. Stuck. I froze. The lightning strike separated me from myself and took me to a different planet, completely alone, disconnected from anything good or familiar. A cold, numb, stunned and lonely pain. Eventually, a midwife pulled him out of me and he was quiet and blue. They rubbed him to life, rubbed the breath out of his lungs and into his brain, and he was brought forth.

But I was ossified. I couldn't move, I couldn't seem to turn to him. They placed him on my back. Eventually I managed to sit and hold him, euphoric. I noticed the water in the pool was very red.

After birthing the placenta, I was examined and the midwife thought my perineum needed a proper examination. An ambulance was called and I was separated from the baby, which was brutal.

In the hospital, my legs were placed up in stirrups, black and thick, and doctors discussed whether I'd had a third- or fourth-degree tear, otherwise called an Obstetric Anal Sphincter Injury (OASI). The baby's elbow—which was up by his head—had ripped through my perineum, rupturing and tearing through the muscles and walls of the anal sphincter and pelvic floor.

The hemorrhaging of blood was worrying the doctors so I signed consent for a blood transfusion and was swiftly wheeled into an operating theater, given an epidural, and operated on by a surgeon. Over the hour or so of the operation, I was attended to by kind nurses and healthcare assistants who stroked me, held my hand, buzzed to and from the baby to tell me he was OK. Within their care, their compassion, I began to heal.

Despite having given birth twice, I did not know before that moment that 3–6 percent of women suffer anal injuries during birth and that third- or fourth-degree tears are always through the sphincter.[45] A proportion of those women will have serious, life-changing, long-lasting complications. The issues worsen over time: over a quarter of women aged forty who have sustained sphincter injuries in childbirth will experience bowel incontinence, which rises to a third of women aged sixty.[46] Almost half of those women suffer postnatal depression. I did not know that midwives are not trained in perineal clinics. Or that being in water—where I was encouraged to be, and wanted to be, for pain relief—means that the midwife can't manually protect the perineum, an action that can prevent severe tearing. I did not know that the bigger the baby, the later the baby, the higher the risk of a significant tear. None of this information is given to women before birth.

I wonder if, as a culture, we will ever be able to take a realistic view of the pain and risks of childbirth. Perhaps it triggers such primal fear that we will never be able to consider it objectively. Do we avoid and deny the reality of childbirth, the pain and injuries it can cause, because we can't cope with the thought of what our own mothers might have gone through to have us? Perhaps we can't bear to imagine them overpowered by pain.

O

The long-term effects of birth and pregnancy on the body are rarely spoken about. When I started talking about my experience with others, I realized how common pelvic floor dysfunction such as prolapse was, and how inadequate postpartum healthcare is. I realized, too, that warnings about the dangers of epidurals were overblown. I felt, in some ways, a fool. Had I accepted the agony of childbirth without pain relief because I thought it was my due suffering, as a woman? Was this some kind of quasi-religious masochism, or deep-seated lack of self-respect and esteem?

Ranee Thakar has been a consultant urogynecologist for twenty years in Croydon, South London. In that time, thanks to the pioneering work of Thakar and her husband, Abdul H. Sultan, the recognition and repair procedure for birth injuries has changed and improved in hospitals and NHS trusts in England, and in other countries around the world. Sultan's research showed that anal and perineal injuries during childbirth leading to severe life-diminishing symptoms (such as fecal incontinence) were being missed by clinicians at the time of birth. Thakar and Sultan developed training courses to teach health professionals to recognize anal sphincter injuries and repair them properly. In doing so, they have vastly improved the quality of the lives of countless women. If the tear I suffered hadn't been surgically repaired, the impact on my day-to-day life could have been grim. In support groups I joined, the experiences of women who could barely leave the house because of anal incontinence were heartbreaking.

Speaking to Thakar from her office in Croydon, I asked what was standing in the way of giving women all the information *before* they gave birth. I was surprised to find out about a long controversy around checking for anal sphincter injuries: many midwives refuse to check a woman's rectum after birth. "It's not been an easy task because there's been a lot of professional opposition saying that it's very interventionalist," she told me.[47] " 'Why do you have to do an examination of the anus, especially on an intact perineum?' It's not been without its battles."

As a urogynecologist, Thakar treats women suffering from incontinence and prolapse, which mostly stem from childbirth. She has spent her career treating mothers.

"Still, if you go to our labor wards, obstetricians and midwives focus on delivering the baby. They want a happy mother, happy baby. No one thinks about the perineum and what its long-term consequences of pelvic floor dysfunction are."

In my (mostly very good) interactions with (mostly very good) midwives, I felt that there was an absence of knowledge about how severely a bad tear, or an episiotomy, or, for that matter, childbirth, affects the body and the mind. In one conversation, a midwife mentioned that women did all kinds of "crazy," irresponsible stuff when they were recovering from birth. Some were using a particular spray which was giving them infections, she eye-rolled. Afterwards, I wished I'd said, why aren't you telling all the women under your care not to use that spray? I knew that infections in the perineal and vaginal area were hard to avoid, and that getting one could lead to wound dehiscence (or breakdown), which could lead to defects in the sphincter, which would make life very difficult. Wound breakdown happened to me and I was prescribed the wrong treatment by a doctor. It was frightening.

Thakar's wish, she said, was that all healthcare professionals involved in helping mothers give birth would come and sit in a perineal clinic and listen to women with injuries to the sphincter and vagina, and learn what can happen to them in the long term. This could then feed into prenatal care, and shape how the risks of vaginal birth are discussed in mothers' meetings with midwives.

Is part of the problem that health professionals don't want to scare women? I asked, according to the theory that fear can inhibit birth's "natural" process.

"Women today want to know what can go wrong," said Thakar. "We don't want to sit around and expect things to happen and then be told afterwards."

In the research Thakar's team conducted, mothers said they would rather know that they are at risk of having tears, so they could make an informed decision about mode of delivery.

"Women said, as long as an explanation is provided we don't mind having a rectal examination. But, of course, you should obtain informed consent! If you touch someone's head, you explain what you are doing."

But what about the theory that fear makes birth harder? I understood the need that some women feel to shut out any negative birth stories while pregnant, in order to feel positive about giving birth. I was trying to work out how prenatal information could be more accurate while respecting these sensitivities.

Thakar told me her work had been questioned on this basis. It was thought that if mothers were told about tears, or rather, the truth about tears, they would want to have Cesarean sections.

"Guess what?" she said. Having informed pregnant women about perineal injury, "Cesarean rates did not go up. Our research has shown that women want to know."

Two things, Thakar suggested, were preventing honest discussion of the risks in prenatal clinics. First is the worry that if you tell women the truth, they might be frightened and want to have a Cesarean. Second is a widespread lack of knowledge. She compared it to Pandora's box. Once it's opened, there will be lots of questions, and healthcare professionals might not know the answers. Then there's the lack of time and resources. The appointments pregnant people have with their midwives are short. The maternity crisis in this country means that midwives are already often stretched to the breaking point. In 2022, there was a shortage of over two thousand midwives in the NHS, amid a recruitment, retention and overwork crisis.[48]

Thakar believes that multidisciplinary education of doctors and midwives, and empowering women with knowledge are the keys to overcoming the problem—a problem that affects hundreds of thousands of women in the UK alone. Here, as in other countries, it is harder for women from minority groups. Some of Thakar's patients are Muslim and for them, the challenge is huge: "For Muslim women it's very important because they can't pray unless they clean themselves.

"Women don't seek help because they are embarrassed and ashamed. They think it's part of childbirth. Many say they went to their doctor and the doctor said 'Well, that's what happens in childbirth.' " The women can be made to feel stupid.

But, Thakar pointed out, "Only when women start asking questions are people going to say, 'Ah, this is important. I've got to learn about it.'

"As healthcare professionals, we are brought up to be kind," she said. "Sometimes we become paternalistic, you don't want to hurt people.

"But I say, sometimes you have to be cruel to be kind, and just say it as it is."

○

Instead of being given proper information about postnatal care, we were advertised to. After the birth of my daughter, I spent a day on the hospital ward. I was relieved when we left. It was noisy through day and night, with the sound of machines, visitors, people speaking loudly on the phone. It was light, hot and hectic.

At one point, we had an unknown visitor. Hello, said a woman, bounding into my cubicle with a large bag and a big smile. Congratulations! What's the baby's name? Would you like a photo taken of the baby?

She started opening her bag and removed a package before I could answer. I've got some freebies for you, Mum. I just need to get some information. But first, I'll take a photo of the beautiful bubba. What's her name?

OK . . . I said. What is this? A midwife?

I'm from Bounty! We go around taking photos for all the new mamas. I just need your names, address, emails, phone numbers and for you to sign here. She handed over a clipboard. I couldn't move to reach it because of the pain of my bludgeoned vulva. She moved closer.

It started to dawn on me that she was trying to sell us products and take our data. But I realized too late. Until I unsubscribed, I received emails almost every day. Twenty percent off a teething mitten. Fifty percent off an audio monitor. Thirty-three percent off bibs.

I wanted to get home as soon as possible. My experience was turning out to be very different to the week my mother had spent recovering in a private room in the 1980s, and the two weeks women of my grandmother's generation were given in hospital to recover in the 1950s. But, I reminded myself, my experience was also very different to that of my great-grandmother, who lived in a poor tenement in London where maternal mortality was over a third and infant mortality was over half. I thought of another great-grandmother whose baby was taken from her on delivery because she was conceived out of wedlock. Looking back, I saw how medicine had greatly improved our lives, and the survival of women, babies and children; that societal expectations had become kinder, less cruel. A culture can choose what it diminishes and what it grows.

○

Back at home with our daughter, just one day old, I found that our flat felt different, as if I'd stepped through a portal into a parallel universe, or onto the set of a film.

In my arms, a collection of trillions of atoms that had cycled through generations of ancient supernova explosions.

We were both so old, made from stars born billions of years ago.

We were both so new, she, breathing, outside me; I being made again in matrescence.

I couldn't believe my eyes. I couldn't sleep for the beauty of her. Little pink mouth. Doughball cheeks. Plant-stalk soft bones. Her astral holiness.

Body of my body, flesh of my flesh.

I heard the contraction and expansion of the universe bouncing into existence, new galaxies, axons, dendrites; cells and love, cells and love.

PART III

Colony

The Portuguese man-of-war is not a jellyfish. It is often called a jellyfish, the most venomous jellyfish in the sea. But that is not what it is. It is a colony of animals, a society. Each man-of-war is made up of a number of zooids: small individual polyps, which have their own functions, such as breeding, feeding, floating, capturing prey. The siphonophore can't move independently. It is swept along by currents. As each part works together, the organism operates as one creature.

The top section is called a pneumatophore. It is a fan-shaped, grooved blob streaked with pink or purple or blue. This part is the float or sail, and it holds the organism above water. But it belies the volume, number and complexity of interactions keeping it alive, under the surface. Cooperating, bearing venom, stinging, trapping, paralyzing prey, digesting food. It can't survive without its colony. It *is* a colony.

5.

Feeding

The thing about breasts is that they are part of someone's body, and if you're not treating that person's perspective as important, you're missing the point.

Rabbi Ruti Regan

After childbirth, she "went owt of hir mende."

The Book of Margery Kempe (1436–38)

Strategies to boost my milk supply
Goat's rue tea
Fenugreek smoothies
Pumping
Hand expressing
Hot compress
Warm showers and squeezing
Looking at a picture of the baby
Smelling the baby
Feeding on demand, around the clock
Switching between each breast three times
Taking a "nursing vacation," canceling all visitors and going to bed to feed for the weekend

Breastfeeding support groups
Breastfeeding books
Breastfeeding helplines
Breastfeeding Facebook pages
Triple-feeding (breastfeeding, then pumping, then bottle-feeding)
Milk
Water
Protein
General carbs
Porridge
Flapjacks

As much as the first part of motherhood is an intimate, personal experience, it is also a social one. And as soon as a child is born, one ubiquitous assumption is made: that he or she will be fed with milk made by the mother via her breasts. This expectation is broadcast in prenatal information and through initiatives in hospitals and postnatal visits. Breastfeeding, I had been told, would make my baby cleverer, physically and mentally healthier, less likely to be obese and more emotionally stable because of the attachment breastfeeding uniquely fosters. The slogans on the official NHS breastfeeding posters were clear: "the gentle art of caring," "this mum knows best."[1] "There is almost nothing you can do for your child in his whole life that will affect him both emotionally and physically as profoundly as breastfeeding," say La Leche League, an international breastfeeding support organization.[2] By contrast, formula was demonized. By law, supermarkets and chemists can't give customers loyalty points (or allow them to redeem points) on formula milk, putting it in the same category as tobacco-related products and lottery tickets. My baby's health and very survival, I understood, depended on her being exclusively breastfed.

There is good evidence for some early-life advantages to breastfeeding. The American economist and writer Emily Oster reviewed the literature for the many claimed benefits of breastfeeding, looking for causal effects, rather than mere correlation.[3] She found that "[b]reastfeeding seems to improve digestion in the first year, lowers rashes for infants and is especially important for preterm babies." It also seems to help reduce ear infections in young children. For mothers, the potential benefits are more significant: breastfeeding can help protect against breast and ovarian carcinoma.

Many women enjoy breastfeeding and it can be convenient. It's also free, if you don't need a pump and you're not counting the time of the mother. Women and babies need policies and systems that support breastfeeding. But, on the whole, the claims about breastfeeding's long-term health benefits are overblown.

Today, we are obsessed with exclusive breastfeeding. Why? My grandmother didn't breastfeed any of her four children and my mother didn't feed my sibling for long. Somehow, though, I had been programmed to believe that it would be unthinkable not to breastfeed, almost a moral failing.

O

In 1990, the WHO and UNICEF recommended that all infants should be fed exclusively on breast milk in their *Innocenti Declaration*, an international text which set out rules for enabling breastfeeding. All babies, they decreed, should be fed "frequently" and for "unrestricted periods" for at least six months. "Almost every mother can breastfeed successfully," it declared.

The historical moment matters: this drive was an understandable reaction to unethical marketing practices by milk formula companies, particularly in developing countries, which had recently been exposed. For decades mothers around the world had been sent home from the hospital with a tub of formula.

But the WHO and UNICEF campaign didn't mention how a woman in the US who had no paid leave could feed a baby "frequently" if she had to go back to work. Or where a woman could feed a baby when public spaces were so often hostile to breastfeeding. Or how it would work for women who can't physically feed, or for adoptive parents, or gay couples, or trans fathers. It didn't mention how a mother could feed a baby "for unrestricted periods" if she was looking after other children.

The decree has been implemented in individual countries by the Baby Friendly Initiative (BFI), run by the WHO and UNICEF.[4] The program was set up in 1991 (1995 in the UK) to "support" women as they breastfeed. It is a staged process by which hospitals are awarded accreditation according to Baby Friendly standards. Hospitals can have their accreditation suspended if care falls below the criteria. Currently, 91 percent of maternity services in Britain are working towards Baby Friendly accreditation and 64 percent have achieved full accreditation, according to the "Ten Steps to Successful Breastfeeding," which include no formula unless medically indicated, communicating the "risks" of bottles, teats or pacifiers, and enabling "rooming-in" twenty-four hours a day, which means enabling mother and baby to stay together.

There is nothing in the Ten Commandments, I mean Steps, that directly addresses the mother's health and well-being at this most vulnerable time.

O

Maternal Mental Health—Women's Voices, a report published in 2017 by the Royal College of Obstetricians & Gynaecologists (RCOG), suggests that attitudes to feeding are a significant cause of anguish for new mothers.[5] Many of the women surveyed found pressure to breastfeed "overwhelming" and the "judgement and stigma" that came along with not breastfeeding their babies "hard to cope with." Many said it affected their mental well-being. A study published in 2015 found that mothers who'd intended to breastfeed but weren't able to had an increased risk of postnatal depression.[6] In 2019, a metasynthesis of five qualitative studies by psychologists at the University of Liverpool found that "current delivery of BFI may promote unrealistic expectations of breastfeeding, not meet women's individual needs, and foster negative emotional experiences."[7]

I spoke with Alain Gregoire, who was then–consultant perinatal psychiatrist with the Hampshire Perinatal Mental Health Service. He explained how, if you're feeling strong and chipper, you can shrug off the fact that you're having difficulties with breastfeeding and accept that it can't be helped. But if you're depressed—which is not uncommon in the postnatal period—you see things in a more negative light. "Pressure [to breastfeed] increases the stress and, probably, from clinical descriptions of women, does increase their likelihood of feeling depressed and being anxious."[8]

In the UK, the drive to increase breastfeeding rates has meant that the health literature has tended to gloss over the possibility that new mothers might not produce enough milk and need to opt for formula or mixed feeding. In prenatal classes, the focus is squarely on the benefits of breastfeeding, rather than what happens if it goes wrong. You would have no idea that just 1 percent of babies in the UK are exclusively breastfed at six months and 73 percent of babies in England are given formula by six weeks.[9,10]

In England and Wales, the rate of breastfeeding at birth has climbed steadily over the last half century. In 1975, 51 percent of women initiated breastfeeding; in 2010, the rate was 81 percent. However, the number of mothers still breastfeeding exclusively at six months in Britain is one of the lowest in the world, at around 1 percent. With pregnant women being told that exclusive breastfeeding for the first six months is nonnegotiable, that's up to 99 percent of all mothers feeling like they haven't given their baby the "best" start in life. It is estimated that 5 percent of these women are unable to breastfeed at all, which equates to 35,000 mothers who give birth in England and Wales each year. Since eight out of ten women want to breastfeed, that means nearly thirty thousand women feel as though they've failed their baby at the first hurdle. The phenomenon isn't new: "lactation failure" is mentioned in one of the earliest medical encyclopedias—the Papyrus Ebers, written around 1550 BCE—and the practice of wet-nursing goes back to the ancient world.[11]

Sadly, the suggestion that if a woman can't breastfeed she's lazy or selfish or just not trying hard enough is common; many women in the RCOG's *Women's Voices* report felt blamed when breastfeeding went wrong. A friend was approached by a breastfeeding consultant at a playgroup and asked why she was bottle-feeding her daughter. "When I said I had struggled with not having much milk, she said that I shouldn't have given up so easily." Another was tutted at when she mentioned that her baby had to have formula in intensive care. Another told me that a midwife cried at her bedside because she so wanted her to breastfeed.

○

The incentive for hospitals to achieve BFI accreditation is the kudos, midwives tell me. If a woman breastfeeds at the beginning, then the hospital receives an award, and can add it to their stats for info-graphics on social media. But does this mean a tick for breastfeeding on hospital targets can be prioritized over and above an individual woman's needs?

"Trusts get clear, good recognition if they have a Baby Friendly award, but that does mean that they encourage breastfeeding far more than maybe is great for some people," said Dr. Leila Frodsham, a psychotherapist and consultant obstetrician and gynecologist.[12] In her view, there is "undoubtedly" a link between the guilt of not being able to breastfeed and postnatal depression; she reported having seen women for whom the psychological impact lasted years.

Meanwhile, the complex reality of breastfeeding itself is under-reported. The conventional portrayal of breastfeeding is, at best, incomplete. For some, it is a relaxing, snuggly, easy act. But it can also be upsetting, stressful, awkward, painful, time-consuming and tiring.

Research conducted by sociologists Deborah Lupton and Virginia Schmied found that while some women experienced breastfeeding as "connected, harmonious and intimate," the majority found the breastfeeding relationship "difficult to reconcile with notions of identity that value autonomy, independence and control."[13]

○

As soon as the cord that connected us was cut, my daughter was placed on my breast and started sucking. I breastfed her through the night at the hospital—the fact I had been awake for sixty hours was not mentioned—and a midwife told me I was doing really well. The latch looked perfect, she was feeding beautifully, she said. Phew. We were instructed to feed on demand, which meant whenever the baby wanted to. From what I'd read that would be every couple of hours or so, but babies love suckling so I should expect more for the first while. "Just feed, feed, feed, feed, feed," I was told.

We spent the first few days in the house, marveling at our daughter. I was feeding around eighteen times in a twenty-four-hour period, sometimes for an hour each time. It's going well, I thought, because she is latching on, though I was hallucinating and feeling odd, and she was crying a lot. A few times, I woke and wandered the flat looking for her, while carrying an imaginary baby in my arms.

On the fifth day, a midwife arrived to weigh her. She had lost more than 10 percent of her birth weight, which was worrying because of her jaundice. She gently taught me how to lie down to feed and bring the baby tighter into the breast. Start the baby on the breast you finished on last time to get the hind milk, she said.

The hind milk?

It's the milk with the higher fat content, she said. The fore milk, which comes first, is waterier, and helps baby hydrate. I wrote down what she said.

The following week, another midwife came over. The baby's weight was still low and dropping. I was starting to obsess about how little she was putting back on, trying to make sense of the number of grams on the snatches of sleep I was getting. I felt highly anxious. Was it possible to not have enough milk? I couldn't find anything in any of the NHS leaflets about this possibility, but I ordered galactagogues I read about online in case. I made oat smoothies and drank lactation tea. The flat smelled of toasted fenugreek and a wisp of fear.

In the back of my mind, there was a growing dread: my body couldn't give her what she needed.

We left the house to walk to the local shop for the first time with our baby wrapped in a sling. I was on high alert and scanned the streets for threat, like a bodyguard. I squinted into the sharp light of the sun, jumped at a dog bark, shuddered at a car horn. I felt as if I was on another planet; the street I'd lived on for years was new and blinding and dangerous. I imagined the ground bursting and cracking below us. I had lost a membrane of protection between myself and the world; my nerve endings felt exposed and fraying.

A couple of days later, we saw another midwife. My daughter's weight was still dropping despite my feeding her around the clock. I was advised to hand-express 60 milliliters of milk and give it to the baby in a cup after each feed. I tried to squeeze milk out of my breasts. It took an hour to get 10 milliliters. I began to panic.

A friend sent over an expensive electric breast pump in a taxi for me to borrow. It sucked my breast into the tube, malforming the flesh into a sausage. It sounded alive, like a farmyard animal honking its last. The poet Camille T. Dungy described the experience best: "I felt like a nameless character in a science fiction movie where things end badly for the women."[14]

It stung but I stared at pictures of the baby to help the milk flow, as I had read online, and hoped for the best. Droplets. I kept trying, using a hot flannel and relaxation exercises. A teaspoon's worth. I was appalled. Had I been starving my child? I was failing at this primal, essential part of motherhood, the *most important* thing I could do for her in *her whole life*.

Did you feel your milk come in? asked a midwife. Not really, I said. A bit. Do you feel the letdown, she asked? I'm not sure, I replied. Sometimes they feel hard and then afterwards they feel soft so there must be something there?

A few weeks in, the baby was still not at birth weight and still jaundiced. A health visitor turned up and said, Sometimes breastfeeding doesn't work out.

I felt a wave of terror. What?

I referred to the NHS hospital booklet again in a daze of fatigue. "Bottled formula milk destroys the protective coating in the baby's gut that the breast milk makes," it said. Well, formula milk wasn't an option, then.

Destroys. I fixated on this word. I didn't want to destroy the protective gut coating of my precious baby. Destroying anything about her was not an option. But how, then, would I keep her alive?

I tried reading scientific studies, the papers I was used to interpreting in my work, but nothing made sense. I was baffled by the volume of information, the conflicting advice, the lack of sleep. I was trying to locate this famous maternal instinct, my apparently innate ability to know how to behave, how to respond to my child's needs. But apart from an urge to protect and care for her, it felt diffuse and wan.

I downloaded a book, published by La Leche League, called *The Womanly Art of Breastfeeding*. The cover showed a beautiful woman with long, flowing curly red hair, wrapped in a white sheet. This book will teach me the womanly art, I thought. "Breastfeeding doesn't give you brownie points. It's simply the normal way to raise a baby," I read.[15]

The authors quote our old friend Dick-Read: "The newborn baby has only three demands. They are warmth in the arms of [his] mother, food from her breasts, and security in the knowledge of her presence. Breastfeeding satisfies all three."[16]

Yikes, I thought. I'd better get this right.

I started spending a lot of time at all hours on a website called KellyMom.[17] "As long as baby is allowed to nurse on cue, your milk supply will typically accommodate baby's needs," it said. Then why wasn't my body doing what it should?

Desperate, I called the hospital helpline, worried about what I'd been reading about the dangers of prolonged jaundice. Our daughter looked skinny and her skin seemed a little loose. She was screaming. I spoke to a woman who sounded older, Irish and kind. She advised topping up with formula after each feed.

At a breastfeeding support group the next week, I cringed when I whispered that I was "topping up." A woman opposite me said her nipples were bleeding when she expressed, and the milk was pink because of the blood. Her face was blank. The feeding consultant advised her to take a painkiller. Another woman next to me looked spaced-out with sleep deprivation or shock. Her face was puffy and blotchy, her eyes were hooded and bloodshot. I eavesdropped as her partner beseeched the counselor, could he give the baby just one bottle at night so she could have some rest? The counselor listed all the reasons why formula was not a good idea for the baby. I felt my stomach flip with guilt and shame. My thoughts descended into darker places. I've failed her already, I thought. At the first hurdle. I was hurting her. I was making my baby ill through my own insufficiency. These thoughts kept gnawing away, tearing strips off my confidence.

And yet there was something else. As much as I obsessed over the requirement to breastfeed exclusively, some part of me started to recognize coercion and manipulation. Faintly, I smelled smoke.

Around that time, in a doctor's surgery, I watched a video which said, "As long as your baby is well positioned on the breast, he will be getting plenty of food." I flared with anger at the inaccuracy.

○

The obstacles to breastfeeding weren't only physiological. One day, I took the baby to the shopping mall in town, to find stimulation, company or something to keep me awake after being up most of the night. We walked to a café in a local clothes store. The only seat free was in the middle of the room, and there were pairs of elderly people drinking tea and eating scones. I planned to eat a cake while she was still asleep. I was becoming well trained at eating in a manic, animal fashion, pushing the food to the back of my mouth and chewing with my molars just enough to let me swallow, quickly vacuuming up the sustenance before she needed me again.

As soon as we sat down, she started waking. Within minutes she was crying and screaming. She was hungry.

I had been topping up with formula, so I took out the bottle and a small sterilized Tupperware of formula and rushed to the barista for boiling hot water. I made a bottle at the table as quickly as possible so I could transition seamlessly from breast to bottle if she needed it.

Her screams were pulsing louder and people stared at us. I unbuckled her from the pram, pulled down my top, unclipped the nursing bra and latched her onto my breast, hoping that it would settle and satisfy her. But she shook her head and moved off. Maybe I was too hot and sweaty. I felt conscious of eyes on us, watching as I tried to get my nipple into her mouth again. My forehead was sweating. I felt vulnerable, exposed, paranoid, judged. Half-naked, I was failing my baby in public, unable to perform this most "natural" of motherly actions. The adrenaline rose in my body and my heart beat rapidly. I tried to latch her on again, but for some reason it wasn't working. I tried again and again, wanting to cry. Her distress felt accusatory. Everyone's stares felt accusatory. My back and torso ached from twisting into uncomfortable feeding positions all day. I decided to pack in the breast and brought the bottle out. She drank happily and I sat there, relieved and ashamed. I was furious with myself. I glanced up at people's faces and read cruel thoughts into them. I would never go to the café again.

O

It's a paradox. Society wants women to breastfeed, but doesn't want to see them doing it. A survey conducted by Public Health England (PHE) found that 63 percent of women would feel embarrassed breastfeeding in front of people they don't know; 59 percent felt the same in front of their partner's family.[18] A separate PHE poll found that 21 percent of women felt people did not want them to breastfeed in public.[19] Mothers were made to feel "marginalized and ashamed" when they fed in public: stared at or tutted at or seen as "weirdos" or "hippies."

In 2018, two women were asked to stop breastfeeding their children in a swimming pool in Stoke-on-Trent. An author called Virginia Blackburn compared the act to urinating in public on the television program *This Morning*. "I do think it's on a level with it actually," she said. "You have a path that leads to anti-social behaviour and I think it's on the same path."[20]

Women are asked to leave shops or restaurants if they are breastfeeding, even though it is legal to breastfeed in public and protected under the Equality Act 2010. Babies need to feed regularly, and sometimes suckle almost constantly, so for a woman to feed her baby breast milk and also spend time outside her house, she requires places that are welcoming or, at least, not hostile to breastfeeding. Such places, in our society, barely exist. For me, they were the library, under trees outside, or at playgroups, but not in public as a rule. In the feeding literature, women report feeling more comfortable feeding in parks than shopping centers, but more comfortable feeding outside in groups rather than alone.[21]

Where does the stigma come from? Breasts, in Western society, are predominantly sexual objects. In eighteenth-century European art, images of the nursing Virgin Mary were replaced with the crucifixion, as the breast became a symbol of the erotic.[22] Indeed, today, one in six mothers reports receiving unwanted sexual attention when breastfeeding.[23] It only became illegal to photograph a breastfeeding woman in 2022 after a campaign led by MP Stella Creasy.[24] The way breasts are sexualized fuels the taboo, and the behavior of sexist men prevents women from feeling safe feeding their babies.[25]

My experience was that it wasn't as simple as popping a nipple into the baby's mouth. Sometimes she would pop on and off like a woodpecker and I'd have to squeeze and contort my nipple to help her latch. I would also need to compress the breast—manually squeeze it—in order to start the milk flowing. Displaying my bodily fluids, especially in front of elderly gentlemen, was too much. I had been socialized to be conscious of people's needs, and I didn't want to make anyone feel awkward.

So, most of the time, I stayed at home.

A US design company came up with a solution to reduce barriers to breastfeeding in public: lactation pods.[26] The pods are opaque enclosures that can be erected in a public space for parents to breastfeed and pump milk. Currently, they are in museums, zoos, airports and malls. I would've liked to have had this option, I think. But we need more solutions than a box to sequester mothers away in, alone.

O

At the postnatal check, the GP said, we'll do baby and then quickly do you. When he asked briefly about my mood (how is mum?), I faltered, but didn't feel permitted to take up any more time. The baby was fine and that was what mattered. I needed to get her home to feed her. It was difficult if she needed feeding when I was out and about. The shame of breastfeeding; the shame of formula.

I decided to write an article about my experiences of infant feeding and afterwards I received a number of letters from readers. Women shared their own similar struggles to breastfeed, desperation to feed their baby, and how bad advice and critical judgment affected their early motherhood experiences. The letters were mostly from women whose babies were born decades ago. "After 30-odd years, I still feel guilty," wrote one. "I still bear the scars," said another, thirty-five years on. Another described struggling to breastfeed twenty years ago after a Cesarean, and being told "if you really wanted to breast-feed you would be able to." A letter by a mother who had given birth that year said that moving to formula made her feel like a total failure.

To understand more about the shame I was witnessing, and had begun to experience deep within myself, I contacted Dawn Leeming, a former NHS psychologist turned academic at the University of Huddersfield. Leeming specializes in maternal shame and infant feeding. Her initial interest was sparked thirty years ago, when she was working on a PhD exploring the management and repair of shame in a range of situations. She had had children and struggled with breastfeeding, and she looked for psychological research in the area. There wasn't any. To fill the gap, Leeming and a couple of other health psychologists devised a study on women's experiences of breastfeeding. As it progressed, she became aware of the relevance of shame. It was central to the experience of many mothers who were facing difficulties—difficulties that today would be labeled depression or social anxiety. Leeming is now one of a growing number studying how narratives around infant feeding—particularly breastfeeding—impact new mothers and their mental health.

Through her decades of research, Leeming has come to see the value of talking as a means of repairing shame. If people speak about their shame, they are taking an important step on the path to being validated, to finding an alternative way to think about themselves. "Unless you speak about it, it can't be normalized and demystified and it becomes this big, terrible secret," she said.[27]

Given that shame around infant feeding is so common, it is strange that it has been overlooked in the research for so long, and that it is still so absent from discussions of feeding by health professionals.

Leeming had, she told me, been involved in a bid to set up a network of policymakers, senior midwives and health visitors to explore how breastfeeding support can be helpful and unhelpful, and the meaning of an empathic woman-centered approach. They couldn't secure support from a funding body so it had been put to one side.

O

The silence around mixed or "combination" feeding—feeding a baby with breast and also formula milk—was odd. I found more accurate information about mammals and lactation when I spoke to my mother's boyfriend—a farmer who would tell me that, naturally, some mother sheep just didn't produce much milk—than in any of the health literature. There was so little information about it in prenatal classes or literature; if it was mentioned, it was waved off with warnings of "nipple confusion." Infant Feeding Surveys, which the NHS conducts every five years, didn't even mention how many mothers feed their babies both breast and formula milk. It may be that the mixed-feeding method is kept quiet because it is thought to affect milk supply. Still, I fed our daughter a combination of formula and breast milk and it worked well for us. One afternoon while I was feeding her a bottle, she looked at me and smiled her first smile. The smile seemed to go on for ages, our eyes locked, my heart felt like it was detonating with joy and she went back to her drinking.

It's easy to see why breastfeeding is strongly encouraged: if it works, it's lovely, and there are some health benefits for mother and baby. But the current advice fails to acknowledge the whole picture. In the drive to normalize breastfeeding the pendulum has swung too far, straying into misinformation and deceit. In the zeal to reform, the reformers have become fanatical. Individual women, their mental health and the barriers to breastfeeding within patriarchal, late-capitalist society get overlooked. Gregoire decries the fact that mothers are still not told that mixed feeding is an option. "The literature is poor but the clinical advice is even worse," he said, adding that "the benefit to the baby is pretty much as good as exclusive breast milk."[28] He thinks that feeding support, instead of specifically *breast*feeding support, would improve the situation.

Once I had made peace with what was happening and accepted mixed feeding, I enjoyed aspects of breastfeeding. Sometimes, when it went well, a sense of opiate-like peace and contentment swelled within me. In bed on winter afternoons, or in the dead of night, the intimate connection was deeply bonding.

The cry the turn the pull the stroke the warmth the dark the nose
the nipple the tummy the tummy the curl the head the crook the
mouth the wide the angle the clamp the suck the latch the draw the
suck the calm the soft the hand the back the pull the close the knees
the feet the box the safe the house the smell the suck the smell the
sigh the skin the suck the smell the sigh the sleep

O

With my second child I had a similar "journey," with one difference. Sometimes, when he latched, my mood suddenly, abruptly went dark. The world was sucked of color and joy. It lasted for only a minute but it was disturbing.

On further reading, I came across the term DMER, or Dysphoric Milk Ejection Reflex, which described the experience. It was one of the seemingly endless examples of strange and unknown health conditions that happened to women's bodies in matrescence. Fistulas, rectoceles, mastitis, blocked ducts, diastasis recti.

I read one of the only reports I could find.[29]

Although there hadn't been any formal study, it is thought that the dysphoria is caused by an abrupt drop in dopamine when the milk release is triggered. Someone described it as similar to the effect of the joy-sucking dementors in Harry Potter, and I winced in recognition.

A few years later, I discovered that I likely have hypoplasia, a type of breasts which means I would never be able to make much milk. I have a key marker—a significant gap between the breasts—and I read that if it is a certain width, that usually means there is "insufficient glandular tissue." I ran around the house looking for a tape measure to measure the gap myself, my heart thumping, to measure the amount of guilt I should be feeling. I haven't felt nearly as much sorrow and guilt about my breastfeeding failures since finding this out. I wish I had known about it before.

O

So much of women's reproductive health is hidden or unknown—the first women's reproductive mental health textbook was published in 2022—but the more I learned after the birth of my daughter, the less insecure I felt.[30] I began to enjoy investigating the changes I was undergoing. My new body became a site of fascination for me.

I'd been told breast milk was creamy and sweet. It is often called "liquid gold." When I tasted my own, though, it was quite watery and sometimes even salty. I was in awe of it.

I'd also noticed that I smelled different, right from the start of my matrescence. The sweat under my arms had become stronger and earthier. It wasn't just because I wasn't washing as much nor wearing deodorant so it didn't get into the baby when I was feeding her. It was disconcertingly unfamiliar.

My pheromones, my smell, I learned, might have been altered or become more pronounced in order that the baby could recognize me. Babies may have an early sensitivity to their mother's smell, and recognizing it probably plays a part in the mother–infant attachment process, going both ways. Olfactory learning starts young: babies can recognize and are attracted to the amniotic fluid smell they grew within. Studies have shown that both mother and father can recognize the smell of amniotic fluid, which may be similar to the mother's odor.[31]

But I wanted to know more about what was behind the change. What was happening in my body to augment the bond between us? Had new microanimals joined the microbiome that already lived in my crevices? What new living creatures were now part of me?

I found no research into the area so I decided to do it myself with the help of a microbiologist friend. I ordered a compound microscope, petri dishes, seaweed agar and gentian violet. I didn't have a sample from before pregnancy, so I couldn't truly test my hypothesis, but I would be able see who or what was living with me. In a small saucepan, I mixed agar powder with water and a quarter of a crumbled stock cube. I poured the mixture into a petri dish. Once cooled, it looked like the palest brown jelly. With a ball of cotton wool, I swabbed my armpit, dabbed it onto my culture medium and put it in the boiler cupboard with a sample from my husband as well.

A few days later, white spots—my bacteria colony—were proliferating, and after seven days I removed the dishes. My bacteria had a green area, unlike my husband's. The growths looked like blooms of jellyfish, many were perfectly spherical and three-dimensional. Dotted minims of creamy bacteria.

To make distilled water, I turned a lid over on top of a saucepan of boiling water so the water droplets could roll from the handle into a small ceramic bowl. I pipetted a few drops onto a thin glass slide and let it dry. Using the cooktop, I heat-sterilized a needle, and pried a few wodges of the colony off the dish and smeared them onto the slide. To make it easier to see, I dropped gentian violet onto the slide. It was electric purple and stained my fingers. I passed the slide through the flame three times to heat-fix it.

I loaded the slide into my microscope, turned on the light and focused the dials.

Both our colonies had a mixture of gram-positive and gram-negative bacteria. Some looked like jumping beans or Tic Tacs, others looked like the outline of jelly beans. Mine, though, had clusters of a round, dyed bacteria. I consulted my microbiologist friend and he told me it looked like *Staphylococcus aureus*. It's a bacterium found on 20 to 40 percent of human skin, but it can also become an opportunistic pathogen and cause a wide range of disease and health conditions, from pimples to sepsis, boils to meningitis. I felt uneasy, and humbled, in the face of my pathobiont. Were they my guests, or was I theirs? Are they me, or am I them?

Othermothers

A behavior among female vampire bats has been newly observed by researchers.[1] A mother bat—"Lilith"—died eighteen days after giving birth, but her friend "BD" adopted the baby bat and raised it as her own. The researchers had tracked the interactions between "Lilith" and "BD" after the baby was born, and observed "BD" helping take care of the bat pup: grooming it, even nursing it, and sharing food with her sickening friend.

Previously, scientists assumed female bats living in "maternity colonies" raised their young individually, but growing research suggests non-kin adoption in a variety of species may be common. Foxes raise their young in groups, with allomother female vixens helping the mother from the cubs' birth. Gorillas parent orphaned infants as a group. In French Polynesia, a bottlenose dolphin adopted a melon-headed whale calf. Humans, who evolved in collective care structures, are not the only species capable of altruism and non-kin family-making.

6.

The maternal brain

Care (noun): "burden of the mind"
from the Old English word cearu (sorrow, anxiety, grief)
from the Old German word karō (lament, trouble, care)

A survey of the natural world through the lens of this life-historical approach reveals just how special a creature the self-sacrificing mother envisioned by men . . . must be.

Sarah Blaffer Hrdy, *Mother Nature: Maternal Instincts and How They Shape the Human Species*

As my daughter began to unfurl, we started to experience more of the world together. Much of our early care work was devoted to learning what she needed to be comfortable and happy. Learning how she behaved when she was tired, and what could help her sleep. Learning what position she needed to be in after being fed. Learning how much stimulation was enough, or when she needed more engagement. We were finding it challenging to adapt to our new world. She expressed her feeling about the transition through smiles and coos and tears; I didn't know how to express mine at all.

One day, in the early months, we took the train to London to meet up with a friend in a café on the river. I was looking forward to hearing about adult life and sinking back into the world of writing and journalism.

I had filled my bag with objects that could alleviate her potential distress: bottles and milk powder, diapers and wipes, toys and spare clothes. Looking after her at home was easier, but I hadn't been out for a while. My husband would often leave for work early in the morning and return later in the evening. I missed people.

My role as protector was different outside the house: there were more threats and dangers. The road seemed louder and busier than it did before she was born. My arms were taut around her, my claws ready to gouge an eye. I was sprung, primed. My gaze was fixed on her unless I needed to sweep the area for fire or plastic flotsam or small batteries or wolves or kidnappers. I smelled for gas, for illness, for tobacco on fibers.

(Somewhere subconscious, there was an anxious flicker: might there be danger within me, too?)

This hyperaroused, vigilant state would last for many months—and in a less tense form for years (all time?). Later I would learn that hypervigilance can be a symptom of PTSD following childbirth, which, it is thought, 9 percent of women in the US—over 300,000 women a year—suffer from.

My brain vividly conjured frightening scenarios: how she would be flung out of the pram if a car hit us, spinning like a rugby ball; how her skull would crack on a marble floor; how her sweet little body would look if she fell off the changing table. My brain would play out a scene in visual detail, leaving me feeling shaken, horrified, even more vigilant. When I started reading and talking to other mothers, I found that many women experience these "intrusive thoughts" in the early months of motherhood, meaning images and fears of the baby hurting itself or even of their intentionally hurting the baby. It seemed to be so common that I wondered if there was a protective mechanism in the postnatal brain which helped mothers to predict hazards and keep the baby safe from them.

The train stopped for a while and I noticed the trees on the banks of the track. They looked wobbly and spindly. Could they fall on the train? I swiftly assessed the distance and length of the trunks. Yes, they could. I looked around at my fellow passengers: Was anyone else worried about these trees? Why wasn't anyone else looking at the trees? If they fell, they would definitely kill us.

The world roared. Potential dangers were turned up to a newly high volume. I saw peril where before I had been oblivious, light-footed, assured of my safety. I was starting to glimpse what the word *careworn* might mean.

When the train started to move I sighed with relief, and kissed and sniffed the baby's head.

In London, I showed her the river, the winding muddy boa. Memories of sitting with friends drinking, smoking, talking, laughing, watching the current move the water. I showed her the trees, which she seemed to like looking at. Her eyes were drawn by the movement of the gulls, which I paid attention to for the first time. One landed nearby and I saw its black-and-white spotted back feathers, the blackened tip of the orange beak, its red-rimmed eyes.

We met my friend in a cheerful café and ordered a sandwich and a drink. I felt happy to see her, but suddenly shy and withdrawn. I found it harder to make conversation now, as I was adapting to spending most of the time alone (well, not technically: the strangeness of caring for a young baby is feeling alone, while never actually being alone). My friend started to speak and something strange happened. I found I couldn't fully concentrate on what she was saying. Every sound or movement the baby made drew my eye to her involuntarily. I kept trying to focus and interpret my friend's anecdotes and questions as I would've done before matrescence, but the baby was demanding my eyes. She was demanding my voice, my touch. My complete attention. If I didn't look at her when she made a sound or a movement, her insistence grew stronger, and louder. She squawked and bellowed, and looked at me imploringly with her large, denim-blue eyes. I felt torn between wanting to catch up with my friend, who had traveled a ways to see us, to nurture a relationship I cared about, and this new person, who required utter devotion. I felt frustrated. Why couldn't I simply talk to a friend? Why couldn't I override this occupation for an hour? I hadn't yet realized the relational reality of our dyad; that, really, I was no longer the individual I thought I once was.

I noticed this happening regularly. With family for Sunday lunch, everyone was talking and eating, but my eyes were fixed like glue on the baby, who was being passed around. When I was among relatives I didn't feel embarrassed about my focus being on her rather than the conversation, but I was aware that there was something robotic, automatic happening. It took effort to tear my attention away. My gaze naturally rested on her. It was a brooding, trancelike stare: comfortable, clicked-in. I began to realize that motherhood is a watching. I was, first and foremost, a sentinel. Her sentinel.

Something similar would happen at night. When she cried out, I registered the sound in my cells, my body, before my consciousness, and it would jolt me awake. It was as if I was being zapped by an electric eel through the wall, a bespoke ultrasound. I would pad to her room, entranced. Despite my exhaustion my body took me to her, zombielike. Even if we had had a hard day, leaving me worn out by the crying, a whole night without her would feel too long. Even when I thought I couldn't get up again in the night, after fractions and snatches of sweaty sleep, my body could do it. I found new pools of strength, of addictive love.

When I tried to take some time away from her, I found I was never comfortable or relaxed. I was always pleased to see my friends, but the experience itself didn't feel wholly pleasant. The handful of times in the first couple of years when I was in another town or city, it was as if my intestines were stretched like elastic leading from me to her, over the fields and rivers and motorways and towns, and the farther away I was, or the longer I spent separated from her, the tauter and more nagging they became. Each time I returned, I was as desperate and panicked to get to her as if she were a ticking bomb I needed to defuse. I would run back to her down the road, jonesing, as if meeting a lover.

In the early months of her life outside the womb, it started to become clear that she had never completely left my body. I felt her as I had when she was physically inside me, but in a different, more carnal way.

It made more sense when I discovered that my brain had changed beyond recognition.

○

During pregnancy and the early weeks and months of motherhood a blitz of birth and death was taking place within my brain. Cells were being born and cells were dying. Areas of the brain were shrinking, and others were growing. Juiced with a multitude of hormones, I was being newly sculpted.

For the first time, evidence that pregnancy has a dramatic, long-term impact on the human brain is starting to be published.

I had a hunch that my brain was being altered in pregnancy, but the oft-repeated cliché of "baby brain" did not resonate. Before matrescence, all I knew about the maternal brain was that "momnesia" or "mum brain" might mean a blanket forgetfulness or scattiness.

This concept has its roots in old and erroneous ideas that women were intellectually enfeebled by their ability to bear children. The nineteenth-century philosopher Herbert Spencer, who coined the phrase "survival of the fittest," left a dark legacy with his theory that women fall short in "intellectual and emotional" faculties because their evolution is arrested to save "vital power" for reproduction.[1] We can see the remnants of this strange idea that motherhood turns the brain to mush in the modern day, in internet memes and media. You can buy a number of T-shirts or mugs online with the slogan "I used to have functioning brain cells but I traded them in for children."

Is there any evidence of an association between matrescence and memory loss? Most women do report some memory deficit but, according to the leading neuroscientist Dr. Jodi Pawluski, it is likely better than we think. In fact, some women find *improvements* in different kinds of memory, including visual memory.

"The narrative of motherhood and memory stays the same because that is what we know, that is what history has told us," she writes, in the *Journal of Women's Health*.[2]

A study published in 2022 suggests that the reductive myth that women are essentially brain-damaged by motherhood affects how women see themselves.[3] A group of mothers self-reported their memory as worse than non-mothers despite no actual difference in cognitive performance. The researchers found evidence of subjective but not objective cognitive deficit.

Apart from sustained periods of sleep deprivation and irritating verbal and short-term memory lapses, my ability to think, solve problems, learn, analyze and hold multiple thoughts at once sometimes felt enhanced in matrescence. It was as though my brain had become newly receptive to the world around it, and above all to the baby. New research suggests it likely did. A study of pregnant women conducted by Bridget Callaghan at UCLA found evidence of enhanced learning, memory and cognitive plasticity.[4] Towards the end of 2022, a team led by the neuroscientist Winnie Orchard of Yale University analyzed the literature on brain connectivity in matrescence—how different regions of the brain communicate. Outside the context of being exposed to their infants, they found evidence that motherhood tunes the brain to be "more flexible, responsive and efficient."[5] Orchard, in the first major scientific review with the word "matrescence" in the title, argues that the lifetime impact of motherhood on cognition and the brain may be positive.[6] The "cognitive load" of adapting and adjusting to the needs of a growing child and adult over time may constitute an "enriching environment" which makes the brain more resilient. Orchard points out that this would be expected for caregiving parents of all genders.

Although much more research is needed, "mom brain" is, clearly, an outdated misnomer. As Pawluski and colleagues wrote in a review published by the American Medical Association in 2023, "the idea that motherhood is wrought with memory deficits and is characterized by a brain that no longer functions well is scientifically just not so."[7]

○

In a landmark study published in *Nature* in 2016, researchers led by Elseline Hoekzema, a neuroscientist from the Netherlands, and Erika Barba-Müller, a neuroscientist working in Spain, provided evidence, for the first time, that pregnancy renders pronounced, consistent changes in brain structure.[8]

Before I read the paper, before I became pregnant, I did not know that my brain would undergo any lasting, let alone significant, structural changes in matrescence. I thought that the hormonal impact of pregnancy was a one-time, transient event, to enable the baby to grow, and then, once out, that's it. It is no surprise that I thought this: we knew virtually nothing about the maternal brain until the 2010s.

Hoekzema's study includes images of brain data that I spent some time looking at. Each brain looks like a walnut, with crumpled mantles. The lined-up brains are gray, with darker or lighter shadows showing their dimensions and folds.

The brains of the control group—who haven't borne children—are solely gray. But the brains of the mothers are dotted with pools of yellow-orange to indicate the regions that are structurally different. The colored parts show areas of shrunken gray matter, in multiple brain regions, including the frontal and temporal cortices as well as the midline.

The yellow-orange areas aren't small pinpricks; they are noticeable, multiple and extensive. The changes are so blatant that the women in the study could easily be identified as having been pregnant or not based on the scans.

My brain was now literally a new brain. The surface area and cortical thickness had changed shape. The sulci, or furrows, were altered. The folds, or gyri, had changed.

It was a relief, to me, to look at these images: to see, in black, white, yellow and orange, that the hunch that I had become, was becoming, a different creature wasn't in my imagination. The data anchored me. This was the metamorphosis of matrescence.

Shrunken gray matter? Decrease in cortical thickness? It sounds as though the brain might be deteriorating, or losing some of its abilities. Instead, the lead author, Hoekzema, explained to me, volume loss can show a "fine-tuning of connections." Synaptic reorganization and fine-tuning, it is thought, make the brain more efficient and streamlined in what it needs to do to care for a baby. Or as Pawluski puts it, "to make sure we, and our child, survive parenthood."

"In adolescence, this is regarded as a specialization of brain circuits, where weak connections between nerve cells are eliminated to fine-tune networks," said Hoekzema, now director of the Pregnancy and the Brain Lab at the Amsterdam University Medical Centers.[9] It is a critical process for cognitive, emotional and social development when a human turns from child to adult.

Although the underlying cellular processes are still to be discovered, "it could very well be that the changes we observed across pregnancy represent a specialization of a woman's brain that helps the transition to motherhood," Hoekzema told me.

Her lab found various indications supporting such a hypothesis, for instance that stronger volume losses predict stronger mother–infant bonding and functional activation in the mother's brain towards her infant.

The changes are most prominently located in regions of the brain associated with theory of mind—the ability to understand and work out what someone else is thinking, feeling or needing. This area is, naturally, of high importance for caregiving and developing attachment. Indeed, when the researchers tested the data further, they found signs that regions of the brain where changes occurred also showed stronger responsiveness towards the mother's baby.[10] When mothers were shown pictures of their own babies, the ventral striatum—where the nucleus accumbens, a core part of the brain's reward system, is found—would light up. Animal studies had already shown that babies become even more rewarding for mothers than cocaine, and this reward system is thought to trigger the drive to care and nurture.[11]

The significant changes in this area of the brain were associated with an alteration of the reward system to include stronger responsiveness to the baby. Pregnancy may update the reward circuit so that the mother can respond to her child, the group concluded.

This may explain why my husband and I would often spend time in the evening, our limited leisure time if we had it, looking at photos of our baby daughter, and why I could repeatedly get up in the night even when dog-tired.

The changes the pregnant brain undergoes have been underestimated, Hoekzema told me, "as hormones and their impact often are, and thought of as something akin to an extreme menstrual period, while this is of course on a completely different scale." It is likely the most drastic endocrine event in human life.

But people think of new motherhood as mainly an external, environmental change, she said, preceded by the transient biological effects of pregnancy, which do not last.

"In fact, we ourselves have also changed."

She told me that, as a mother herself, she likes experiencing the "powerful biological drive."

"I've never smelled anything as wonderful as my babies' heads, for instance. Some of these things seem to be evolutionarily conserved and engraved into our brains.

"This is unlike any other brain changes I've investigated before. Something very powerful is reshaping our brains."

I had thought that my disrupted sense of self, my notion that I'd become a new hybrid creature, must be in some way fanciful. But, in fact, as these early studies of the maternal brain show, it was the idea that I was ultimately an independent individual that was fanciful. According to a paper by Hoekzema, the neuroscientist Susanna Carmona and others in *Archives of Women's Mental Health*: "A distinct neural plasticity characterizes the female brain during this period, and dynamic structural and functional changes take place that accompany fundamental behavioural adaptations." Together, these changes stimulate mothers "to progress from *an individual* with self-directed needs to being responsible for the care of another life."[12] Orchard describes the process as the mother's sense of self extending "a little further."

This groundbreaking science is getting more attention. Like Hoekzema herself, the neuroscience world was struck by the strength and extent of her findings, and the paper was covered widely. It was impactful on the wider scientific community because it made people realize how significant the changes are, Pawluski told me. Hoekzema's pioneering research was recognized with a €1.5 million grant for further work from the European Research Council (ERC) in 2020.

Soon after Hoekzema's work was published, Carmona and her lab in Madrid found that the impact of pregnancy on the brain is as significant as the impact of adolescence. The group compared the brains of twenty-five first-time mothers with twenty-five female adolescents; the brain changes were extraordinarily similar. Each group had reductions in cerebral gray matter volume at the same monthly rate. Both showed changes in cortical thickness and surface area, and depth, length and width of sulcal grooves (the lower part of the Viennetta-like ripples of the brain). "Our findings are consistent with the notion that the brain morphometric changes associated with pregnancy and adolescence reflect similar hormonally primed biological processes," the team concludes.[13]

There is now a growing number of neuroscientists in laboratories across the world studying how various areas of the brain may be altered by caregiving, and working out the implications of these neural changes for new mothers. As the data increases, researchers cross-pollinate each other's work.

This new frontier of discovery could have an enormous impact on the health and well-being of mothers, and their infants. The more scientists know about the physiological, endocrine and neural changes of pregnancy and early motherhood, the more we will know about how these processes can trigger mental illness, and how we can improve postpartum care.

At the end of 2022, a new comprehensive study by Hoekzema and her lab was published.[14] It is the first neuroscience work that speaks directly to the hard-to-describe sense of change that mothers experience: the sense that the self has become something new, that the old identity is over. The state of being in chrysalis goo. Hoekzema's study—of women before conception, through pregnancy and in the postpartum period—found that significant changes in the brain happened in the Default Mode Network (DMN), an area associated with processes like the perception of the self, self-referential processing, self-related mental explorations and autobiographical memory. The observed brain changes were linked to pregnancy hormones, particularly third-trimester estrogens.

"I think the most important findings of this new study are that pregnancy also changes brain function," Hoekzema told me. "And that the observed brain changes are linked to all kinds of perinatal processes in the female body and behavior, for example, their physiological responses to infant cues, their nesting behavior and their bonding with their infant in the postpartum period."

The changes, they found, "alter the neural basis of the self."

O

Finding out that the matrescent brain undergoes a radical metamorphosis was, in itself, reassuring for me. It wasn't just me overreacting: there were substantial changes unfolding in the nucleus accumbens, prefrontal cortex, dopaminergic response system, amygdala, hypothalamus, ventral tegmental area and ventral pallidum and no doubt in more areas that are yet to be discovered.

But it isn't just birthing parents or biological mothers whose brains change in multifaceted ways. We all evolved in collective child-rearing networks.

Over the last few decades, the work of the groundbreaking French-American biologist Catherine Dulac has altered the received wisdom that biology is destiny. It *is* destiny, she says, but it's also flexible.[15] In her studies on mice, she found that both male and female animals had the physical brain circuitry for both male and female behaviors. When a particular pheromone-sensing circuit was repressed, the male mice became maternal and looked after the pups instead of trying to kill them, while the female mice acted like the males and engaged in typical mounting behaviors towards each other. The implications for humans are that caregiving neural circuitry exists in both male and female brains.

Early neuroscientific research on humans is now showing that caregiver brains experience significant plasticity, even without the experience of pregnancy. Hands-on caring shapes brain circuitry and causes other biological changes. In 2020, a groundbreaking study showed that having a baby changes a father's brain anatomy.[16] The brains of men were studied before their partners became pregnant and after the baby was born. First-time fathers showed a significant reduction in cortical volume and thickness. The higher the volume reduction, the stronger the father's brain responses to pictures of his baby. Other studies found that the hands-on time a father spends with an infant, and even how affectionate he is, is associated with different hormonal and neural changes, such as the reduction of testosterone, and increases in oxytocin and the level of activity in the brain's reward systems.[17,18]

Studies of brain activity in fathers in heterosexual partnerships, gay fathers and nonbiological parents show that the adult caregiving brain is highly adaptive and will change in response to the demands of an infant. Many of the neurobiological mechanisms associated with nurturing in mothers—the presence of oxytocin, prolactin, vasopressin—are also present in fathers and non-birthing parents. Neuroscientists Eyal Abraham and Ruth Feldman, of Reichman University in Israel, concluded two decades of behavioral and imaging work with a paper published in 2019 saying that the malleability of fathers—and other caregivers—"may be built on an ancient alloparenting evolutionary substrate that supports a role of both male and female as direct caregivers."[19] It is the infants' abilities to elicit care, which reorganize the caregivers' brains and bodies. Parents (usually women) who are pregnant and give birth have an incomparable neuroendocrinological experience but they are not unique in their biological ability to adapt to look after babies or children. It's a good thing, too, considering how common maternal mortality has been until very recently.

I observed this in my husband. As he began to spend more time one-on-one with our daughter, I could almost see his reward pathways firing more strongly and rapidly before my eyes. As time passed, his response to her cues, her cries and her needs became quicker and more skilled. I also became more adept at caregiving over time, but the cries felt like an absolute emergency to me from the very beginning; my intense preoccupation with her had started in pregnancy. In the first year or so, he didn't wake up in the same way I did when she cried or made a sound in the middle of the night. Now, years later, he wakes up and attends to our children much more quickly and easily. The more caring he did, the more attuned he became. Studies suggest that contact with children does reconfigure parents' brains. When babies and adults make eye contact, for example, their brainwaves become more synchronized.[20]

O

With the endocrinal storm of pregnancy, mothers do undergo the most dramatic brain changes, and Hoekzema's research helps explain why new mothers may feel altered. It may even give a neuroscientific explanation for the psychoanalyst Donald Winnicott's famous theory of "Primary Maternal Preoccupation." This, in Winnicott's interpretation, is the state that follows childbirth when a mother becomes preoccupied with the baby to the exclusion of anything else, giving her a heightened sensitivity and empathy to what the infant needs. It "would be an illness" he wrote, but for the fact of pregnancy.[21]

After the initial shock of new motherhood had passed, the feel-good effects seemed to grow and grow, albeit depending on how much sleep I was getting. My dopamine response to smelling the baby's head, or hearing her first words, or watching her first drawing, seemed to become stronger over the years of my matrescence. It's possible my dopamine levels had already been altered: Alison Fleming's animal studies suggest that baseline dopamine levels may be lowered in pregnancy, so a burst of dopamine in the postnatal period becomes more thrilling and addictive.[22] I felt—and often feel—that I am physically addicted to my infant children, falling in love with them more deeply each day, and, as this research shows, in some ways, I am.

The maternal brain continues to change after the baby is born. One study found that the brains of women four to six weeks after giving birth looked five years younger than they did at the birth.[23] Other research has shown that cortical thickness increases in mothers during the months after the birth, so it is possible, as Pilyoung Kim of the University of Denver puts it, that the maternal brain "waxes and wanes."[24] Indeed, the relationship between pregnancy, child-rearing and the brain seems to be in flux throughout the life course. We don't know if matrescence really ever ends. Middle-aged and older women who have had children show less brain aging and cognitive decline than those who have not given birth—and the positive effect may increase with the number of children, though it drops a little at four.[25]

It's not all good news for mothers, though. In early 2021, the journal *Frontiers in Neuroendocrinology* published a comprehensive review by Kim revealing how stress can affect brain adaptations to motherhood.[26] She details how pregnancy and the postnatal period is a vulnerable window in which the plasticity of the brain makes it particularly sensitive to severe stress. Of course, some level of stress in life is normal and required. An ability to sense threat or danger is crucial to keeping a young baby alive. But severe stress is a different matter. There are three types of severe stress that can negatively affect a woman's transition to motherhood. First, environmental stress such as poverty, unsafe neighborhoods, marital conflict, racism and discrimination. Second, adverse childhood experiences, such as neglect or abuse (in the UK, 47 percent of people experience one adverse childhood experience). Third, stress related to childbirth and parenting. Just as in adolescence, when the brain is plastic and changing, it is more vulnerable to stress. A dampened response in an area of the brain associated with reward—the amygdala—was found in women living with socioeconomic stress. Childhood adversity has been found to increase the stress response in the hippocampus to negative infant cues. Parental stress—such as parenting a child with a "difficult infant temperament"—is found to reduce activity in areas of the brain, such as the amygdala, associated with aspects of motivation and reward.

Again, more research is critical but the science of the maternal brain published to date tells us that mothers in this vulnerable period need care, and particularly protective social policies. The one strategy which seems to inoculate most new mothers against mental illness is social support. Social support, according to scientific tools and scales, includes emotional and practical support from a partner, family and non-family relationships, support from coworkers, support with routine home duties such as watching children, traditional rituals, reassurance of worth and companionship. Wider social support looks like infrastructure for caregivers, such as libraries, childcare centers and child-friendly transport networks, affordable childcare and investment in perinatal healthcare.

This is illustrated by the success of Mom Power, a groundbreaking psychotherapeutic initiative in Michigan. It was set up in 2009 to help new mothers who were facing severe stress, or had histories of trauma. Not only did participants in the program show reductions in depression, PTSD and parenting stress, but functional changes in their brains were recorded by researchers.[27] This was the first time that a program supporting maternal mental health had been documented in this way. Mothers who completed the program showed greater activity in brain circuitry involved in empathy. The psychotherapy they were given—the group used CBT, DBT and attachment-theory skills—helped reduce stress levels. The ten-week, thirteen-session format has since spread to thirteen areas of Michigan and nine other states, with 350 individuals being trained.

It is exciting to see how powerful social support can be for new mothers. But perhaps it shouldn't come as a surprise, considering the extended social networks and caregiving cooperatives that we evolved within.

○

Costs, benefits and trade-offs are a hallmark of the natural world—and humans are no exception. To be a smart species—to be able to learn and read and write and draw and solve and build and invent and empathize and imagine—humans have to be born vulnerable.

Few other species of animal on earth are as helpless and immature as human babies. The brains of other primates are much more developed at birth. Humans are one of the only mammals with brains that grow so significantly outside the womb. The benefit of this early helplessness is that it means the brain can adapt and rewire as the infant grows.

And who soaks up the cost of this vulnerability in humans? Mothers.

As the Canadian neurophilosopher Patricia Churchland explains, "the biological solution seems to have been to modify the emotions associated with self-survival (fear when threatened, discomfort when hungry) so they are also aroused for baby-threat and baby-discomfort."[28]

That sounds familiar.

Social vocalization and audible communication may have evolved in mammals so that mothers could find a lost infant. "Language is born of absence," wrote Roland Barthes.[29]

"In effect," Churchland says, "the mammalian mother feels her babies are part of her . . . evolution expanded the ambit of 'me' to include 'me-and-mine.' "[30]

How did this happen? The "underlying genetic trick," to use Churchland's phrase, was the expansion of the territory of the hormone oxytocin to the brain from the body.

Throughout pregnancy, the pituitary gland expands, and extra oxytocin receptors set up shop in the brain and uterus, where oxytocin has an important job to do. The word *oxytocin* is from the Greek *okus* for "swift" and *tokos* for "birth," which is a way of describing oxytocin's role in triggering the uterus to contract and push the baby through the pelvis and birth canal and into the light.

We might know oxytocin as the "love hormone," and be aware of the activities associated with its release: sex, cuddling, hanging out with friends, stroking a pet. Oxytocin triggers the release of neurocannabinoids that make us feel high. In fact, it is much more complex than this, but oxytocin is broadly associated with bonding and attachment.

Our knowledge of how oxytocin may interplay with attachment circuitry has emerged through the study of prairie voles, small rodents with shorter snouts than rats and fatter bodies than mice. Their fur is light brown and speckled with gray and their eyes are dark and ink-like. Scientists have studied prairie voles with interest over the first decades of the twenty-first century because of their long-term pair bonding. Why do prairie voles attach for life when their cousins, meadow voles, don't? What are the neural circuits which prime prairie voles to attach?

Neuroscientists found that if a vole was removed from its mate, and then stressed out with loud noises, then, on its return, its unstressed mate would lick and groom it.[31] When the voles were first returned to one another, the corticosterone levels—commonly referred to as the stress hormone—would match up across their brains. Both voles were experiencing the same level of stress; both were demonstrating anxiety behaviors and fear responses despite having experienced very different conditions. When the researchers blocked the brain receptor for oxytocin, the mate's consolation behavior stopped.

Oxytocin doesn't just make animals like humans and prairie voles feel warm and gooey; it forms the basis of our ability to interact socially, work together, cooperate and compromise. These ancient neurochemicals and processes that I am feeling—the fears and discomfort, the love and attachment—were fundamental to the evolution of humanity.

In those early months, I became aware that expressing love and affection through physical touch would have a pleasant, soothing physical effect on me, as if my body was being juiced with a feel-good chemical. The effect seemed to intensify as the months went on. The baby's thighs were increasingly addictive. Her eyes gave me butterflies. I would sniff her skin with urgency. I was awed by her pudgy little body and her face was—is, with her brothers'—the most beautiful thing I have ever seen. As our attachment grew, and she grew too, she responded by winding her little arms around my neck, by stroking my hair when she fed, by becoming calmer when I held her or carried her around on my hip, by smiling when she heard my voice. I'd stroke her head and hair automatically. I'd kiss and caress her and she'd smile and laugh and it was—is—the highest high.

O

Still, as she grew, the loss of autonomy began to gnaw at me. Primarily, my inability to do the basic essentials. I wanted to be able to sleep more than a few hours a night, go to the loo when I needed to, shower and brush my teeth. But she was often unsettled and I didn't want to put her down.

I saw everything through the gauze of her needs. Some days I felt obliterated by it. I was melting into her, and she into me. I wasn't sure where I ended and she began.

Increasingly, I had a creeping sense that I wasn't wired for this. I was a lone mother in a nuclear household and, despite my infatuation, the shock of the baby's needs—called nurture shock, I would later learn—was challenging.[32] Increasingly, when I was desperate to sleep or so tired that tears were close to the surface all day, I didn't feel certain that I could meet her wants. After a day of her crying, my reserves of patience and empathy would be depleted. I was surprised by this: my understanding was that there should be no such thing as a limit when it came to maternal care.

The lack of sleep continued, and I spent more time on my own with her. The crying and isolation started to wear me down. Even though I had a loving, supportive marriage and family, I started to wonder whether this pattern of caregiving for twenty-four hours a day, mostly on my own, was sustainable. Was there something wrong with me? We were fortunate to live near our wider family, but I was struggling to accept that I could let other people take on some of the care work. I didn't want to be a burden or an imposition; I didn't feel like I could admit that I was starting to struggle. I didn't know how to ask for or accept help. The idea of doing so felt horribly uncomfortable: my primary way of relating to people was to attempt to make sure everyone around me was OK, to be emotionally self-sufficient. But I knew that this wasn't right; my female ancestors hadn't mothered this way, alone and indoors.

O

I may share a neurobiological and emotional legacy with my ancient ancestors, but there is a major difference between my experience of motherhood in one of the so-called WEIRD countries—Western, educated, industrialized, rich and democratic—and that of most of human life.

For most of our evolutionary history, humans lived in small groups. Mothers lived in small social communities. Crucially, this meant that they mothered alongside others. Over hundreds of thousands of years, women foraged, together, with their babies close by. Our brains, our nervous systems, evolved in collective child-rearing societies.

For millennia, mothers relied on the help of others to rear infants. Research undertaken by the primatologist and anthropologist Sarah Blaffer Hrdy suggests that women needed help simply to feed a baby and ensure its survival through childhood. A lone foraging woman would not have been able to supply the ten to thirteen million calories a human child would need to eat before it could find food independently.[33]

So wherever they safely could, human mothers handed babies over to alloparents—"other" parents or fathers.[34] They weaned children early, swaddled them and hung them from doors. Mothers in foraging societies across the world still do.

I started to realize that the ideal of continuous, exclusive, one-on-one contact between mother and child is a modern fairy tale. It's one which clashes exquisitely painfully with contemporary work culture, with its lack of flexibility and family-friendly workplaces, with its long hours and expectation that new parents return to work quicker than many would choose.

New research into the neurobiology of parenting and caregiving helps explain why alloparenting succeeds in different cultures. We are learning that a person doesn't need to be pregnant for the brain to reconfigure into an infant-caregiving brain: hands-on parenting can rewire a male brain in a similar way to the effect of pregnancy and childbirth. And, as Hrdy puts it: "Female primates have always been dual-career mothers."[35]

O

When people say "enjoy every minute"—the stock phrase repeated to all new mothers—they must've forgotten, or not experienced, what it's like to spend hours with a crying baby every day. What it's like to listen to your crying baby, especially when alone.

Some babies cry a lot more than others and this is often called colic. The etymological roots of "colic" are in the word for colon, and the term referred originally to abdominal distress. Now, colic is a catchall term for babies who cry a lot without an obvious cause. The NHS definition is three hours a day of crying, for three days a week, for at least one week. In the first few months this is also called PURPLE crying (peak, unexpected, resistant to soothing, pain-like face, long-lasting, evening) and up to half of babies suffer from it, crying for long, inconsolable stretches in this period.[36] Some types of infant cries elicit greater responses in different brain areas. Preterm babies and autistic babies have been found to have more "aversive" cries in the first year which can negatively affect maternal mental health.[37]

The maternal brain adapts, as we have learned, to be able to respond quickly to an infant's needs. Which is good for the infant. But what about the impact on the mother?

I hadn't anticipated how excruciating and torturous the crying would be, nor did I know that sometimes there is nothing a person can do to help or soothe a baby. I hadn't realized that some have more sensitive temperaments than others, and that this can make the experience of new parenthood more stressful. I was starting to understand that the experience of matrescence is deeply heterogeneous.

This crying in early infancy is sometimes called "developmental," I learned. This interested me. My daughter, who seemed to cry a lot in the early weeks and months, even when being held or rocked, wasn't necessarily hungry or thirsty or tired or needing physical contact; she may have been in "developmental" pain or anguish, her brain growing and changing rapidly, fearing separation, which would mean death (babies are close to that portal, and the primitive need for survival). This period of inconsolable crying could start at around two weeks and continue until three to four months—with a peak at around four to eight weeks. I read—and saw—that there were other stages where an infant might be more "clingy," and need carrying around more, or to sleep close by, shortly after which she would often be able to do something new. The baby might just be finding being in the world, and growing in the world, stressful, and all she could do was cry, even if all her obvious needs were met. It might mean that she was simply processing the world, and the rapid changes within, and crying was the only way to communicate. I began to realize that I wouldn't ever be able to take all her pain away. The ideal of the mother who could solve all problems by always being there was, perhaps, a myth: even when I was there and able to give my all, sometimes it just wasn't enough. Sometimes I couldn't be the medicine I had been led to believe only I, her mother, could be. This crushed my naive understanding of a "maternal instinct."

At times I wondered if the experience of birth had affected her. The psychoanalyst Otto Rank believed that babies are traumatized by their experience of being born. His guiding principle for *The Trauma of Birth* was Freud's theory that birth, and the experience of near-asphyxiation in the birth canal, is the primal human anxiety.[38] I tried to imagine what it must have been like for her in that long labor, to be squeezed repeatedly by the pushing uterus muscles, to hear my strange bellows, the repetition of thick, hard walls closing in, and then her head moving through a tight hole—the cervix—over her nose and cheeks, my hot wet muscles turning her into the birth canal, and then the taste of metal, sweet blood, and a crushing and shunting, back and forth back and forth, for a couple of hours and then into the light and the air. A new element.

After birth, Rank believed, human life is spent trying to return to uterine bliss, to find the comfort and security of the maternal womb in the world. He built on Freud's idea that the anxiety of a child alone in a dark room will quieten when the child becomes conscious of the voice or touch of a loved one. Rank thought that humans repressed the traumatic memories of being born after the blissful prenatal state, but that the anxieties birth generated would play out throughout life. He thought, for example, that fear of small animals such as frogs, toads, mice or beetles occurred because of their "peculiar ability" to disappear into holes in the ground. "They therefore exhibit the wish to return into the maternal hiding-place as completely accomplished. And the feeling of dread which clings to them arises because they materialize one's own tendency, namely, to go back into mother," he wrote.

Rank might well have pushed this too far. Evolutionary biology suggests that my baby crying in this way was normal. Babies have evolved to demand more than they need. To compete effectively with the parent, the offspring must attempt to induce more care, attention—investment—than the parent is selected to give. The "squeaky wheels" get the milk, to use the American evolutionary biologist Robert Trivers's phrase.[39]

It is not unusual to find nurturing difficult. If humans did it automatically, babies would not need to be so attuned and discriminating, writes Hrdy.[40] Just as the baby in the womb plays tug of war with the mother's body and resources, so the infant in the world uses techniques such as vocalizations, tantrums and other behaviors to get the resources it needs.

This was the most intense period of learning and knowledge-acquiring of my life, and the baby was my teacher. As the months passed, she taught me nonverbal communication and how to take turns with noises and sounds. She taught me how to speak baby. She showed me that bathing in warm water was soothing, that impressions of snoring were funny. She reconfigured my brain.

I sometimes felt shipwrecked by the tumultuous changes I was undergoing. The health visitor arrived to see how we were. Any questions? she asked. But I couldn't express what was on my mind. Was it normal to feel turned inside out? Was this new hybrid self what my life would be now? Is everyone frightened every day that their baby will die? How can I soothe my inner baby while soothing my actual baby? Would my nervous system feel on edge forever? What is the word for the realization that your society has left you ill-equipped for a major part of the journey of your life? When a mother cries, is it also developmental?

Aurora borealis

Auroras appear when the sun changes. The sun sends out heat and light, but also energy and particles, which the electromagnetic field of the Earth protects us from. This solar wind is blown out into the solar system, a million tons a second, traveling three hundred miles a second.

As the sun's particles, or plasma, break through, and travel down the magnetic field canals at the poles, they mingle with the Earth's atmosphere: oxygen and nitrogen. These interactions produce extra energy which is released as light: when the oxygen interacts with the solar gases it emits green and red light, and the nitrogen glows blue and purple. The colors wind and snake, rhubarb and kryptonite, transforming the canvas of the sky. The aurora is millions of collisions, illuminating the Earth's magnetic field lines.

7.

Motherhood and sociality

The isolated parenting that women do in this society is not the best way to raise children or treat women who mother.

bell hooks, *Feminist Theory: From Margin to Center*

What do playgrounds say to women? They say—"You know what, just fuck you! You haven't anywhere to change dirty diapers—fuck you, deal with it. You and your babies don't count enough for us to put in the plumbing. Are you going to sit for hours under the boiling sun? Okay! Because you don't count. This work doesn't count."

Naomi Wolf, Interview with the *Guardian* (2001)

Before matrescence, I didn't really know what child-rearing entailed. I didn't know how vulnerable human babies are, how much we needed, how much our mothers had to give us. I thought looking after children was easy.

What I knew about mothers and infant care was basic, even superficial.

This is what I thought I knew. Babies are sweet. Babies drink milk, travel in prams, sleep in cots, and need cuddles and kisses and diapers. Sometimes, they cry. Mothers can "naturally" soothe them. Mothers mother intensely for nine months of statutory maternity leave and then return to working more or less as normal.

But, on closer inspection, it became clear that a further set of assumptions about motherhood had lain dormant inside me. When the baby was born, they reared up, reinforced by what I read and heard. Good mothers are content and grateful, undemanding and unambitious. Good mothers are fulfilled by their children. Mothers shouldn't pursue their own interests: they are morally obligated to put themselves to one side, especially in the early years. Mothers are the most important people in an infant's life and they alone carry the responsibility for the health, well-being and security of their child. Mothers serve the family.

Until matrescence, I had sought to live a life like my father's. Now I found myself living my mother's life. I had switched from protagonist to stagehand. But I went further than my parents and their generation, who made their children work around them, rather than the other way round. I had internalized a set of expectations about my new role that were significantly more child-centered and mother-abnegating than the maternal ideal of the 1980s, when the most popular book for my mother and her peers was called *How Not to Be a Perfect Mother*.

O

As the months passed, it dawned on me that my mother went through a lot to give birth to me, and then to look after me as an infant, and then to raise me through childhood. When I visited her in Scotland, I kept furtively looking at her stomach and thinking, I came from there. That is where I came from, where I began.

I started to see her in a new way. I was glimpsing how much vaster and harder the undertaking of motherhood is, how much she had had to do to keep me alive and to love and care for me. I couldn't believe I had so little idea of what child-rearing entailed: that it is a doing, rather than a being, and a doing around the clock, without end. She had a life before me! She was a person before me! I considered this, really, for the first time.

While staying at her house, I found my own baby record book.

The cover is duck-egg blue, with lined sketches of seven children at various ages. Originally published in 1950, *The First Seven Years: A Record Book for Mother & Child* was reissued in the 1980s, around the time I was born.

I scoured it for information that could suggest when my daughter and I might start getting more sleep. I looked through the notes my mother had jotted down about when I started sleeping for longer stretches and then sleeping through, about my first foods, favorite toys and first words and phrases.

I flicked through the Introduction, which discusses the unalterable foundations of "mothercraft." "They will always be serenity, humour, affection and understanding, and in a mother's protective care and love the fragile bundle of helplessness will grow into a healthy happy child."

This chimed with my pre-matrescent image of a mother. Effectively, she was Mary, the mother of Jesus, her expression matching the gold icons we had on the walls and mantelpieces of my childhood home. The baby Jesus, on her lap, was never having a tantrum. His swaddling clothes were immaculate. Motherhood looked chill.

I turned to the section on feeding. Weirdly, the advice was completely different to the instructions I had been given. It advised feeding every four hours on a strict schedule rather than "on demand." It also recommended a little orange juice between feeds. I had been told that if I gave my baby anything but breast milk before six months it would be a catastrophe. The book talked about routines, and how they are good for babies, which sounded like the Gina Ford school of baby care, which I'd sensed was a "bad thing." I'd gathered from a few parenting Facebook groups and Mumsnet threads that Ford's methods did not align with good mothering. A health visitor had told me that she and her colleagues would hide Gina Ford books if they saw them in charity shops because they disagreed with her ideas so vehemently. (When she next came over, I would turn the copy on my bookshelf around so she wouldn't see the spine.)

The majority of mothers I had met didn't follow Ford's methods—

or wouldn't admit to doing so. I found her overall approach too rigid, but her suggested schedules were useful and I liked that she considered maternal sleep and well-being, which was a lot more than most authors on parenting did. Instead, the dominant mothering method in the wider culture around me was focused on forming a secure attachment with the baby in the early months, influenced by child-centered parenting gurus such as Dr. William Sears, Penelope Leach, Sarah Ockwell-Davies and Janet Lansbury. Posters and leaflets in the doctor's surgery or at mother and baby groups were about baby-wearing, breastfeeding on demand and child-led weaning. The messages that I heard decreed that the right way of mothering was to adopt this baby-led, instinctive mode. Mothers needed to be in near-constant physical contact with their baby, letting them suckle and feed whenever they wanted.

My eyes narrowed when I got to this part in my 1980s baby book. "From birth to two months he should sleep twenty out of twenty-four hours." What? My daughter was sleeping around half of that amount because I couldn't put her down without her crying, nor would she sleep for long when she was resting on one of us. I smiled at the next line. "He . . . should sleep out of doors all day winter and summer. The only weather which is really unsuitable for baby is fog."

The section on emotions was very different to what I was being taught: mirroring and containing the child's emotions, no matter how explosive or inconvenient, and affirming and validating with plenty of patience and delight. "The important thing to remember is that all emotion, either of pleasure or annoyance, must be banished, and a calm, wholly dispassionate attitude adopted which takes for granted the child will do what is expected of him."

Looking over the old baby record book, a seed was planted: standards of infant care were culturally relative. Perhaps, then, our ideal of motherhood was constructed, too. Maybe there was no truth, no single way of raising a healthy baby, of being a good mother. Maybe I should stop reading so many parenting books.

○

But still, I wanted to get it right, so I did keep reading books and articles and forums manically, this being the way I had always solved problems and learned about the world. My brain started to frazzle from the conflicting advice about sleeping and feeding. I figured there must be a solution to the puzzle; there must be evidence-based answers. I wanted to follow my own instinct but it was proving hard to locate. The one element the books all had in common was the claim that their way was the only way and, if you deviated from it, your child wouldn't sleep, eat properly or be happy. Looking back, I think my hyper-receptivity to external influences and social judgment may have been a result of the increased plasticity of my brain.

One morning, after months of my getting only a few, broken hours' sleep each night, the health visitor came over. I had read that picking up a baby whenever they were crying wouldn't help them in the long run: they needed to learn how to "self-soothe" and fall asleep alone. The French, I'd heard, had a tactic called *le pause*, where they would leave the baby protesting for a minute or so to see if she could settle herself.

I could barely see straight when the health visitor arrived. I had been awake since 2:00 a.m., knocking back sips of coffee like tequila.

How's Mum? she asked. I hadn't yet got used to being called Mum, rather than my name. Tired, I said, with a wan laugh, trying to chase away the lump in my throat. She is still quite nocturnal and it takes a while, sometimes hours, to settle her back to sleep in the night after a feed. She cries even while being rocked and held.

Very normal, said the health visitor. Have you started a nighttime routine with a bath?

Yes, I said. Actually, I've been thinking about how much I'm picking her up, and rocking her, I ventured, tentatively. I'm wondering if it's OK to leave her crying for half a minute to see if she'll settle herself, or if I should pick her up immediately? I rubbed the baby's back and kissed her ears, feeling guilty about even mentioning the idea.

Baby needs Mummy, she said. If she's crying, it's because she needs you. She's trying to communicate and needs picking up. She might be hungry, or need her diaper changing, hot or cold or needing a cuddle. Baby needs Mummy.

Yes, yes, I trailed off, extinguishing the remaining tiny flame that my need for sleep could be of some importance.

You can never cuddle a baby too much, she added. Don't listen to anyone who says otherwise. Babies are only little for such a short period of time, why wouldn't you just cuddle them constantly?

O

Around this time, I started to worry that the baby might have acid reflux. She would cry for hours each evening and no amount of rocking or cuddling or soothing seemed to help. I hadn't realized that I was powerless to soothe her. Baby needs Mummy. According to an app on my phone, which tells parents how a baby should be behaving from day to day, week to week, according to "leaps" and "regressions," we should be enjoying a run of sunny days.

We went to see the doctor. Suddenly I became conscious of how I must look. I was wearing a pajama top—I needed a top with buttons to breastfeed, and all the others were dirty—and drawstring trousers. The slackening elastic of my large underpants and a slab of their graying lilac and green flower design were visible. I pulled my trousers up quickly. I looked down and saw runs of milk down my chest and bits of cereal or lint and unexplained stains on my top. Sweat patches were probably visible. I smelled acrid. My hair was tied back. It had been falling out and now the small bun was more like a new potato with ratty short bits peeling off. When I ran my hands through my hair, clumps would come off in my fingers.

I stood and rocked the baby to and fro. Every cry felt like she was revealing to the doctor that I couldn't mother her properly. I'm worried she has reflux or is in pain, I said, my head thumping. Wild-eyed, sweating, bobbing up and down as I was, the doctor deduced I might not be feeling great, too.

She's picking up on your anxiety, the doctor said. Babies can sense if their mother is feeling anxious or worried, and it can make them anxious, too. Babies are very intuitive.

Oh sweet Jesus, I thought. I gritted my teeth. I am making her anxious, because I'm anxious. How on earth am I going to solve this one?

But she might have reflux, too. I'll look at her. We left, without a prescription, but with me now harboring a growing sense of guilt and horror that my emotional life could be infecting her. The only way through, I thought, was to repress the anxiety, pretend it didn't exist. I could do this; I had had years of practice. I had to be stronger, more emotionally self-controlled, more resilient. I willed it.

I began reading a baby book by the popular child-rearing guru Penelope Leach in which she lays out the imperative that mothers adopt an attitude of calm. I can do this, I thought, though inside I felt like a ship in a storm. I was becoming accustomed to splitting myself, to acquiescing to the wider culture's requirement for a kind of passive silence and a rictus grin. I acted as though I was managing. I read Leach's description of the "brief drama" of labor and it made me feel like I mustn't dwell on the violence of birth. (Only later would I start to sense a revisionist agenda in a lot of the stories people tell of their births: they can't all have been "brief dramas" when 45 percent of women find birth traumatic.)

Over this period, I spent more and more time walking around the local shopping mall, giving the baby a chance to sleep in the pram and meeting my desire to be around people, even strangers. The mall was the heart of the town we had moved to, geographically and symbolically. On the platform of the train station, a big sign proclaimed that the town was "Home to Festival Place." Festival Place—the mall—was a temple to consumerism. It housed millions of products, from bath bombs to plugs, pens to books, pickles to doughnuts, vases to lipsticks. It was warm and bright and aseptic: a place of potential, of objects which promised something. Although it was not a place of community or connectedness, it was the nexus of activity in the town and it had a library and coffee, so it was where I ended up.

Being in shops and supermarkets reminded me of being a child and going shopping with my mother: the smells of each aisle, of magazines, bleach and pastry. I got a mild buzz from buying a packet of seeds or a cookie, which broke up the monotony of caregiving. I would walk slowly around, admiring piles of colored, beautifully folded towels, all clean and neat and perfect. Red, orange, yellow, green. I liked how ordered they were compared with how disordered our house and my mind were starting to feel. But it didn't have any lasting, nourishing effect. The more I wandered the shops, the more a craving for people—for relationship with others, for ecologies of care—set in.

Any social interactions that I had were usually with middle-aged or elderly women, eyes watery and wistful, who invariably said "enjoy every moment, it doesn't last." Or "make the most of it, it goes so fast." They would stare at the baby and I'd feel proud and in some way connected to a kind of wider matrilineality, but also guilty that I wasn't enjoying every moment. It started to weigh down on me, this constant mandate to enjoy it all. I wondered why it was such a common trope. Had they not made the most of it? Were they trying to make sure I didn't make the same mistake? Why was it so important to people that I saw these as the best days of my life? It left me with a note of fear: when my children left home, would I be the one wandering around the shopping mall, staring nostalgically at babies, wishing for the past?

O

I began to notice, when I was out and about pushing the baby in a pram, a change in the attention my body drew from the world. When pregnant, I had felt conspicuous: everyone's eyes fell on my growing womb. When the baby was out, I became invisible: I could move around without any attention being paid to me at all. I realized then that I had never seen mothers or women with young babies or children. I had never *seen* them. But now I saw that the world was full of them. It was a lurching change of consciousness.

It was relaxing, in a way, to be invisible, particularly to certain men. Not that I expected sexual interest anymore, but no one ever badgered me or told me, "Smile, love, it might never happen." I was no longer spoken to in ways that used to drive me up the wall. The presence of a pram declares sexual nonavailability to most people.

But I looked different, too, from before, and the disconnection I felt with my new maternal body affected how I moved through the world.

When I saw myself in the mirror, I would wince. I was someone else. My stomach was an empty cocoon, doughy and spent. I was larger: two stone heavier, more. My hips and thighs were buttered with new layers of fat. I had thickened. *Matronly* might be the word for it. My shedding hair—which I didn't have much time to wash—was newly shorn. There were red, sore patches of eczema around my mouth and cheeks. My eyes, puffy. One eye had a red vein across it, drawn by her newborn nail. Thrown by all this change, I would tiredly chuck on baggy tracksuits, holey jumpers, utilitarian striped tops, old T-shirts, leggings, to hide my bigger shape. Sometimes I carelessly bought items of clothing which screamed of an identity crisis. Bizarre oversized dungarees. A horrible silken shirt. Ugly dresses I thought a mother would wear.

In adolescence, our changing bodies were collectively adorned: we customized our clothes, borrowing and sharing wardrobes, finding our new identities with the styles and the colors we liked. But in matrescence, well, the clothes were shit (maternity clothes are floral, ultrafeminine or very expensive).

As the baby grew, I realized I was starting to dress a bit like the clown that she loved on the children's television channel. My rib cage was bigger, my hair darker, my waist gone. The moles on my face had changed. It wasn't me.

I knew what I was supposed to look like. New mothers are supposed to "ping" or "snap" back, to use media parlance. Maternal bodies are not beautiful. Just look at recent headlines in the most popular newspaper in the country and you'll see hysterical updates about Elyse's "impressive slimmed down post-baby figure," Emily flaunting her "VERY slender midsection just two months after welcoming her child" and Danielle's "taut stomach" and "no signs of tiredness."[1,2,3] The narrative in each one of these articles follows the same formula. The celebrity "flaunts" her taut abs "just" two, seven, eight months after giving birth. As much as I rejected this kind of media, an internalized sexism and misogyny whispered to me: you know what you're supposed to look like. I was supposed to "get my body back" and shed any signs of matrescence. The media reports didn't say "Rowena flaunts her VERY roly-poly midsection just two months after welcoming her child" or "Gia flexed her jiggly-wiggly tummy" or "as she stepped out Poppy made sure all eyes were on her stretch-marked and saggy stomach in the Balenciaga bra showing deep signs of tiredness with a pallid complexion and perfectly greasy hair." No—new mothers are supposed to swiftly reverse our metamorphosis.

I hadn't realized that it is unlikely that after pregnancy a woman will ever return to pre-birth fitness. I didn't know how profoundly pregnancy affects the body, from cardiac health to musculoskeletal performance. A study by researchers at Martin Army Community Hospital in Fort Benning, Georgia, showed that women who became pregnant while in the military, even with regular training throughout pregnancy and the early postnatal period, struggled to get their bodies back to prepregnancy fitness. "It can take a long time—if ever—for them to get back to how they were before," says Wendy Brown, at the University of Queensland in Brisbane, Australia.[4]

Increasingly, when I looked in the mirror, I'd search quickly, fearfully, trying to find myself in my new face, my new body.

Wrinkles and lines were bedding in, from laughing and smiling and singing and cooing and whooping and frowning and wide-eyed enunciating.

My teeth had yellowed. More coffee, less time for brushing.

My breasts were misshapen from breastfeeding and scrawled with stretch marks. For months and months after I stopped feeding, they would still contain drops of milk.

The skin on my knees was beginning to toughen like elephant hide, a thicker, rougher skin from time spent on the floor with the growing baby. Crawling and peekaboo. Kneeling and holding. Picking up toys. Spinning from one stance to another, responding, reacting, changing.

Eventually, I stopped looking.

○

For all the new characters who had appeared and seemed to be invested in my day-to-day—the health visitors and parenting gurus and kind old ladies at the mall—this was the loneliest time of my adult life.

Before my matrescence, I had been accustomed to meeting friends for coffees and dinner, walking with friends, dancing with friends, chatting with friends, swimming with friends, watching films with friends, cooking with friends. Time was suspended in my twenties: mortality didn't figure. I'd been attending alcohol and drug recovery meetings for around four years before I got pregnant and I'd relied on those social networks for my sanity. My young adulthood was defined by a rich social life, by adventures and travel and independence. Regular social interactions were as necessary as food and sleep and oxygen.

Once matrescence hit, most of my social support came virtually, through Instagram accounts, parenting podcasts and in messages from friends on my phone. I counted down the hours to the lunchtime call from my husband and then to his arrival home from work.

Life became quieter.

The soundscape of the early months of motherhood, apart from the crying, was soft rhymes, faint feathery sounds, coos and gentle knocks between lip and lip and tongue and roof of mouth, using mouth and air and cheeks to soothe and entertain. Putting bottom lip to top lip with a little pressure and inhaling slightly, bringing air into the mouth. I stopped listening to music. I didn't know what to play. I didn't know who I was.

○

I noticed that friends and family members who were part of a church, or from cultures in countries such as Nigeria or India where a family member—a mother or sister, usually—would come and stay for a number of months, seemed to adapt better to matrescence than I did, immersed as I was in a white Western culture without formal rituals and traditions, without a culture of asking for and accepting help.

I was raising my child in a country where thousands of children's centers and Sure Start centers—public places parents could go with babies and young children for play, support, social connection and interaction; places simply to go and be with others—had recently been closed, merged or defunded.[5]

I was moving through built environments—public spaces and transport networks—that had been designed by men, not caregivers, in a male-dominated, profit-driven world. Pavements are narrow; curbs aren't always pram-friendly. Cars dominate, so children can't play together freely or safely.

When I spent time in public spaces, places hostile to the anarchy of infants, I found that I felt ever more abject and transgressive. I sniffed bums in public and wiped snot from noses. The baby sucked from my tit; I sang in public. My breasts leaked milk. I made animal noises on the street. Perhaps this was what Marguerite Duras meant when she said motherhood makes you obscene.[6]

O

As time passed, this new isolation and alienation chipped away at my sense of self. It felt as if I was dropping out of society entirely.

Saying yes to invitations wasn't simple. I was anxious about losing the little sleep I was getting. The baby was highly sensitive to different environments and sensory stimulation. I didn't know what to talk about. I didn't know what to say about looking after a baby all day. Matrescence was another country, another planet. I didn't know how to talk about the existential crisis I was facing, or the confronting, encompassing relationship I was now in. I didn't know what was happening to me. I was ashamed that I felt so overwhelmed.

Often, I simply didn't have the energy to talk.

Without speech, I lost speech. I struggled to react quickly and grew acutely conscious of my responses. It felt as if I'd lost any crumbs of social ease I had earned.

The less I talked, the more the silence grew. So, for a while, I withdrew.

O

Increasingly, social isolation and loneliness are recognized as risk factors for mental and physical health problems and early mortality. Loneliness is as damaging for health as smoking up to fifteen cigarettes a day.[7] Although we know that it can increase during transitional periods of life—for example, during adolescence, illness, bereavement, retirement—researchers have only recently started studying loneliness in the perinatal period.[8] In the last decade or so, the first work has been published recognizing that women experiencing loneliness in pregnancy and new motherhood are more likely to suffer from mental illness.[9] Studies suggest that loneliness also exacerbates symptoms of depression in fathers. The findings suggest serious fault lines in our society. It is striking that we've so forgotten our interdependence that we need scientists to prove to us that we need other people to survive.

Loneliness is more prevalent in new parenthood than in the general population, and is even more common among young parents (aged sixteen to twenty-four), immigrant parents with less language proficiency and transgender male and nonbinary parents. Immigrant and refugee mothers are at higher risk if displaced from their communities.[10] Surveys vary widely but suggest that between 28 and 90 percent of new mothers experience loneliness. Mothers, across the literature, describe motherhood as an experience "imbued with loneliness."[11] Half of depressed new mothers, according to a Netmums survey in 2018, believed isolation was the main cause. Almost half of all new mothers, according to the Red Cross and Co-op, feel lonely "often" or "always." New mothers spend significant time alone—around 38 percent spend more than eight hours alone each day, according to one study—which doesn't seem at all ideal for a species that relies on social contact for health, well-being and survival, and on social learning for development.[12]

The isolated nature of this relationship is new. For millennia women and children were part of an "actively busy social cluster," as Adrienne Rich puts it. "Work was hard, laborious, often physically exhausting, but it was diversified and usually communal . . . Nor were mother and child circumscribed into an isolated relationship."[13] The institution of motherhood in the UK, the US and other European countries is a recent—failing—experiment.

An extensive paper led by the clinical psychologist Billie Lever Taylor at Kings College London illuminates the relational aspect of postnatal mental distress.[14] Many of the women interviewed "experienced a sense of failure or inadequacy that could prevent them from connecting to others." All mothers felt shame and anxiety about being judged "inadequate" but mothers from ethnic minority backgrounds, from deprivation or who were single or young felt a stronger fear of being judged to be "bad mothers."

"There was a sense of loneliness in the mothers' beliefs that they were alone in their feelings, and ought not admit to them, preventing honest, authentic interactions with others," write Taylor and her team.[15] Shame is dangerous because it makes people feel that they are on the outside of the group, causing them to hide away and isolate from others, as Professor Brené Brown has explained. She coined the term "mother-shame" to describe the particular intensity of societal expectations women face around parenthood.[16]

In Taylor's study, a mother who identified as Black African and Muslim compared the social support for mothers in her home country in Africa with the lack of support in England.

"If it's back home now, you know, your parents, you give them your children sometimes. Two days, three days, they would be with your parents. You have a little rest. But here there's nobody."

Another spoke of feeling abandoned by her midwife, whom she had formed a strong bond with, and who had become like a "wife and sister."

Women felt pressure to be the primary caregiver and to be "perfect," but they also felt dependent on others. "I just wanted to be looked after," one said.

Other reviewers found the causes of loneliness include a lack of recognition of the difficulties of being a mother, the burden of childcare, and an absence of community and social networks.

Millennial caregivers, those born between 1981 and 1996, experience increased isolation and loneliness compared with previous generations, with other stresses including financial strain and lower rates of home ownership. Some may also be "sandwich caregivers," looking after children as well as elderly parents or relatives.[17]

Researchers found a pattern whereby new mothers who felt distressed would actively withdraw, and "silence the self" through fear of "being a burden" or judged as inadequate.

In a study of women who regretted motherhood, conducted by the Israeli sociologist Orna Donath, mothers described a feeling of being "obliterated," "fading away" and "disappearing." They felt that in matrescence they had become "deficient."[18]

O

At the mother and baby groups I attended, it seemed more and more as though we were all colluding not to say much at all, aware of the panopticon of surveillance, with society in the watchtower, waiting for us to slip up and fail.

One playgroup was in a spacious community hall with areas of toys for different age groups. Trucks, tunnels, soft toys, building blocks, plastic animals. At a hatch in the corner, a volunteer made teas and coffees and offered biscuits. Women sat on gray plastic chairs with shiny black legs, huddled around hot mugs, watching their children, talking. In the baby corner, mothers sat on cushions on the floor with their younger babies lying down on mats. There was usually one father. In the back room, older women helped new mothers with breastfeeding difficulties.

We avoided talking about ourselves and focused instead intently on the babies: how often they slept, how often they fed, whether they were using a pacifier, if our partners had gone back to work. We rarely talked about childbirth or how we were coping with sleep deprivation or how we were coping at all.

I would often leave these groups feeling bereft, frustrated and even lonelier than if I'd stayed in the house. I started to think there was something weird—wrong, even—about me.

We new mothers didn't have the words to articulate the existential and emotional crisis of matrescence. I hadn't yet come across Rich's concept of the Institution of Motherhood. Without the words, I sank into a shameful, silent unhappiness.

What we said at baby groups

It's obviously the best thing that has ever happened to me.

Everything is great, really great.

I'm hoping she might sleep through the night soon but she's so little.

I'm topping up with formula because I didn't have enough milk but *I'm still feeding as much as possible.*

It's going well. It's all fine. The baby is really well. Yes, feeding well. It's all fine. The lack of sleep is fine. The crying is totally fine. The screaming is fine. The thoughts of death are fine. We are so fine! They are so sweet and only young once so it's all fine. Best thing that ever happened to me.

What we didn't say

I am being sucked dry.

I am drowning.

I love the baby so much it hurts, it actually hurts (how will I ever be OK?).

Every day I think, she could die (how could I ever be OK?).

I'm trying to work out how not to lose myself.

This love sometimes feels closer to terror than bliss.

Is anyone else's heart broken open?

One day, I tentatively asked the mother next to me how her birth was. Fucking awful, she said. Her two words turned the key of a lock inside me. We laughed darkly. We shared our stories. We bonded. Swapped numbers. The pressure lifted for a moment.

But then we went back to the silence of our sealed-off, nuclear houses and submitted again to the myth of independence and self-sufficiency and individualism.

O

Over the course of that first year, I increasingly felt that I needed my mother, who lived around three hundred miles away. My nerves were worn down. I wanted someone to tell me everything was going to be OK. I needed to be able to be honest about how bad I felt, how exhausted I was. My husband had a busy work period and I was tired of pacing the streets, trying to settle into these new skills, this new solitude, this frightening new existence.

I didn't drive at that point, so we would take the train to visit her. We would travel up through the green fields of Oxfordshire, the hills of the Lake District, the peace of Oxenholme, past the silvery firth near Liverpool, the red brick factories of Preston and Carlisle, the horizons of Annan, to the ever-changing light of Galloway. It's an eight-hour journey, more or less.

In preparation for our first journey up, I had asked an online parenting group for tips on traveling alone with a baby not old enough to sit for long distances. Working prams are not permitted on trains in England: they must be folded up because there is no designated space for them on board. One commenter suggested I buy a seat for the baby using a Family and Friends railcard, although children aren't required to have tickets until they are five. The rest of the advice I was given was military in its precision. Wheelie bag. Easy-to-access pouches. Cold coffee. Sling. I bought two tickets, left the pram at home, and assembled my tool kit. I packed the bag with toys, books and snacks, and dressed light to avoid overheating.

On the train, the first hour or so was fine. She stood on my knees and looked out at the other passengers. I noticed how she tried to make eye contact with everyone she could. Some smiled back and made funny faces. Others were engrossed in their phones and laptops. She was keen to connect with the strangers around us. It seemed instinctual and important, as if she was trying to win the trust of the group.

But, soon, she (we) grew uncomfortable. I stood in the corridor, trying to soothe her, attempting to rock her to sleep, avoiding looking at people. She was tired, hot and screaming. I took her in and out of the sling. "You're brave," said a woman, walking past.

I was angry with myself for putting her through the journey, angry with the train company for making the experience so challenging. I packed up our stuff, ready to change trains at Wolverhampton for the next three-hour leg. The fresh breeze on my face on the platform was welcome. We were over halfway.

Missing a nap, being awake for hours and the overstimulation meant that she was just as upset on the next train. I brought out a book to try and calm her and focus her attention. It dropped into the alleyway. I couldn't bring myself to pick it up immediately and I looked out the window to compose myself and hide my stress. Suddenly, I realized a woman across the way had picked the book up and was reading it to my daughter, pointing to the mouse, the fox, the snake, the owl. It's not easy, is it, she said. I exhaled properly, for the first time that day.

In England, it is easier to travel with a bike than with a baby. One train company has a dedicated space for four bikes, or two tandems, that cyclists can book in advance. Tandems have more rights on the trains than young humans. New mothers are often found sitting on the filthy floors with their infants. The situation is different in other countries. Switzerland's trains have a family zone, with space for pushchairs, with play areas and games tables. France's trains have dedicated family areas for buggies and a power source to warm bottles. Finland's family sections have slides, toy cars and a castle to play in.

The hostility of the train network didn't come as a surprise, however. On a bitterly cold day a few weeks earlier we had taken a train for the first time to see my father. The sky was as dull as office blocks, our breath visible in the air. When I got on the train, I'd aimed for the disabled area, ready to move if need be, but it was occupied. I hid with the pram in a vestibule next to the loos, hoping the train guard would take pity on me if he or she came by.

When we arrived in Slough, we made our way to the lift. It wasn't working. I would need someone to help me carry the pram up the stairs. The platform was empty apart from a guard so I walked up to ask if he might assist me.

Not allowed, he said. Health and safety.

It had started to sleet and icy rain was swirling around us on the platform. I had covered the baby with a soft white blanket, tucked into her sides, but she was rousing. The air was pinching, and I felt chapped by the wind and stress of it.

How can I get out then? I asked. The lift is broken.

You'll have to wait for someone who can help you, he shrugged.

He walked off. My stomach churned. I loitered at the bottom of the stairs waiting for someone to offer, too embarrassed to ask. Eventually someone stopped and offered their hand.

Ecdysis

Just before snakes shed their skin, they become angry or defensive. Snakes become anxious because their vision is impaired during the shed. The shed is called ecdysis.

8.

Sertraline and sleep deprivation

> But then, on becoming carers in our own right, we are catapulted right back into our own preverbal primary bodily processes . . . Beguiled by baby-soft tenderness, pristine smooth on our rough skin, the infant's raw emotions permeate into us . . . which throw us back into subsymbolic formlessness.
>
> Joan Raphael-Leff, *The Dark Side of the Womb*

> Fact: death too is in the egg.
>
> Anne Sexton, "The Operation"

It hadn't crossed my mind, before giving birth, that by bringing a life into the world, I would also be bringing about a death.

In the first weeks of early motherhood, I had visualized the same scene repeatedly: an enormous, thick, purple velvet curtain hung from ceiling to floor in a cavernous temple, ripped from top to bottom. It took a while to remember it was an image from the Bible. The curtain of the temple is torn in two after Jesus dies. "The earth shook and the rocks split," writes Matthew, in his Gospel.

I found myself drawn to seedpods: dried, empty, desiccated, dead. My phone filled with photographs of brittle, geometric shapes. (During the pregnancy, it had been buds about to unfold or shoots pushing through.) It was surprising to grow obsessed with death and deterioration when faced with new life.

In the first months, when I couldn't sleep at night, I pictured small coffins, car accidents, choking. My mind became a theater of all the possible scenarios that could go wrong. My phone filled up with thousands of photos of her, using up the memory, but I couldn't delete any of the images in case something happened.

I kept it to myself, of course. My morbid thinking was abnormal, shameful, I thought. But anger was simmering, too. So I'm meant to be self-controlled and serene when there are dangers and hazards around every corner?

There was no outlet for my anger, nor could I properly articulate it, so I stuffed it down. And, like anger often does, it festered away over time, and my mood started to drop.

O

I took the baby to the doctor again when she was a few months old because I was worried about her crying. I sat there, tears running down my cheeks, trying to soothe her cries, so tired my skull was throbbing.

How is your mood? the doctor asked.

I looked up and squinted into the sunlight piercing through the window.

Not great, I said, rubbing the tears away with a disintegrating old tissue I found in my pocket, looking at a painting of flowers on the wall. I'm very tired.

I'd been treated for periods of clinical depression and anxiety in young adulthood, but, after years of regular psychotherapy and a newfound emotional stability after entering recovery for drug and alcohol addiction at twenty-seven, I thought I was healed. How could it have returned now, at what should be the happiest moment of my life? I had what I had always wanted, a baby. Why would I be depressed? I couldn't be. I refused it. She handed me a questionnaire to fill out, the Edinburgh Postnatal Depression Scale. I had to choose how much I agreed or disagreed with ten statements.

I was confused by the third.

3. I have blamed myself unnecessarily when things went wrong
Yes, most of the time
Yes, some of the time
Not very often
No, never

Unnecessarily? But if something was wrong with the baby it *was* my fault, my responsibility, so if I blamed myself that couldn't be *unnecessary*? Not enough breast milk? Difficult birth? Baby with colic? Baby doesn't sleep? The mother's fault.

I stumbled on statement 4.

4. I have been anxious or worried for no good reason
No, not at all
Hardly ever
Yes, sometimes
Yes, very often

For no good reason? I looked up at the doctor. What did it mean, no good reason? I wanted to ask but didn't. But really—I had a tiny baby to look after. Most days on my own. In a world facing climate chaos and extinction. That seemed like a good reason to me. Not to mention the dangers of bringing up a girl in a society that doesn't properly condemn violence against women. Was that a good reason? This felt like a trick question. I was anxious and worried, but justifiably so. A life is in my hands and, as Winnicott said, if I get it wrong she will be "falling for ever . . . all kinds of disintegration . . . dying and dying and dying."[1]

5. I have felt scared or panicky for no very good reason
Yes, quite a lot
Yes, sometimes

No, not much
No, not at all

What did they mean? Did we live on the same planet? A world which isn't ultimately safe? A world where bodies fail and children die? Where accidents happen? Does my child growing up in a world that could be three degrees warmer by 2100 count as a very good reason? Or the fact that babies die in the night? What about meningitis? Or sudden death? Or car accidents?

6. Things have been getting on top of me
Yes, most of the time I haven't been able to cope at all
Yes, sometimes I haven't been coping as well as usual
No, most of the time I have coped quite well
No, I have been coping as well as ever

On top? I pictured a hat, a heavy military-like helmet. Then, a number of hats piled up, one on top of another. Mother, wife, worker, child, friend.

I didn't know how to answer this one honestly. On the outside, I was coping. I was able to look after our baby and present a happy face to most people. On the inside, I was in turmoil, and I wasn't sure how I could continue.

How do you live with your heart ajar?

I left the doctor's surgery with a prescription for 50 milligrams of the SSRI antidepressant Sertraline and a diagnosis of postnatal depression, although I have come to think it was more anxiety that I was struggling with. In the first few days I felt like I'd taken an Ecstasy pill. My brain was fizzing, I felt dizzy and spaced-out and I was swallowing a lot. But I wasn't coming up in a nightclub. I was sitting in Rhymetime at the local library or at soft play, waiting for the shelter of my mother's little helper like the almost-majority of new mothers I knew who took some medication to get through the day.

Our little Lorazepams
Our Nytols and wine
Our Amitriptylines
Our Zolofts, Prozacs
Our Zopiclones and
Oh, our Citaloprams
Sertralines, semibreves
of Detachment. Once:
Cocaine, Speed, Gin.[2]

O

A few months later—deeply, thickly sleep-deprived—I started to see things. Ants, beetles, earwigs in the carpet, in the corner, out of the corner of my eyes.

But when I fully focused they disappeared. Were they there at all?

An unusually windy storm had blown in. Power cuts. Trees fallen. Car alarms. In the sky, the wind was throwing gulls around. Out walking, I spotted something that caught my attention in the corner of a field. It looked like a newborn baby on the ground.

Alarm rose in my body. I could see what resembled arms and legs and a stomach, a form lying on its back. My stomach twisted. I looked behind me and around to see if, what? Its mother, I suppose, was somewhere. What would I do? Call the police? I stopped a meter or so away and realized it was a large vegetable root.

My eyes were sore and dry. On the radio, a program had started about a doctor who harvested thousands of organs and body parts of dead children. I half listened while I took care of the baby, snatching bites of chocolate from the drawer, gulping them down half-chewed, and slurping cold coffee from yesterday's cafetière.

"Being tired won't kill you," I read on a forum.

But it felt dangerous, the anxiety and isolation and sleep-deprivation feeding each other, sluicing around. I wasn't sure how I could keep going. I found it more and more upsetting that I was unable to soothe the baby. I was nettlish with my husband.

"Some mums found ways to just get on with it," a sleep researcher said in a video I watched later about sleep deprivation. "Even though it might not have been pleasant they perceived it as something they had to work around."

The nights were anarchic and I felt body-bruised by fatigue. As the sun set, I'd enter a boxing ring and in the morning it hurt to walk from one room to the other, to open my eyes, to speak. I was violently tired. Sometimes, there were no nights, no days, it was one, a twilight zone.

11:25 p.m. 1:15 a.m. 2:30 a.m. 3:48 a.m. 5:30 a.m.

Six months in, I hadn't slept for more than five hours or so a night, and very rarely in a four-hour chunk. We were at the doctor's again.

How old is the baby?

Six o'clock, I said. Six weeks. Erm, six months.

I had started to misspeak with sleep deprivation. Every day hurt.

O

Sleep deprivation is different to feeling tired. It's like being underwater, in a new state, another element.

To keep myself awake when I was feeding the baby, I would pinch the flesh on my arms, frightened that if I fell asleep, she could come to harm. I'd slap my cheeks, hard, slap my legs, then pinch, pinch. I once fell asleep while giving her a lunchtime bottle; it fell out of my hand on to the floor as I dozed off. Jump! Shudder. These days of exhaustion were frightening: they didn't feel safe. On the floor, playing with her, I would feel myself wanting desperately to fall asleep. I'd jump up and do a few jumping jacks. Drink coffee. We'd pace the streets. Coffee. I'd open the back door for a blast of fresh air to keep me awake. Coffee. Chocolate. Coffee.

I found the hours I spent awake in the dead of the winter night the hardest, when I was unable to settle her and desperate to fall back into the dark womb of bed. Or falling into delicious blackness for twenty minutes and then wakening again to the cries. JUMP.

FLASH! INTO ACTION. The blood in my limbs would squirm like hot jam.

Around a year into the sleep deprivation, I signed up to a gym across the road. It was a spit-and-sawdust place where people lifted weights and pushed tires. I was booked in for a "biosignature" appointment and one of the trainers used callipers to record my body fat. The metal claws clamped down around my flesh as he measured and wrote down the number.

When he got to my knees, he stopped after recording the number, looked at me quizzically, and asked how much sleep I was getting.

Your knees are carrying more fat than is normal, he said, which is a sign of chronic sleep loss.

O

In 2004, the reality show *Shattered* was canceled after its first season. It collected a group of people and challenged them to go without sleep for seven days. The prize for the winner was £100,000. There was uproar from counselors and health professionals, and viewers complained to Ofcom. One of the contestants hallucinated that he was the prime minister of Australia. "You felt your life was ending," he remembered.[3]

It's unlikely *Shattered* would be made again today. We know much more about how dangerous lack of sleep is. The WHO has now formally classified night-time shift work as a "probable carcinogen" because the evidence that links sleep deprivation and cancer is so strong. *The Guinness Book of World Records* doesn't include attempts to break sleep deprivation records anymore, because they pose too high a risk to health.[4] Governments have stopped using sleep deprivation as a technique of torture. In the United States, the military was still using sleep deprivation in 2004, although detainees were supposed to be given "four hours of continuous sleep every 24 hours."[5] This is more than many mothers will regularly get in the first year of looking after a new baby.

We are all physically and emotionally dependent on sleep. Sleep loss inflicts devastating effects on every part of the human body. It is linked to multiple neurological and psychiatric conditions, almost any that you could name: cancer, diabetes, heart attack, obesity, immune deficiency, anxiety, depression, suicide, chronic pain. The impact on the brain is startling. In sleep-deprived people, the ventral striatum—an emotional center of the brain associated with dopamine, which we encountered in chapter 6—becomes hyperactive in response to rewarding experiences. The heightened sensitivity is also associated with loss of control from the prefrontal cortex. Was that why I was eating so much sugar? Sleep deprivation even impacts DNA and learning-related genes in the brain involved in memory-making. Was that why other mothers didn't talk about the reality of early motherhood or childbirth? Because they hadn't made the memories?

The neuroscientist and sleep researcher Matthew Walker argues that sleep loss contributes to numerous psychiatric illnesses we don't give it credit for. Sleep loss and mental illness are a "two-way street of interaction."[6] He believes that sleep loss is a neglected factor in numerous psychiatric illnesses.

One reason for this might be the lack of REM sleep. Dream research suggests that REM sleep is important for people to make sense of emotional events, and life itself, and to protect against anxiety and depression. Without the chance to dream, was I unable to make sense of this major life transition?

In early matrescence, I was in a constantly adrenalized state, harried, on edge. This might have been related to another detrimental effect of sleep deprivation: prolonged activation of the sympathetic nervous system, known as the fight-or-flight response. People who get too little sleep have overactive sympathetic nervous systems, which can cause damage throughout the body. Crucially, it attacks the heart and degrades cardiovascular health. It also shuts down surges of healing growth hormones, which are more active at night. In a survey I conducted among new mothers, sleep deprivation was voted the most emotionally challenging aspect of new motherhood, alongside loneliness and isolation, loss of time and the difficulty balancing work and parenthood.

There is limited evidence about the long-term effects of sleep deprivation, because, says Walker, "we feel it morally unacceptable to impose that state on humans—and increasingly, on any species."[7]

Except new mothers.

O

It was a cold morning for May. The sky was gray as lead. It had been gray for weeks. I struggled to maneuver the pram out of the house. I slammed the door closed and twisted around the bins. Kicked the gate open. Money was tight but I had enough for a can of coffee and a small packet of tobacco. I hadn't left the house much for a while. It was a mess and I was sick of the washing up lying in the sink, the milk-flecked rooms, the smell of the diaper bin. The antidepressants didn't seem to be working anymore.

The baby was nine months old. My statutory maternity pay from the government—around £560 a month for self-employed workers—had stopped, and I would soon need to start working and earning properly again. I felt conflicted about paying a childminder or a nursery to look after the baby. Although most of my friends had happy children in nurseries, I couldn't quiet the influential external voices which said she was too young not to be looked after at home. We needed my earnings to pay our mortgage, and I was contracted to write a book, but I was plagued with the fear I would be letting her down by not looking after her.

I couldn't reconcile the need to care with the need to earn. I didn't know who I was anymore. I felt increasingly insecure, psychically disintegrated.

I winced as I saw my reflection in the windows of a shop. Disgusting. My face was large and unrecognizable. I scowled. I wanted to scratch my skin off. I stepped over smears of dog shit on the pavement, swerving the pram to keep the wheels clear.

In the department store, I wandered in a daze around the home furnishings. Soft carpets, patterned curtains. Lamps and lights of all sizes. Frames and prints and cushions. Thread, needles, ribbons. A clock, shaped like a lighthouse, in seaside colors, on sale. That will look nice in the baby's room, I thought, and stuck it under the pram.

At the till I swallowed my shame as I asked for tobacco and rolling papers. Avoided eye contact. Paid. The clock was still in the bottom of the pram, concealed. Outside, I opened the tin of cold coffee, downed it, and trudged wearily home.

The baby woke as I started walking. She began screaming. To get her home as fast as possible I picked her up and carried her the twenty minutes or so up the hill. There were no designated spaces on the buses for prams and if I got on I could be kicked off so I didn't bother. At the top of the hill, she started to quiet so I put her in the pram again and played peekaboo. We smiled and laughed and sang, and I stroked her gently and cooed. I felt at peace for a moment. Her eyes closed again in slumber. I stroked her cheeks, liquid-soft. Love swelled in my body like ink in water. She drifted off to sleep. We got back and the house was silent. I was stiflingly hot. Sweat on my top lip. I flung my coat and sweater and scarf and bag on the floor. Kicked it all to one side. Carefully, quietly put the pram in the living room so the baby could stay asleep and removed her hat so she didn't overheat. I went to the cupboard and took out three mugs. I walked to the back door, stepped outside, shut the door and threw the mugs straight down on to the concrete patio. One by one, one after another. They made two sounds: a harsh, strong break and a muffled crunch.

I went back inside and saw the bottom of the pram. The clock was still there, ticking.

My friend, a mother and psychotherapist, wondered if I stole the clock because I wanted to take time for myself. I think actually I wanted to stop time.

O

I returned the clock to the shop and called the doctor's surgery. My antidepressant dose doubled and I started weekly cognitive behavioral therapy at the perinatal mental health services in a dour, brown building opposite a wine merchant and next to a halfway house.

We spent some of the sessions talking about guilt, self-loathing and why I didn't feel like I could spend any time looking after myself, from showering to regular exercise or seeing friends. Every choice I made now impacted the baby, even a choice to rest or take a bath. Doing anything for myself was in conflict with my maternal role. We made a pie chart of my time. There was no sliver for me to look after myself. That's a problem, she said. But I didn't know what to do about it. I didn't know how a mother should be.

The notion that I must be with my baby permanently, alone, and sacrifice my needs had got firmly under my skin. As had the self-critical voices. I'd become paranoid and thought everyone was judging me.

Around that time, I came across an interview with the eminent British sociologist and author Ann Oakley in which she questions the prevalence of postnatal depression diagnoses, and says that the feelings experienced by many new mothers are of "normal human distress" brought about by the demands of looking after young children.

"It's a medicalization of normal human distress," says Oakley, referring to "the experience of sleep deprivation, responsibility of a new job for which one has no training, i.e. being a mother and in charge of small children, loss of status, career change, not very much money often, and no social support."

In my low, paranoid state, I felt berated, irritated, and interpreted her words to mean that women like me overdramatized our situations, or could pull ourselves out of our mental distress by the bootstraps.

"The diagnosis of postnatal depression which was handed out to me and continues to be handed out to thousands of women, is in most cases, I'm quite sure, a misnomer," says Oakley.[8]

Now, though, I think there is something to her point. As much as I'm grateful to modern medicine—for the antidepressants that have lifted me out of psychic darkness—it can be used as a sticking plaster in the absence of deeper social change, as a way of patching up rather than addressing the underlying issues that can lead to postnatal mental illness (and much other mental illness) in the first place. Up to 10 percent of new mothers are prescribed SSRIs, despite the fact that, though they are effective, nobody really understands how they work. Is this primary intervention treating the symptom, but not the cause?

Oakley argues that women are experiencing a form of bereavement or grief for the change in self, and the loss of their previous life of independence, equality and freedom.

"All of these things create a situation in which we wouldn't be human if we didn't have a reaction to that."

We wouldn't be human. This is what it felt like. That I mustn't be human, mustn't grieve the loss of my former self, but instead be a mothering machine, without emotion, complaint or expression.

Later, with distance, I could take what I'd read, and ask the question for myself: Is the problem the individual woman who is pathologized for having "PND," in its diminutive and popular shorthand, or is the problem a society which utterly fails to support women in this major life transition? Was I disordered or dysfunctional, or was my social environment? I had entered matrescence from a relatively privileged position. What must it be like for less privileged women, women who have society's dysfunctions and inequalities stacked up against them even before they become pregnant?

We badly need a biopsychosocial approach to matrescence and maternal mental health. While the official figures suggest that up to a fifth of new mothers experience mental ill health, the actual number is likely to be higher for a constellation of reasons. The concept of "mental health" is understood differently in different cultures, and women from different demographic groups are less likely to ask for help. Black women are at higher risk of developing postnatal depression but are the least likely group to be identified as depressed. In her book *My Black Motherhood: Mental Health, Stigma, Racism and the System*, Sandra Igwe recounts her experience as a Black woman becoming a mother in England. Three hours after her first child was born, she was told she had been referred to social services by the midwife she had seen throughout her pregnancy. "Terror almost paralysed me," she writes. "Were social services coming to take my baby?" When the social worker, who was also a Black woman, arrived, she said to Igwe, "I know exactly what's going on here and I'm sorry this happened to you."[9] The NHS trust wrote her a letter of apology but the damage had been done: Igwe didn't trust healthcare professionals and was understandably unwilling to ask for help when she was struggling postnatally because of the fear of being judged for the color of her skin.

O

Environmental and social factors are major components in maternal mental health and illness. Income inequalities, living conditions, life stress, domestic violence, systemic racism and geographic location have large effects on the prevalence of postnatal depression. But, as we've seen, we are now learning how significant the neurobiological changes are in pregnancy and the postnatal period, and how these changes increase all women's vulnerability to psychological illnesses. Even in countries with more and better social support for new mothers, they do still become ill, though in developing countries the contributing factors and environment will be different. We are also learning more about epigenetics and mental illness, and epigenetic inheritance. Given the dramatic neurobiological changes of pregnancy, some occurrence of postnatal illness seems to be inevitable.

To find out more, I contacted the neuroscientist Liisa Galea, who has studied the maternal brain for decades. She talked to me from her home office in Vancouver. Behind her was a print of a brain, in blue and purple, and a large photograph of her daughter taken on holiday on the Isle of Skye.

Galea's research focuses on how the hormones of pregnancy affect the mother, particularly the hormone estradiol.

"We know that hormones increase dramatically in pregnancy," she said. "The placenta, a new endocrine organ, is pumping out hormones, some of which are unique to pregnancy, at amazing levels, sometimes two hundred or three hundred times normal levels, even higher than that."[10]

In pregnancy, the increases are enormous: estriol rises a thousand-fold. Testosterone by six. Progesterone by fifteen.

"The big thing," said Galea, "is that these hormones dramatically increase for months at a time, not for a couple of days, like the menstrual cycle."

And then, when birth happens and the placenta is expelled, the hormones dramatically decline to very low levels. There is a huge drop of progesterone and estradiol, as well as other hormones.

"It's like a withdrawal," said Galea. Scientists think it's this withdrawal that can create fluctuations in mood and increase susceptibility to mental illness.

This fits in with the evidence we have of how premenstrual dysphoric disorder (PMDD) and premenstrual syndrome (PMS) affect women's mood changes. Women with PMDD might suffer more from hormonal disruption.

"Some people get upset about this," said Galea. "That somehow we're tied to our hormones, but I think it's important to know about it. That's how we're going to get some therapeutics behind it, and understand how our body impacts our mood."

Also, she pointed out, men are as hormonal as women. In parenthood, new fathers have lower levels of testosterone and studies suggest testosterone and estradiol drop even before a baby is born.

There are some treatment pathways beginning to emerge. In March 2019, Brexanolone, a novel treatment for moderate to severe postnatal depression, was approved for distribution in the United States by the FDA.[11] It is a neurosteroid administered through injection into a vein over a sixty-hour period. A derivative of allopregnanolone, which modulates brain function, it is thought that it works by modulating the HPA axis, which mediates the response to stress and inhibits anxiety and depression. The three randomized controlled trials found a much quicker response and recovery than with traditional antidepressants, working within twenty-four to forty-eight hours rather than two to four weeks.

The price tag, however, dims the excitement. It costs $25,000 to $35,000 per dose, so would be available for very few women. It's the most expensive antidepressant treatment currently on the market.

In June 2022, zuranolone, the "little sister of Brexanolone," was found to have promising results in its trial data. Zuranolone is also a neuroactive steroid but it can be taken orally for fourteen days rather than through an injection, which would reduce the cost. The FDA approved the drug in August 2023.[12]

I know it's an impossible question to answer, I said to Galea, but, given what we know now, how much maternal mental illness is inevitable and how much is preventable?

Matrescence "is a perfect storm that creates the right climate for mental health disorders," Galea explained. "There are all these natural changes that we can't control." Pregnancy requires a certain set of changes to occur, she told me, which are also found in depression. In both depression and pregnancy, for example, there is an increase in cytokines, the inflammatory signaling markers in cells. Other, similar changes are seen in serotonergic pathways, which are involved in mood and mood disorders.

Alternative ways of mitigating postnatal depression are appearing, too. Research by Dr. Jeffrey Meyer at the University of Toronto found that probiotics stimulate the gut hormones which contribute to serotonin, which enhances mood.[13] Galea was a reviewer for a paper which looks at the effect of a blueberry-extract probiotic mixture on postnatal women, designed to boost serotonin levels and gut heath. "The endorsement of depression symptoms really went down," she says.

Crucially, there is plenty of evidence that social support also plays a major role in protecting women from maternal mental illness. Interestingly, the placebo curve of the graphs in the studies on Brexanalone also showed a marked decrease in depressive symptoms—suggesting that the care and attention the women were receiving thanks to their participation in the study was acting on their symptoms, too. Social support has been found to both reduce symptoms at the time of illness and *prevent* postnatal illness, even in the most severe mental health condition women can suffer from after childbirth, postnatal psychosis.

As Jodi Pawluski, the neuroscientist who runs the Mommy Brain Revisited podcast, told me, "We know that social support can really reduce our stress.

"A lot of solving problems around mental health and maternity is support," she said. "We have a lot of interventions. We know a lot, but we don't put them in place—the money, resources, training."

There is a highly complex dance between the intrinsic, biological processes triggered by pregnancy and extrinsic environmental factors that "translate into internal signals," as Pawluski and colleagues put it. It is not one or the other, it's a mixture of both, which interweaves to create each individual matrescence.

So, as much as the advances in medicine are hopeful, a focus on care before, during and after pregnancy in order to prevent illness is critical, too. The researcher Elizabeth Spry, and a team in Australia, found that women with depressive symptoms before pregnancy are five times more likely to suffer afterwards, but that effective intervention and social support—such as peer support and family-focused, partner-inclusive care—could dramatically reduce that risk.[14] The more we acknowledge the hard and potentially dangerous side of motherhood, the better we could be at caring for those who need it.

We need to acknowledge that pregnant women and new mothers are highly vulnerable to mental illness. Thoughts of suicide and self-harm in new mothers are relatively common, at 5 to 14 percent.[15] Forty percent of women with postnatal depression have never had depression before, but may go on to have it again. Many, if not most, new mothers I know have had a significant systemic response to childbirth and becoming a parent, including the most life-threatening conditions: psychosis, sepsis, severe depression. I think of the woman with the clitoral tear, and the one with the bladder prolapse, and the rectal prolapse, and the fistula, and the suicidal ideation, and the bowel perforation, and the PTSD, and the psychiatric stays, and the one whose intestines fell out days after birth, and wonder: Why are we sending a high-risk group off to spend an unknown period of time at home alone, where they must look after vulnerable infants and recover from the trauma of giving birth, while burdened with loneliness, lack of sleep, and a shedload of impossible cultural expectations, including the imperative to enjoy every minute of it? Are these the actions of a responsible or functional society?

PART IV

Matriphagy

At least six species of spider eat their own mothers. A few other animal species do it, too: the hump earwig, the pseudoscorpion, nematodes and the caecilian. The black lace weaver (*Amaurobius ferox*) engages in this form of maternal care. Once her spiderlings hatch, she feeds the brood regurgitated fluid and then her own body.

I watch a video of the process. The mother has a blue-black body and her legs are brown, akimbo. She is upside down. It's hard to tell whether she's still alive or not. About forty spiderlings, which resemble creamy yellow sea pearls, wander over her nonchalantly, devouring, snacking, nibbling, pulling bits of her flesh into their tiny mouths. Some of the babies are still, replete, close to the mother. Others are busier, hungrier. Do they know what they are doing? What is it like to have your mother in your mouth?

(I'm surprised by how uncomfortable I feel watching it. Usually I love anything to do with arachnids. But this feels too close to home. Voyeuristic. Intimate. Like I shouldn't be looking. I don't like seeing the helplessness of the mother, her extreme altruism.)

Later, a spider appears in the toy box when I'm tidying up. I look closer. It looks similar to the spider from the video. I had thought that these matriphagous happenings would be in a country far away. Australia, or an island in the South Pacific. I look up a photo of the black lace weaver and compare the two. Yes, there are the faint, pale markings on her back. Oh, God. I'm not sure I want matriphagy in my house. I look around the wicker basket for spiderlings. She's safe. For now.

9.

Maternal ambivalence

ond his modor þa gyt,
gifre ond galgmod, gegan wolde,
sorhfulne sið, sunu deaðwrecan

But now his mother
Had sallied forth on a savage journey,
Grief-racked and ravenous, desperate for revenge.

Seamus Heaney, translation of *Beowulf*

The only thing which seems to me to be eternal and natural in motherhood is ambivalence and its manifestation in the ever ongoing cycles of separation and unification with our children.

Jane Lazarre, *The Mother Knot*

Shards of shell prickled the soles of my feet as I walked into the waves. I knew I didn't have long. The sea was the color of whale skin, ale, snow. The foam sprayed up and into my eyes and my nose. I had to stop myself looking back to the beach. The water at my navel, the cold feeling good against my warm stomach. I paused, made a bowl with my hands, splashed the water onto my arms. A quick glance back. The baby is OK, distracted.

I stood in the sea, feeling the power and strength of the current. A wave almost tugged me off my feet and I liked the sensation, the whispered possibility of being swept away. I saw a large ship, a cruise liner, on the horizon, and what seemed like banks of charcoal cloud, puffing across the sky.

I wondered what I ought to be thinking. I felt disintegrated, like the grit of sand and beads of pebble on the ocean floor. Focusing on the pulsing waves pulling my body around, I submerged myself. I used to like swimming in the sea, the feeling of cold water on my scalp. Underwater, I began coming back to myself. Filling up. No one could get to me here, in this other element. I couldn't help anyone while I was under the water. As I floated, making a star shape with my body, I started to remember. *This is who I am, or once was, or might be again.*

Mama! Mama! Mama! MAMA! Mamaaaaaaaaaaaaa!

My head snapped to the shore. I knew before my eyes confirmed it that it was my baby crying. Her father was trying to comfort her and show her shells to direct her attention away from me, but she was having none of it.

At once, there were fire ants in my blood. Prickling. Stinging. Marching from my gut up through my chest and lungs, through the alveoli and marrow and into the back of my neck and spinal cord. A marching band of fire ants playing percussion—drums, cymbals, whistles, trumpets, claves, gongs—along my veins and nervous system. I stared at the baby, and waved with both arms outstretched, grinning, willing the fire ants to go. "I'm here!" I mouthed, as if in a pantomime. "I'm *right here*!" My heart started beating faster. My throat constricting. My body felt wrong. Everything felt wrong. The fire ants were trying to march me back.

I bartered with myself. One more minute. A swim is good for me. I need a swim. It will make me a better mother today. She will be fine for a minute. I love swimming. I need to do something for myself. I need exercise, I start to plead. I haven't been properly alone for months. I'm desperate for two minutes in the sea. This is crazy. What would other people do? One minute isn't going to harm her.

She is with her father, she's fine. Oh God, are people looking at me and wondering where is her mother and why is she still in the sea and not running to her?

I looked sheepishly around to see if I could observe any judgment from other people on the beach.

Mammaaaa! Mammmmaaa!!!! I could feel her rising distress in my body.

forfuckssake.

I couldn't remain in the sea. I was commanded by her cries. My body stomped me back to the beach, ignoring the stinging stones, my feet thumping angrily on the sand, and bent down to pick her up. I found myself soothing, stroking her hair, swallowing myself again, emptying myself like a bucket of seawater onto the sand.

She calmed, and the fire ants receded, hushed. My body cooled as her cries ceased. My nervous system settled down as we slotted together again. I was relieved, satisfied, high on the smell, the feel of her skin and jellylike thighs, her big eyes, and I forgot my irritation, resentment and myself.

O

I didn't know whether I would keep the "for fuck's sake" line in the finished manuscript. I took it out, and put it back in. Took it out, and put it back in. Many times. Even when writing this, years after I stood in that sea and felt irritated, I am still uncomfortable with airing my irritation, even if it was for a moment, a flash of a thought.

I feared that it might suggest my love for her was wanting.

But it wasn't, and it isn't. So why does the truth feel so uncomfortable? Why is having a mixture of feelings—both good and bad—about matrescence so hard to admit to?

In untangling my social preconceptions about mothers, I realized that I had in mind not one but two basic, limiting and fantastical images of maternity. On one side was, of course, the good mother, who was constantly loving without ever reaching capacity, self-annihilating but blissed-out. She was gentle and kind, intuitively nurturing, and took constant pleasure in her children. On the other side was the bad mother. The bad mother was selfish and discontented, unable or unwilling to give herself over to her child completely, and intentionally or obliviously harming them.

The "happiness imperative," as the psychoanalyst Rozsika Parker called it, rules out the "inevitable unhappiness associated with motherhood."[1] It is central to contemporary attitudes towards child-rearing. Childcare and parenting manuals uphold happiness as an ideal: "Happy parents mean happy babies," says Miriam Stoppard. "If you make happiness for him, he will make happiness for you," writes Penelope Leach. Happiness is not just the goal, it is essential.

When I found the baby's crying intolerable, or the lack of sleep painful, or the breastfeeding struggles upsetting, I blamed myself. I shouldn't be finding this difficult, I thought. But I was.

I started to make secret notes on my phone about the experience. They were filled with contradictory sentences.

I am so lucky; I have everything I've ever wanted and every day is hard.

I have never felt happier or more alone.

The child is a yoke and a rainbow; a total eclipse and an Ecstasy pill.

Late in her first year, the baby got a shock from falling over. Her eyes rolled to the back of her head, her skin turned pale blue and she lost consciousness for twenty or thirty seconds. I thought, in those seconds, that she had died. My body and mind went berserk before, suddenly, she was back. Spaced-out and sleepy, but alive. After seeing a pediatrician at the hospital, and a few more incidents, we were reassured that it was a condition called "blue breath-holding spells" or anoxic seizures, which are benign. It is stressful for the parents, though, said the doctor. The spells then happened every few months, and each time, even though I knew they wouldn't damage her, the experience derailed me. The blue-gray pallor, the limp body and the wait for her to return were so frightening that I couldn't connect my logical brain—which knew I had talked to the doctor—with what my eyes were seeing and my body was reacting to. I was supposed to enjoy every minute of this?

O

The psychic reality of new-mothering life is breathtakingly challenging and complex. How could it not be? As babies can't regulate their own emotions, they project difficult feelings onto an external object, most often their primary caregiver, who is usually a mother. When the baby is frustrated, she brings her feelings to the mother, who empathizes, mirrors, holds, soothes, coos, sings it away. Metabolizes and digests the experience for her. Young babies' needs must come first, above maternal needs for sleeping, eating, defecating. How could that be unwaveringly pleasurable? The world contains myriad dangers for our children. How could that not be frightening? Psychoanalytic thought tells us that how we are mothered is the most important influence on our lives. How could mothers be impassive, emotionally zen, in the face of such a vast responsibility? Being told to "enjoy every minute," while undertaking such psychologically and physically demanding work, is a peculiar type of societal gaslighting.

The only negative emotion in new motherhood that didn't appear to have been outlawed was the "baby blues," but "baby blues" doesn't describe the collision of awe, bewilderment, contentment, delight, euphoria, fear, grief, heebie-jeebies, ilinx, jubilation, kalopsia, loneliness, mono no aware, nostalgia, overwhelm, panic, querulousness, rapture, shame, terror, uncertainty, vulnerability, wonder, *xenolalia,* yearning and zeal that mothers experience. Sometimes, within a day. Enjoy every minute!

I created an anonymous survey to gather qualitative data from mothers in a bid to understand what others were feeling. The women who took part were from a mixture of demographic groups. I made the survey anonymous so they could answer freely. One of the questions I asked was: "What would have helped your matrescence (journey into motherhood) and experience of new motherhood?" The top answer was "opportunities for honest conversations about the reality of motherhood" alongside "more affordable childcare." The other highest-voted factors were being able to rest and recover more after pregnancy and childbirth, longer leave for partners and cultural rituals to acknowledge the transition.

It was remarkable to see a consistent pattern of shock, sadness and regret. I asked respondents how they thought they could have been better prepared or what they wish they'd known. Here are a few of the answers.

> "I wish I had known how much old stuff I'd never really dealt with would come to the fore."
>
> "I just wish I'd known how destabilizing it can be."
>
> "I wish I'd understood more about how childhood trauma (smacking, shaming, being shouted at as most 80s kids were I think!) can manifest and trigger you when you have your own children."
>
> "I wish I'd known how difficult it actually is being a mother. I wish I had more understanding towards other mothers."
>
> "I wish I'd been allowed to see more of the maternal experience out there. Whether on the television, in books and films."
>
> "I wish that some of the brutal truths had been discussed with me in more depth."
>
> "In some ways I wish I'd known that it would make me question so much of the world and of my own childhood and family upbringing."
>
> "I wish I'd been better psychologically prepared. Could midwives prepare us more for the brutality of birth?"
>
> "I wish I knew that my identity and independence would be gone."
>
> "Insipid/idealistic portrayals of motherhood made me less interested in it as a young person. I thought it was boring when it's one of the most extreme socio-political experiences I have ever been through."

These women loved their children unconditionally. That didn't mean they loved motherhood unequivocally.

O

According to Freud, ambivalence is at the heart of, well, the human heart. In psychoanalytic thought, ambivalence means the existence of conflicting feelings. It is a hallmark of the human experience, said Freud. To have conflicting feelings about someone or something is characteristic of human consciousness. Where you find love, you will find hate. Where you find hate, you will find love. They are simultaneous and coexist.

"Clinical observation shows not only that love is with unexpected regularity accompanied by hate (ambivalence), and not only that in human relationships hate is frequently a forerunner of love, but also that in many circumstances hate changes into love and love into hate," he wrote.[2]

The idea is illustrated well in a contemporary exchange which went viral online.

> "You're offered £50,000, but if you accept, the person you hate most in the world gets £100,000—are you taking it?"
>
> "Yes, why wouldn't I want £150,000?"[3]

Melanie Klein believed ambivalence to be a sign of healthy development in her studies of children. The child, who would once see a "good breast" that nurtures and gratifies it and a "bad breast" that is frustratingly absent when desired, heals the split into one integrated person and comes to see that the mother contains both "good" and "bad."[4] Only then can the child begin to accept the ambivalence and ambiguities in others and the outer world.

This acceptance, which Klein calls the "depressive position," involves sadness and mourning, and is critically important in early-years development. "When in the baby's mind the conflicts between love and hate arise, and the fears of losing the loved one become active, a very important step is made."[5]

Klein was concerned with the experience of young children, but others—most notably Rozsika Parker in the 1990s, and Joan Raphael-Leff, whom we met earlier—have developed her theory from the particular point of view of the mother. Parker, in her seminal book *Torn in Two*, coined the phrase "maternal ambivalence," defining it as the "experience shared variously by all mothers in which loving and hating feelings for their children exist side by side."[6]

While Parker and others have attempted to release mothers from the sentimentalized portrayal of the mother–infant dyad, we remain largely unwilling to let mothers experience the full range of their emotional life.

Part of the issue is the limitations of our language. Parker concedes that the word "hate" is problematic, and this I agree with. "Hate," to me, sounds too fixed, more like a permanent state than a rising emotion. It is too blunt and ugly a word, especially when associated with lovable babies. While love and hate are used in psychoanalysis, for the layperson, I think, hate can be a violent and off-putting word, and even ambivalence isn't perfect. In the survey I conducted for mothers, about a third didn't know what "ambivalence" meant. Some thought it meant being undecided, or unsure, about becoming a mother.

Still, it is a useful phrase in the absence of anything else. The mothers who knew the phrase wrote that it was a comforting and helpful description of "the tension," the "push and pull of a mother–child relationship," the "tidal" nature of the maternal experience.

"That sort of feeling when you can't wait for your baby to be asleep because it's actually really boring being with a baby and you just crave your own time," wrote one. "It helps to hold the nuance of the experience and counters against the prevalent idea of mothers as pure/perfect/always maternal," said another. It is interesting, too, that it even has to exist at all.

O

As a society, we just don't seem to be very interested in the actual flesh and bones of the maternal experience. Maternal subjectivity has, until very recently, been almost entirely absent from Western philosophy, literature and culture. I hadn't read about it in any of the core texts in my English literature degree. Siri Hustvedt has called it "the forgotten land of the mother and mothers . . . A territory Western culture has studiously repressed, suppressed, or avoided to a degree I have come to regard as spectacular."[7]

As my matrescence progressed, I started to look out for cultural representations of mothers. Walking through the Tate Britain one day, I noticed that almost all the mothers in the paintings gazed downward, while their children looked directly out of the canvas. I walked around quickly, searching: I wanted to look into the mothers' eyes, to see what they were thinking, but I couldn't. It reminded me of the "hidden mother" phenomenon in Victorian England, whereby mothers would be covered in a blanket while they held their children for photographs. I looked at icons of Mary, the Virgin mother of Jesus, and found her passivity newly chilling and frustrating. She is there as a container, a prop, a dummy.

It was interesting to me that this state that I now knew intimately—the closest I had ever been to death, to birth, to growth, to the coconscious, to rapture, to rupture—was, according to the world around me, boring, or at least not worthy of serious artistic or critical attention until very recently. Aren't we all obsessed with our mothers? How are these stories so few and far between?

Looking at these paintings, it struck me that our society is very like the Kleinian baby: it aims for unlimited gratification, seeking an "inexhaustible and bountiful breast." It cannot tolerate absence; it can't allow mothers to express their own needs. Here, in image after image, were mothers as idealized objects; nowhere could I see mothers as subjects, as agents of their own lives.

Klein believed that if a person couldn't integrate their feelings of love and hate they would remain in what she termed a "paranoid-schizoid position" where the good and bad are split, torn between idealization and scapegoating.[8]

Are Western societies stuck in the "paranoid-schizoid position" in relation to motherhood? Is that why we are so intolerant of mothers feeling their feelings? Are we, as Julia Kristeva suggests, trapped in primary narcissism, collectively idealizing our primal relationship? Are we trying to deny the ambivalence we felt as babies towards our own parents?

Kristeva writes that the fantasy of the perfect mother is more an idealization of the relationship itself—the "lost continent"—rather than of the mother.[9] We want mothers to be perfect because we want, or wanted, our own mothers—and the security they offer us—to be perfect and unlimited. Parker suggests that the intimacy between mother and baby brings the mother's baby-self, and memories of her inevitable frustrations and challenges, to the forefront of her being. "Her own infantile neediness merges with her needs as a mother, intensifying the feeling of not being met," she writes.[10] How could that not be disturbing?

Hrdy brings some common sense to the issue. "We should be asking ourselves how we failed to expect these ambivalent emotions in their every nuance," she writes.[11] "There are good reasons why infant demands sometimes seem so insatiable, and there are equally good reasons why mothers sometimes find such servitude overwhelming and resist them."

Even so, in 2021, an article in the *International Handbook of Love* took a severe, decidedly midcentury view of maternal ambivalence, stating that it "may contribute to profound, lifelong implications for maternal and child mental health."[12]

O

Sentimentalizing motherhood and running the reality underground might seem relatively harmless, but its effects can be dangerous. According to psychoanalysts such as Parker, maternal cruelty may be the result of unmanageable ambivalence. When unreconciled feelings of love and hate go unaddressed, they can intensify, and then explode into helplessness and violence. Certainly, the conditions of mothering today make it almost impossible to acknowledge normal ambivalence, leading many to feel unbearable guilt and overwhelming persecutory anxiety.

For Parker, the anguish of maternal ambivalence—an example

she gives is of an urge to smash an untouched plate of food in a toddler's face—is something that mothers, and surely all parents, need to be able to think about, rather than suppress. It "keeps the heart alive," she writes. "It is the mother's achievement of ambivalence—the awareness of her coexisting love and hate for the baby—that can promote a sense of concern and responsibility towards, and differentiation of self from, the baby."[13]

If suppressed, the anger and difficult feelings might also turn inwards. Parker theorizes that maternal masochism is related to unmanageable maternal ambivalence. The negative emotions or impulses—anger, resentment, rage, hate, boredom, impatience, despair—fill the mother with guilt and, to "gain absolution," she can become excessively giving and hyper-altruistic. Without an outlet, she may turn the anger on herself, leading to masochistic martyrdom.

(What's rich is that psychoanalytic theory, which has been so keen to police mothers, suggests that anger and aggression are normal parts of life, and their suppression is damaging. "Unexpressed emotions will never die. They are buried alive and will come forth later in uglier ways" is a quote commonly attributed to Freud.)

The assumption that ambivalence is abnormal has also affected the direction, framing and focus of science. Hrdy points out that exactly *how* infants evolved to have such power over their caregivers, with their clever traits and attributes and addictive deliciousness, has received remarkably little attention. It also, she says, boxes maternal ambivalence into the study of "the odd" (psychoanalysis), rather than the study of "the natural" (evolutionary biology).

Klein believed that attempts to make humanity more peaceable failed because the depth and vigor of instincts towards aggression—innate in each individual—are not yet understood. "Such efforts do not seek to do more than encourage the positive, well-wishing impulses of the person while denying or suppressing his aggressive ones. And so they have been doomed to failure from the beginning."[14]

This, too, sounds like our unrealistic, overly prescriptive norms for maternal behavior and expression. Parker writes of the importance of "owning up" to the emotional impact of children, which is impossible to do when the mother is an "icon of adult restraint, moderation and thoughtful control."[15]

Some women have done this, responding to being silenced by speaking out—and one particularly high-profile case shows that there is little our culture abhors more than a mother expressing herself.

In *A Life's Work: On Becoming a Mother*, published in 2001, Rachel Cusk depicted the "psychical events" of childbirth and early motherhood, with all its ambivalence and pressure.[16]

The fallout from the book was significant. Cusk was vilified. In an article written years afterwards for the *Guardian*, entitled "I was only being honest," she defends herself and critiques the damning reviews of the book.

"I was accused of child-hating, of postnatal depression, of shameless greed, of irresponsibility, of pretentiousness, of selfishness, of doom-mongering and, most often, of being too intellectual," she writes.[17] Sections of her memoir were picked out by reviewers to make a case that she was a "bad mother."

In an interview, she reflects on the violent reaction to her story of early motherhood. "I had touched a nerve," she says. "People disown dangerous feelings." On the pressure of conformity in new motherhood she says, "anyone who complains is ejected."[18]

O

In the 2020s, more diverse reflections of maternal experience have started to appear. Many of the most popular portraits of maternal ambivalence use humor, such as the best-selling book series *Why Mummy Drinks* or the television series *Motherland*. Evil Witches, an online community for mothers run by the Chicago-based writer, essayist and self-defined oversharer Claire Zulkey, is amusing, but also engages in an expansive exploration and discussion of the maternal experience. Her website and newsletter are irreverent, sardonic, witty and soothing, described as being for "grouchy" mothers of all stripes (biological, step, adoptive): "Grouchy, like somebody did not give us all the information about motherhood/womanhood before we got into this but we don't know who," the website reads.[19]

Zulkey set up the original Facebook page as a way for mothers to share "wisdom and empathy and humor and irreverence." In her newsletter and website, she deals in hilarious GIFs, interviews with experts and also painful subjects such as miscarriage and divorce. I wanted to talk to her because I was interested in her refreshingly unapologetic writing about motherhood, and wanted to know how she had found the energy to create a useful community for so many people.

She told me how it started. "You have everything. You have this beautiful family and a kind husband who does his best. Your mother-in-law might not want to hear that your husband is a fucking infant who can't solve a problem but you want to complain about that. Your friend who is struggling to get pregnant might not want to hear that your kid is being an idiot but you want to complain about that.

"It's space, also, to be around people too who also understand that you are actually a really great mom. That's the thing that's undersold, or the undercurrent. The fact that you care about this and you're processing this, you are a great mom, you can set that aside, you don't need to apologize for yourself."[20]

Zulkey's unusually judgment-free, welcoming atmosphere punctures the usual expectations of maternal behavior.

"There is so much parenting content that's like, what would a good mom do? Or is it normal to do this? Or I confess that I hide from my kids. I want to move beyond that and let's just take it for granted that we all do that," she said.

We discussed making sense of the modern motherhood crisis. Who are the culprits, who should be in the dock?

"Whoever runs the baby industry and makes you think you should be happy and complete after the baby comes, that is bullshit. They should stop telling you congratulations and start saying, are you OK? And what do you need? They should stop saying you're complete now and you've got everything you ever wanted. That's capitalism I'm pretty sure and whoever makes money off selling baby shit."

She also questions the image of the mum who does it all and looks great doing it.

"In reality you're sweating, you want to cry because you can't unfold the stroller and your kid shit his pants, and you're having a horrible time."

O

In 2020, Frida Mom, a company based in the United States that makes products for women recovering from pregnancy and childbirth, created an advert for the Oscars. It was the most viscerally accurate depiction I've seen of the first few days of early motherhood, when matrescence feels cosmic, wild and brutal.

A baby cries in the middle of the night and their mother carefully maneuvers her damaged body out of the bed. She hushes the baby and hobbles to the bathroom in the mesh underpants that are holding her towel to soak up the lochia. She sits on the toilet visibly in pain and squeezes a "peri bottle" onto her undercarriage, winces, and sprays herself with what is probably a witch-hazel spray to help healing before limping with her pants down towards the baby so her vulva will dry naturally and the wound will not become infected. This is the reality for the up to nine out of ten mothers who tear, graze or have an episiotomy during childbirth. Mothers who give birth via Cesarean are also—obviously—in significant pain. Many women have to inject themselves in the stomach with a coagulant for the first ten days or so to prevent clotting.

The Oscars rejected the advert for being too graphic. In an email to the CEO of Frida, the Academy of Motion Picture Arts and Science suggested a "kinder, more gentle portrayal of postpartum."[21] In the 2020s, the maternal body is deemed too offensive for television, alongside guns, ammunition and sexually lewd content.

What did this advert violate? The sensibilities of prudes who didn't want to see a woman in her underwear? Or society's mythical ideas about motherhood?

While Zulkey and others like her are creating spaces that can accommodate the whole maternal experience, the wider culture's conception of motherhood is perhaps more exacting and idealized than at any time in history. This vision of motherhood is also more intensive, with new requirements and mandates and unprecedented pressures for mothers to bear. This is the modern institution of intensive motherhood.

Parasitism

The emerald cockroach wasp (*Ampulex compressa*) has a metallic body that glows turquoise, and bright crimson markings on two of its legs. Found in the tropical regions of Asia, Africa and the Pacific Islands, it is a beautiful insect, but pity the cockroach that crosses its path.

It is one-sixth the size of a roach, but that doesn't stop it. First it delivers a simple paralyzing sting. Then it hijacks the roach's mind, injecting an elixir of neurotransmitters into its brain.

This turns the roach into a helpless zombie. After a quick suck of recharging roach blood, the wasp chews off the roach's antennae and leads it to its nest like a dog on a lead. There it lays its eggs on the roach's abdomen, and barricades it in with pebbles. The hapless roach doesn't even try to escape, even though it physically could. It just sits there submissively, as the wasp larvae eat it alive.

10.

Intensive motherhood

It seems that just as women were making inroads and feeling confident, a new discourse of motherhood emerged that made two things inevitable: that women would forever feel inadequate as mothers and that work and motherhood would be forever seen as in conflict and incompatible.

Andrea O'Reilly

Child-care specialists . . . invented a motherhood that excluded the experience of the mother.

Shari L. Thurer, *The Myths of Motherhood*

Most heterosexual couples I knew had, like us, planned to split childcare and paid work equally between them after the maternity leave period of nine to twelve months. It rarely worked out that way.

Until parenthood, mine and my husband's time, our ambitions and dreams, our rest and well-being, were of equal importance. As soon as the baby was born, that changed. I moved unconsciously into a role in which I would serve the needs of the family above all. It is true that I wanted to be the one primarily looking after our daughter in her early years, but I also felt a powerful and amorphous external pressure to retire from work, take up my place at home and transform into a different type of being.

I felt strongly that the health and well-being of our baby was my responsibility. I saw my husband—who wanted and supported an egalitarian partnership—as an important player, but, from what I'd learned, from early training in psychotherapy, from books, from media and culture, from other people's comments, my mothering was the fundamental factor in her destiny. Everything I read told me that the best way to mother was to be led by the baby, and fit myself around her needs, especially for the first year or two. This would involve studying child development—age-appropriate care, the development of the infant brain, optimal emotional and cognitive growth, nutritional health—so I could be attuned to her and give her what she required. My care should be continuous, tactile, patient, and any absence could be harmful. But when I started working, and then when our son was born, this approach started to seem untenable. How was it possible to live up to this demanding maternal ideal and work at the same time?

In 1996, the sociologist Sharon Hays coined the phrase "intensive motherhood" in her groundbreaking book *The Cultural Contradictions of Motherhood.* She used it to describe the new pressure on mothers to provide constant, exclusive nurture.

Academics such as Andrea O'Reilly, who developed the formal discipline of motherhood studies in the 2000s, chart the development of today's "intensive mothering" ideology back to the late 1980s.[1] It is defined by a number of beliefs. First, that mothering is natural and instinctual to women. Second, that the mother is the primary caregiver. Third, that she should be a full-time mother and that caregiving is all-absorbing. Fourth, that children need copious amounts of her time, energy and material resources. Fifth, that mothers are attuned to their children's cognitive, psychological, social and emotional needs. Sixth, that the mother must be ultimately fulfilled by her role, satisfied, happy and calm.

Unsurprisingly, "intensive mothering," which is now both studied and practiced across the industrialized world, is associated with poor maternal mental health, stress and parental burnout. The sociologist Caitlin Collins, in her study *Making Motherhood Work*, describes how all mothers in her study, from four different countries, shared "one source of stress: the pressure to live up to an idealized definition of motherhood."[2]

This was familiar. The more I learned about the different cultural iterations of childhood and motherhood, the more I realized that my crisis was, in part, the product of a particular historical context. Before I could jettison the "modern maternal straitjacket," as Siri Hustvedt calls it, I needed to understand the materials it was made of, and the conditions that had allowed it to thrive.

O

Maternal ideals have waxed and waned, blossomed and withered, in the postindustrial West according to wider social, economic and political conditions. My daughter's record book, between the sections for recording her first tooth and her first word, quotes the French writer Victor Hugo: "A mother's arms are made of tenderness and children sleep soundly in them." This is a classic portrait of maternal love, and still resounds with us today, but in nineteenth-century France, when Hugo was writing, babies were actually abandoned in numbers that are shocking to modern sensibilities. Up to a fifth of babies in Paris were left in foundling homes or with wet nurses in the countryside, where they often died.[3]

As industrialization set in across eighteenth-century Europe, a larger, healthier workforce was required.[4] This brought the quality of mothering into central focus and invited greater public scrutiny than ever before. There was, increasingly, an onus on mothers to raise healthy children, particularly men, who would be useful, productive workers. "Women are the agents through whom men become either healthy or sickly, through whom they are useful in the world, or become plagues on society," wrote the highly influential Scottish physician William Buchan, in 1769.[5] As the split between public and private life became more pronounced, the home—and the adult inside it, the wife and mother—became a symbol laden with exalted meaning: security, support, a haven.[6]

In England, the process of enclosure, whereby common land was taken from ordinary people and turned into private property, had already reduced women's ability to forage and contribute food and fuel for their families. Working in factories was impossible to combine with the raising of children. The majority of industrial work environments were designed for the male body, not for women or mothers, although children were put to work in various industries.

As women's freedom to work was limited, the family unit became more atomized, reducing women's contact with their wider societal milieu.[7] Mass migration into industrial cities left the "nuclear family"—comprising two adults and their children—more isolated. Mothers would not have had the company and assistance of grandmothers, sisters, aunts and younger children so readily—and this scattering of families has continued with globalization. Even quite recently, when my grandmother had her first baby in Scotland in the 1940s, two of her sisters-in-law moved in to help, but this would be unheard of now.

The notion of a "natural" maternal instinct in women originated around this time, advocated for and legitimized by prominent thinkers such as Jean-Jacques Rousseau. "The true mother," he wrote, "far from being a woman of the world is as much a recluse in her home as the nun in her cloister."[8] This idea continued to reduce women to feeling, instinctual beings, confined—newly—to the home, in opposition to rational man, who belonged in the public sphere.

Alongside their elaboration of a maternal instinct, male writers became authorities on the questions of how a mother should raise her children and how a woman should conduct herself. Through the seventeenth and eighteenth centuries, the growth of publishing, the spread of literacy and the development of epidemiology and statistics—combined with a deep-seated view that women were intellectually inferior—led to the beginnings of a serious child-rearing publishing industry.

"The very first part of their infancy is a season only for those cares which concern their bodies," wrote the churchman and provost of Eton College Richard Allestree in *The Ladies Calling* in 1676.[9] In

1785, Michael Underwood, in *A Treatise on the Diseases of Children*, scolds mothers who "refuse to give nourishment to their tender and helpless offspring" and who "commit this charge to a stranger, give up every other charge with it; and rarely visit the nursery or superintend those they have set over it."[10] He chalked this up to the "depravity of the age," which he considered the "leading symptom of the falling empire." In the late eighteenth century the "how-to" genre of child-rearing took off and, as historian Sarah Knott notes, these books were written exclusively by male physicians. The pediatrician Luther Emmett Holt's *The Care and Feeding of Children* (1894) was a bestseller. "Babies under six months should never be played with; and the less of it at any time the better for the infant," he wrote. Other rules included not taking babies outside for the first three months, along with a warning that "uncontrolled emotions, grief, excitement, fright, passion may cause milk to disagree with the child."[11] Holt promoted eugenics in his role as the president of the American Association for the Study and Prevention of Infant Mortality.

Mothers were commanded to listen to "experts," instead of neighbors or other experienced women in the community, on matters of feeding, bathing, clothing and health. Undoubtedly, scientific-information sharing and the development of medicine led to huge successes in the reduction of infant mortality, but, in giving primacy to the opinions of mostly male doctors, a collective reservoir of women's wisdom, knowledge, involvement and empathy—as well as self-determination and freedom of thought—was slowly emptied. The ground was prepared for the intensive demands of the child-rearing tracts—or rather "mother-rearing tracts," as the sociologist Shari L. Thurer calls them—that have proliferated in recent decades.[12]

O

At the beginning of the twentieth century, there was widespread consensus across the West on the question of how best to raise a baby: through disciplinarian means, as epitomized by the methods of Truby King. Adults were superior to children, and children should be seen and not heard. King advocated feeding babies according to a strict regime, and not feeding them in the night. Soon, however, evolutions and advancements in child development made the new century the "century of the child," as the writer Ellen Key prophesied in 1900. Through the popularization of the ideas and philosophies of Maria Montessori, and later Jean Piaget, a new focus on child-centered learning and creative play emerged in the 1910s, which influenced education systems in Europe and the United States and raised expectations for parents to foster learning and development.

Postwar, child-centered ideas continued to spread. In the 1940s, Dr. Spock's gentler parenting philosophy conclusively supplanted King's strict norms, calling instead for loving, nurturing and mutually respectful relationships with children to keep them mentally healthy. His magnum opus, *The Common Sense Book of Baby and Child Care*, opens with the line, "Trust Yourself: You know more than you think." A little disingenuous, you might argue, considering what follows: in the latest edition, over 700 pages of detailed information. After the Bible, it was the best-selling book of the twentieth century in the United States.[13]

Spock's "enthusiasm for benevolence was in keeping with the mood of the decade," writes Thurer. His maternal ideal was part of a collective fantasy fueled by postwar optimism and an international appetite to recover from the horrors of war and look forward to a brighter future.

While women had been able to work outside the home much more during the war, they were soon required to leave paid employment behind. The ideal of the 1950s housewife was constructed in line with traditional ideas of femininity and Spock's conception of the good mother, and disseminated through TV series such as *The Adventures of Ozzie & Harriet*, housekeeping books and "good wife" guides in popular magazines.

Donald Winnicott's enduring concept of the "good enough"

mother—a phrase he coined in 1953—tempered these glorified ideals, although he still believed mothering meant acting instinctively and compared it to "the power-assisted steering on a motor bus." Besides, although it sounds fine at first, who would really be happy to be "good enough" when the stakes are so high?

O

It was one of Winnicott's contemporaries, John Bowlby, who has perhaps done the most to determine modern conceptions of motherhood and child-rearing. After the war ended, Bowlby was commissioned to study the mental health of homeless children by the Mental Health Section of the WHO.[14] Working at the Tavistock Clinic in London and consulting with researchers in Europe and the United States, he collected evidence for "the adverse influences on personality development of inadequate maternal care" during early childhood. His report would lead to transformed conditions for children in hospitals, children's homes and institutions, and his development of a theory of attachment has shaped our societies' attitudes towards how we relate to each other—and particularly how babies relate to their mothers and vice versa.

Over the course of his career, Bowlby developed a concept of "attachment behavior" which, he argued, was key to survival. It was distinct from the drive to feed and to reproduce (the two drives considered fundamental to humans). Attachment behavior, according to his 1988 book *A Secure Base*, is any kind of behavior that results from "a person attaining or maintaining proximity to some other clearly identified individual who is conceived as better able to cope with the world." The presence of an attachment figure gives a person a "strong and pervasive feeling of security."[15] The strength and quality of the attachment influences whether a person will be able to love, and receive love.

Attachment theory was further developed and clarified by the empirical studies of the American-Canadian psychologist Mary Ainsworth. In the 1970s, based on her observation of infants in Uganda and Baltimore in the 1950s and 1960s, Ainsworth devised what she called the "Strange Situation" to observe attachment behavior between one-year-old infants and their primary caregivers. In plainer terms, she called her study "the growth of love."[16] In the procedure, the attachment behavior of a baby is watched through separations and reunions with their caregiver, over a period of twenty-one minutes. The baby and caregiver are placed in an unfamiliar room, with lots of toys to explore and a stranger, the researcher. The baby's exploration behavior is observed with the stranger present. The caregiver pops outside for a number of minutes and the baby's response is observed. The caregiver returns and the baby's response is observed again. The caregiver and stranger leave the room, and the baby is observed when the stranger returns first.

If an infant has a secure attachment, they explore and play using the caregiver as a "secure base." When the caregiver leaves the room for a few minutes, the child will usually cry and protest and search for her. Ainsworth called this a "heightening" of attachment behavior.[17] When the caregiver returns, the child will seek to be in close contact with her, and be comforted, and their exploratory behavior may be diminished. A child with an insecure or ambivalent attachment might ignore the mother on her return. Ainsworth describes the Strange Situation as a "useful illustration" of the dance between exploratory and attachment behaviors that has evolved in human animals to ensure survival, protection and learning.[18]

The work has been hugely influential. When I had my one-year check from a health visitor in 2017, I noticed she seemed to be informally testing my attachment with our baby. As the baby traveled to and from me, towards her toys and back again, looking at me, the health visitor said we had a good attachment. She was able to use me as a secure base to explore with a stranger present, she said.

Critics of Bowlby's theory have pointed out that a universal attachment pattern ignores cultural variability and the fact that "shared motherhood" is the norm in over a thousand distinct societies around the world. The highly regarded psychologist Heidi Keller shows that the idea of maternal responsiveness is built on a concept of "person and the self" that is different to what good caregiving means in collective societies across the world.[19] In the Philippines, for example, the children of the Agta people are often cared for by other children, in children-only playgroups.[20]

Undoubtedly Bowlby's work has led to improved treatment of children, particularly in institutional care, but some of the guilt carried by mothers today can be traced back to him or, more markedly, to subsequent interpretations of his work.

One of the problems with how Bowlby has been interpreted is that his clear emphasis on the role of society and community is ignored and forgotten: "Just as children are absolutely dependent on their parents for sustenance, so . . . are parents, especially their mothers, dependent on a greater society for economic provision. If a community values its children it must cherish their parents."

Modern mothering ideology—particularly attachment parenting—tends to cherry-pick from Bowlby the conclusion that looking after a baby is a twenty-four-hours-a-day, seven-days-a-week job, and that children require a great deal of time and attention. But they leave out his emphasis that it is "no job for a single person" and that a caregiver needs "a great deal of assistance."

In a lecture given in 1980, Bowlby outlined the crisis of care—one which we still face decades later. In most societies throughout the world, he said, it is taken for granted that children should be raised collectively, so that the primary caregiver is "not to be too exhausted."[21] Society is organized accordingly in most of the world. It is remarkable that the majority of the world's so-called developed nations neglect these basic facts of human need.

Perhaps the biggest culprit in misinterpreting the full picture of attachment theory is the child-rearing philosophy of "attachment parenting." Because of the name, it is often confused with the theory, which lends it legitimacy. It is a philosophy, though, rather than a theory developed through scientific research methods and empirical studies.

Attachment parenting was invented in the 1980s by an American pediatrician called Dr. Bill Sears. At its heart are values that most people would agree are good and fundamental to caring: emotional responsiveness and being sensitive and receptive to an individual baby's needs. But his philosophy takes it further than that, claiming itself to be "the way nature intended." His stipulations include bonding straight after birth, breastfeeding on demand, baby-wearing, co-sleeping, avoiding schedules or routines, and high responsiveness to emotions and cries.

As well as riffing on Bowlby, Sears was inspired by the highly influential book *The Continuum Concept* by Jean Liedloff, who had randomly traveled to the rainforest of Venezuela on a diamond-hunting trip, loved it, and returned to study the Ye'kuana tribe and make quasi-anthropological reports.[22] These depicted happy, well-behaved children who never fought and were never punished. It sounded very different to her own experience of childhood: "turning to my mother always ended in my being hurt."[23]

She found that the children were carried everywhere, breastfed for many years, and slept alongside adults. Childcare was communal and mothers shared their infant care with others, including children. Babies and young children were integrated into everyday social life, and mothers and caregivers were never isolated. Babies were not "left starving for experience" in their own cots, playpens or prams.[24] She had an epiphany: this was the right and correct way to raise children. The book became a cult favorite of the natural motherhood movement.

There are myriad problems and contradictions within Liedloff's book. As the feminist academic Petra Buskens writes, "This is classic romantic nostalgia for the 'noble savage' arising in conditions of destabilizing social change."[25] Liedloff's rose-tinted rendering of "primitive" life is reductive and self-serving. In 1975, when the book was published, the women's movement was driving significant social change. Anxiety about women working outside the home and disrupting the ideal of the 1950s housewife was rising. Liedloff's instructions played into conservative and growing neoliberal ideas of the family, and the individual.

While she is quite clear in her accounts of Ye'kuana life that multiple people cared for babies and young children, when she turns to transplanting their practices on to women in industrialized countries, the focus is *solely* on the mother's adequate caregiving as the singular factor in a child's healthy development. The mother who fails to give her baby the "in-arms" experience—constant physical contact for at least the first six to eight months—is an inadequate mother, and Liedloff spends a long time detailing all the different personality injuries a mother can cause. If "civilized" mothers knew how to parent "in accordance with nature," she writes, they wouldn't leave their babies alone, "tortured by longing for their mothers," for more than one minute.

As the book continues, it crescendos to the point of Liedloff saying that "maternal discretion" and the treatment of infants should be policed by society: "Our society must be helped to see the gravity of the crime against infants that is today considered normal treatment."

This is emotional stuff. It was translated into eighteen languages, reprinted many times, and spawned an international movement. Through its adoption by Sears, it turbocharged the idea that exclusive maternal care eclipses all other factors in a baby's development, despite the fact that this vision of care clashes, for most women, with the demands of modern life.

While the particular practices of attachment parenting, such as carrying a baby in a sling and responding to a child in the night, are likely adopted by many parents who wouldn't even identify as "attachment parents," the widespread influence of the dogma can lead parents—mothers—to be anxious that any kind of absence means deprivation. Reading Sears directly, this is no surprise:

> Most babies . . . have some unexpected need periods and stress periods each day. Being away from him during these times deprives him of his most valuable support resources . . . Children are spontaneous, and parenting [*sic*] means being available when children's spontaneous activities occur. An alternative to part-time mothering is immersion mothering, of being consistently available and attuned to the needs of your baby.[26]

O

Through the 1970s and 1980s, liberal feminism successfully emancipated (mostly white, economically privileged) women from the home and into the male-dominated workplace. As the rollout of neoliberal economic policy and a drive for globalization triggered an increased consumption of commodities, it became possible for more women to enter the workforce, earn money and have a fulfilling career. This greater freedom to determine our own lives was a huge step forward. There was just one problem: having a career wasn't compatible with the prevailing model of motherhood. A full-time job, or even a part-time job, wouldn't allow for the "total" or "immersion" mothering that was now expected of women.

Enter a new ideal, which would neatly square the circle: the woman who "has it all." She works and earns money in previously male industries, but she is also a present and devoted mother. Growing up in the 1990s, I was influenced by profiles of glamorous women in magazines who appeared to have successful careers as well as beautiful families. Somehow these two identities were kept separate: these women never had dried cereal or snot trails on their suits.

Before my matrescence, I had thought that I could be a woman who "had it all." I thought that my husband and I were pretty much the same: that we could both work and care for our children. I was suspicious of maternalism and biological essentialism, having grown up in an all-boys boarding school where I became aware of the limiting and distorting effects of patriarchy and gender stereotypes for both boys and girls. Reading Germaine Greer, Shulamith Firestone and Simone de Beauvoir as a young teen reinforced this view. Though I'd always dreamed of having children, motherhood itself didn't interest me. It was, in fact, almost completely absent from my early feminist education. When I entered matrescence, I realized it was a major female experience where feminism has failed. There seemed to be a distinct biological—as well as a sociological—reality to contend with; one that took me by surprise.

Our daughter seemed to demand more from me than her father,

and I seemed to feel her needs, her pain, her desires in my body in a different, visceral way. She wanted to be held and touched and carried by me to a degree which sometimes pushed my nervous system to the brink of what I could tolerate. Feeling "touched out" is how other mothers have described it. And I found being away from her in the early years physically uncomfortable in a way my husband did not. Even when our work situation changed and my husband took on more childcare, though from the outside it might've looked more equal, I remained the primary source of care.

To emancipate women, second-wave feminists had to neglect motherhood and maternal subjectivity. *Wages Against Housework* (1975), Silvia Federici's brilliant, furious key text of the Wages for Housework movement—formed to dismantle unequal power relations between men and women—focused on attacking "our female role at its roots."[27] But in unbuckling women from the housewife role, the birthing and care of young children was clumsily thrown in with all the other housework, neglecting the fact that it can be more emotionally and ecologically complex, embodied and demanding than laundry, cooking or even the relationship with a husband or partner.

"Because gender difference is seen as structuring and maintaining male dominance, many feminists seek to downplay and disavow anything that marks this difference," O'Reilly writes, noting that the subject of motherhood studies is ignored by much academic feminism.[28] By rejecting—understandably—the reductive primary association of women with their reproductive functions, liberal feminism ended up leaving mothers in the cold, neglecting the maternal experience as an important site of meaning for many women. Late twentieth- and early twenty-first century mainstream feminism then concerned itself with breaking the glass ceiling, "leaning in," being a "girlboss"—surviving in a neoliberal corporate world.

So, today, mothers still do the majority of caregiving, as well as housework and emotional labor. Quality childcare simply is not available, and the use of shared parental leave in Britain by fathers is low. Workplace policies that enable fathers to share in parenting work are sluggish. Mothers spend twice as much time looking after their children every day compared with the 1960s, while also working more. Men today do about as much care work as women did fifty years ago.[29]

I see stress, burnout and guilt in mothers all around me. I see mothers voraciously consuming books, podcasts and online influencers' social media feeds, desperate to learn how to best talk to their children, encourage their healthy development, give educational activities, allow their sense of self to flourish without restriction, and avoid ways of parenting which might be harmful. I see women who are so exhausted and strung out that they might quit work. During the Covid-19 pandemic, with a lack of affordable childcare, women in the UK left the workforce in significant numbers. Having it all, or as the psychoanalyst Jessica Benjamin puts it, *being it all,* is too much.

In some ways, the institution of motherhood looks more punishing today than it did in the forties and fifties, when my grandmother would open the back door, and usher the children outside to play for the day. This may be due, in part, to our fast-paced digital landscape—and particularly Instagram and "momfluencer" culture—exacerbating the problem. It is hardly surprising that a study published in the December 2022 edition of the journal *Computers in Human Behavior* found that social media posts of picture-perfect motherhood could be harmful for new mothers' mental health.[30] In an analysis of depictions of motherhood on social media sites, a group of psychology academics in England found "very normative" notions of "good mothering" which were associated with intensive or immersion mothering.

The dizzying rise of the intensive motherhood model, with its extraordinary demands for maternal altruism, playtime and positivity, has also been interpreted as a backlash to the shift in women (relatively) gaining independence in economic, professional and social terms. Thurer suggests that women's gains in power and the workplace may have "triggered man's atavistic fears of his dependence on her," causing anxiety about her sexuality and autonomy.[31]

But it has also coincided with multiple demographic and social changes. Today, it is becoming harder to have children, with many women trying to conceive later in their lives, once they've established their careers. This means some women may have children in quick succession, which adds to the intensity of early-years child-rearing. At the same time, mortgages and rental costs have risen far more than wages, as has the cost of having children, increasing the pressure for caregivers to return to work, or to work more hours or at more than one job. Childcare is massively underfunded, and there is less social support than ever before. Grandparents tend to be older and may live farther away, meaning they are less able to provide day-to-day support. And the intense competition fostered by predatory capitalism has resulted in a culture of increasing busyness, presenteeism and overwork, which corrodes social relations. Urban design, transport networks, housing design and the design of roads and streets deepen the isolation of caregivers, too. Mothers have been stripped of safe public spaces for play and child-rearing, of collective care structures and public services.

We are more disconnected than ever before. No wonder birth rates have declined so much. Such factors go some way towards explaining what researchers have called the "parenting happiness gap": evidence that parents have lower levels of happiness compared with nonparents in industrialized societies, with the largest gap in the United States.[32]

O

Does it matter that much if a lot of women feel guilty and stressed and overwhelmed? Maybe it depends on what you think about the status quo of gender politics. The modern institution of intensive motherhood silences women, contributes to maternal mental illness, and leaves women too worn out to fight. To fight for what? Potentially transformative policy changes, such as proper maternity leave, flexible working hours, better and more affordable childcare. And even if you don't have any compassion for new mothers, the current lack of support makes no financial sense. The long-term economic consequences of perinatal mental health problems are high, costing society £8.1 billion for each birth-year cohort.[33]

Researchers at the Paris Cité University have found strong evidence to suggest "intensive motherhood" is connected to the persistence of gender inequality and gender-hierarchy beliefs.[34] In an analysis of French "mommy blogs," they found a pattern that mirrored Sharon Hays's description of modern "intensive motherhood." Mothers felt much more guilty and responsible for children than their partners; mothers had a tendency to self-evaluate and self-monitor, in order to improve according to the child's needs; mothers tempered any ambivalence with assurances of unconditional love for their children. Drawing from system justification theory—the theory that defending and bolstering the status quo has a motive, even if it doesn't directly serve the individual—their conclusions suggest that elaborating and intensifying the work of motherhood rationalized and legitimized the status quo of overburdening women with unpaid care work.

The problem is not the needs and requirements of young children. The problem is having to strive for an ideal within societal conditions that make meeting it impossible. Ultimately, the intensive mothering ideology serves those benefiting from the gender gap, those with money and power: in a society with a focus on competition, capital and accumulation, optimizing children fits right into neoliberal economics. There is an unnecessary, insidious cruelty to the societal construction of motherhood. An "invisible violence," as Adrienne Rich puts it.

O

In the last few years, the emotional aspect of "intensive motherhood" has become increasingly pronounced.

Healthy emotional development of children and parents—mothers, usually—has become a part, if not the main goal, of contemporary parenting, thanks to the popularity of "gentle parenting" or "respectful parenting." Broadly, this is a philosophy which offers caregivers tools to parent consciously and intentionally, without physical discipline, harsh punishment or authoritarian treatment, and through mirroring feelings, validation, preempting problems, talking mindfully. In this wave of modern parenting, the overriding focus is on respecting the child as you would an adult and responding to a child's emotional needs with empathy, compassion, understanding and some knowledge of neuroscience and child development. Less of the smacking and "naughty corner," more giving choices and playful negotiation. Discipline—which, interestingly, is a legal part of parental responsibility in the UK—has become a bit of a dirty word.[35] Gentle parenting focuses on methods of influence other than the punishing of bad behavior associated with traditional discipline.

On the one hand, there is a lot of good and helpful information in this movement and, as I've said, it comes from an understandable place. On the other, it can be a lot of work, and it overemphasizes the individual mother's responsibility at the expense of a broader understanding of child development: the roles of genetics, temperament, other family members, the wider community and environmental factors. There is no evidence that "gentle parenting" is better than other approaches—like attachment parenting, it is a philosophy, not an empirical method. But for many people, especially those who may have had more authoritarian upbringings, it is seductive and fraught with strong and even painful emotion.

Many mothers I speak to are highly anxious because they are scared of fucking up their own children. In the survey I conducted, almost half of the mothers said that "triggering childhood issues" was an emotionally challenging part of becoming a mother. They really, really did not want to inflict similar patterns of harm and shame on their children as were inflicted on them. Often those who have had more difficult home lives or relationships with parents seem to find becoming a parent more disorienting. "Being a mother may reawaken devastating feelings of abandonment and desolation," writes the Jungian analyst Lisa Marchiano, thus fueling a desire to get things right.[36]

Adverse Childhood Experiences (ACEs)—events or situations in childhood which are highly stressful or potentially traumatic, including abuse, losing a parent through divorce, death or abandonment, abuse of alcohol or drugs, and exposure to domestic violence—are associated with risks to maternal mental health and, perhaps surprisingly, almost half of the population have experienced one ACE.[37] In a major meta-analysis published in *BMC Psychiatry*, researchers found that "memories and cognitions regarding childhood abuse and household dysfunction" could be sources of stress in matrescence.[38] They argued for more social support and trauma-informed care for women in the perinatal period.

Even for people who aren't "cycle-breakers," motherhood "may sharpen and accentuate the outlines of obstinate traumas," as the sociologist Orna Donath, who studied mothers over a number of years, aptly puts it. [39]

And there has been a major shift in the "cultural acceptability," to use Sara Ruddick's phrase, of how to—and how *not* to—treat children, connected to a greater knowledge about, and prioritization of, emotional health and development. Behavioral expectations are different today compared with "old-school parenting": emotional regulation has replaced obedience as one of parenting's central goals. A "tantrum" is not disobedience or a willful, naughty child trying to get their own way, it's a stress response from a developing brain. People are challenging an inherited culture that denies or dissociates from pain and largely seeks to repress emotions. While once children would fit around the lives of their parents, now parents fit their lives around their children. This is not small work.

Like most people I know who grew up in the 1980s and 1990s in England, my parents used physical discipline when they felt it was required. I polled my close friend group and found that over 60 percent were smacked. The social expectations of children and parents were also very different. Authoritarian parenting was more common: sparing the rod spoiled the child, so you encouraged a stiff upper lip, didn't let a child get their own way, and used force if necessary. Neither I nor most of my contemporaries slept in our parents' beds, as is commonly the case among young families today. Perhaps this was the case in Britain more than in other countries. Schools and institutions that my parents attended, and the school I grew up in, condoned the use of belting, caning and beating to punish and control children, and some of these practices continued until very late in the twentieth century. Parents were far less likely to apologize or engage in the "repair work" common today. Saying sorry to children, in the culture I grew up in, would have been anathema and seen as confusing for the child. Today, parents are encouraged to apologize if they lose it and show their impatience. Once seen as "bad behavior," meltdowns are now considered the normal behavior of a two-year-old with an immature prefrontal cortex, or "a good kid having a bad time," to use a popular gentle-parenting mantra.

Bookshelves and online media today are filled with experts and psychologists and parenting coaches explaining how to mirror your children's feelings, how to contain their emotional outbursts, how to defuse situations using a singsong voice and funny games. A positive alternative to authoritarian parenting, perhaps, but it also adds to the mental load on, yes, mothers. While I spend hours reading and learning about how to raise emotionally healthy children, my husband doesn't, and I don't seem to be a better parent than him. Am I falling prey to the "larding up" of the maternal function, as Maggie Nelson puts it?[40] Do I really need to do a singsong voice all the time?

The American clinical psychologist Dr. Becky Kennedy, known as Dr. Becky, is one of the most influential voices in the new child-centered parenting movement, with over 1.2 million followers on Instagram. Her page features her talking directly to the camera, looking like she's just woken up or come back from the school run—none of the hyper-contouring makeup or high-style outfits that are usual from influencers. She offers quick bursts of advice on topics such as "You Don't Have to Punish Your Child" or "How to Respond to Whining" or "Words to Replace 'Good Job!' " She also runs courses such as "Reparenting Ourselves: Building New Pathways for Self-Care, Boundary Setting, Self-Worth and Confidence." Her book *Good Inside* was an instant *New York Times* bestseller.

She is popular, I think, because she offers a vocabulary and a script for the new generations who want to parent differently and are desperate to know how. "Top hacks" for responding to a child who is upset include phrases like "you didn't want that to happen" and "feelings are your superpower: they tell you what you care about and what you need." She also recognizes and validates the maternal and parental experience, and talks to her audience in a very human and relatable way.

For many people—me included—this is part of a brand-new way of talking, a new way of adults relating to children. Helpful, yes, but also unparalleled in its demands for new relational skills, communication, empathy and fun, humor and play.

O

One of the most popular parenting books over the period of my matrescence has been *The Book You Wish Your Parents Had Read (and Your Children Will Be Glad That You Did)* by the psychotherapist Philippa Perry. Her book was on bestseller lists for years and, like many thousands of other parents, I bought it, after traveling to London to watch her in conversation with the philosopher Alain de Botton. Perry's work suggests that becoming a parent is like an "emotional time warp." "Whatever age your child is, they are liable to remind you, on a bodily level, of the emotions you went through when you were at a similar stage," she writes.[41]

At the time, my daughter was two and a half and I was pregnant with our second child. Something very uncomfortable had been awakened in me. I wanted to look after the children in a way that allowed them to feel what they needed to feel so they wouldn't repress their emotional life. I, like almost every mother I knew, set out with the intention to parent without using force or threat. I knew the importance of clear boundaries and I was wary of becoming permissive, but I wanted my expectations of my children to be age-appropriate and for them to feel witnessed, understood and accepted. I wanted them to know that I could tolerate their difficult feelings without being overwhelmed, so that they would eventually develop the capacity to cope with their emotional life and learn how to soothe themselves.

But I also found the meltdowns stressful. And I was scared of the neuroses or unconscious dents I might inflict on their psyches, or the fantasies from my own childhood that I might try and enact through them. Of the ways I might obliviously harm them. If I was to believe psychoanalysis, and the reason all my friends give for going to see therapists, this would be inevitable.

At the same time, I had had another painful reckoning: my understanding of my own parents had not been quite right. I had overestimated what an adult, a parent, could do. How perfect they could, and should, be. My expectations had not been realistic. Young children could be infuriating! I would have been infuriating!

A two-year-old is wont to push boundaries, I was learning. She could shout and scream, sometimes for quite some time, at quite some volume.

While pregnant, I'd spoken with one of the sonographers about why children behave "worse" around their parents than at school or in public. Why they save up their tantrums and meltdowns for their mothers. "Well, they've got to take it out on someone, don't they," the sonographer said.

I had not expected how challenging the explosive outbursts would be—or the pain and discomfort and urge to dominate they would trigger in me.

One winter day, while pushing my daughter in the buggy up the hill to our house, she had a meltdown. It was pouring with rain and she didn't want to be in the buggy with the rain-cover on. I tried carrying her but she was very upset and flinging her body around, as toddlers do. We were walking next to a traffic jam of cars, windscreen wipers moving furiously, headlights wiggling in the rain. I felt observed, ashamed that I couldn't control my daughter. I needed to get her home and out of the cold and rain. Why am I so shit at this, I thought. I was sleep-deprived, lonely and stressed; frightened of the proximity of the cars and of her wriggling free and running into the road. I decided to strap her into the buggy and march quickly home out of the rain. It was horrible to use force to strap her in. I used the way of talking I was learning. I know this is horrible for you. You are feeling very angry. It is so horrible to be in the rain. I can't let you hit me. But we are going to be home soon. The screams and thrashing continued, and I suddenly had a vertiginous moment, a rising in my body. I had a very fleeting urge to use physical force to make her submit, to slap or hit her. I reeled away, sick to my stomach. But the thought stuck with me like a thorn. I couldn't believe I could consider hurting my beloved child. I had never before felt the urge for violence within me, apart from towards myself. It rocked who I thought I was.

In subsequent, similar moments of varying intensity, I didn't find it difficult to stay calm and contain the emotional outburst on the outside, but inside my nervous system would be screaming, and I would be desperate to run, or freeze. It made me feel a kind of distress I couldn't even describe.

Perry might say these might have been feelings I dissociated from as a child. Infants cannot hide or repress their emotions or emotional needs, which can be a trigger for a caregiver who is emotionally repressed.

But, if this is true, how would I learn to calm my inner child while soothing my actual child? I needed to learn how to regulate myself.

Perry argues that if children's feelings aren't tolerated, or taken seriously, they will become bigger and harder to manage. "The most common cause of adult depression is not what's happening to the adult in the present but because, as a child, they did not learn in their relationship with their parents how they can be soothed," she writes. The stakes, then, are extremely high.

O

So much of the gentle parenting school—Perry, Lansbury, Dr. Becky—is great. Who wouldn't want to give their child the best opportunities in life? Who wouldn't want to learn how to help their child develop emotional resilience? The problem isn't the desire to look after children as gently and consciously and respectfully as possible, it's the fact that this work still mostly plays out along unequal gender lines. The pressure is, as ever, on the individual mother rather than shared among wider social structures. And, sometimes, that mother is sleep-deprived and overburdened. This ideology is too much for one mother to take on.

It will be interesting to see what this generation of gently raised children will grow up to be like. When I talk to my father, he wonders about narcissism. I've wondered about self-discipline, drive and the ability to tolerate having a boss. We won't know what we have done wrong for a while.

Still, a backlash of sorts against the ideology of intensive parenting has begun. One of the best-selling books in the Amazon "Motherhood" category when I write this, in 2022, is called *There Are Moms Way Worse Than You: Irrefutable Proof That You Are Indeed a Fantastic Parent* by Glenn Boozan.[42] It's an illustrated picture book about parenting in the animal kingdom. "Whenever you feel guilty that you haven't cleaned the house: Sexton beetles raise their kids in a decomposing mouse."

Astronomers at the
University of Cambridge have
found a new type of habitable exoplanet.
Hycean planets are warm, covered in oceans
and have hydrogen-rich atmospheres. They are also
potentially habitable. The discovery happened when
astronomers began looking for planets outside the
dimensions of Earth or other planets in the solar system.
The first find—K2-18b—is eight times as big as Earth
and twice the radius. "At the bare minimum,
microbial life should be possible," said
Dr. Nikku Madhusudhan, the lead
author of the research, which is
how life started
on
Earth.

PART V

Mycelium

Through mycorrhizal networks—fungal threads between plants—trees can communicate with seedlings ("family members") and other species. Working with Susan Dudley at McMaster University, the forest ecologist Suzanne Simard conducted an experiment. She labeled the biggest and oldest conifer trees with the most mycorrhizal interconnections—the "mother" trees—by feeding them a radioactive form of carbon, to see if the carbon would be transmitted to a "kin seedling," rather than a stranger. The mother trees seemed to recognize their son, daughter or sibling trees through chemical signals. (One of the chemicals that moves through these networks and underpins the workings of the forest is glutamate, which is also a major neurotransmitter in the human brain.)

The mother trees protect and care for seedlings in need. When there is a frost or a hot day, the mother tree responds to the tough conditions and her care and attention benefit the health and well-being of the entire forest environment. Mother trees are hubs, intricately connected with other species, sharing excess carbon and nitrogen with hundreds of seedlings, which increases their resilience and survival. The "children" of the mother trees receive more carbon, and they will "mother" other trees too. As well as sending resources, trees can also transmit stress signals that trigger defense mechanisms in others, to protect against insect infestation and drought. The trees are not competing, or in contest with each other. Instead they are helping and supporting each other, even if it is the fungi that are pulling the strings.

II.

Recombobulation

To destroy the institution is not to abolish motherhood. It is to release the creation and sustenance of life into the same realm of decisional struggle, surprise, imagination and conscious intelligence, as any difficult, but freely chosen work.

Adrienne Rich, *Of Woman Born*

Finally I came to the thought, All right, then, annihilate me; that other self was a fiction anyhow. And then I could breathe.

Sarah Ruhl, *100 Essays I Don't Have Time to Write*

We found that these online substitute networks were created by women, for women, in an effort to fill much needed social, political, and medical gaps that fail to see "woman and mother" as a whole being, rather than simply as a "discarded candy wrapper."

Lauren Britton, Louise Barkhuus and Bryan Semaan, " 'Mothers as Candy Wrappers': Critical Infrastructure Supporting the Transition into Motherhood"

At home, I take my microscope off the shelf, remove its dust cover, plug it in and place a pinch of lichen from the forest on a slide. As the lenses move into focus, I am exploring what seems at first to be a derelict building. Dark-green, rubbery looking walls open up to see-through canyons. It is squamulose lichen and I pore over the details of its overlapping scales—or squamules—when, suddenly, I see a creature moving. I slow my roaming, watching this lone housekeeper in an abandoned hotel. It has a sectioned thorax, a long body and a long beaky nose. It slips between the squamules and my eye is caught by a cluster of emerald-green spheres. Whose eggs are they? The arthropod's, perhaps.

What looked, to the naked eye, like inanimate plants is in fact a habitat, abundantly animate, and an example of symbiosis. "A lichen" doesn't exist. Lichens are an association, a relationship between fungi and algae and/or cyanobacteria. The relationship is mutually beneficial. The fungi receive food from the algae or bacteria; the algae or bacteria receive protection and shelter from the fungi. The word "lichen" comes from the Greek *leichēn*, to lick, or to eat around oneself.

Aha! A tardigrade appears, waddling around on its eight legs like the water bear or moss piglet it is also called. Although their name, *tardigrade,* comes from the Latin for "slow walker," this one is moving energetically. It looks like a cross between a hog, a manatee and a vacuum bag. Tardigrades are hardy, the most resilient of all animals on Earth. They can survive high and low pressures, temperatures and altitudes; they can withstand radiation (a thousand times' more than other animals), dehydration (they survive a dry state for ten years or more) and extreme impacts. When frozen, they can remain in a dormant state—the "tun" state—for around twenty months, and then come back to life.

In 2021, a group of physicists at Nanyang Technological University in Singapore claimed to have quantum-entangled a tardigrade. It was the first time a multicellular organism was able to be placed in an entangled state, they said. Although their paper was received critically by other physicists, who questioned whether it was actual quantum entanglement, it caused a stir.

Quantum entanglement is hard to get to grips with. The Royal Society calls quantum effects "weird." "Spooky action from a distance" was how Einstein described it. Quantum entanglement involves two or more particles becoming connected to each other in such a way that their properties cannot be described *individually* anymore. Once entangled, changing the properties of one of the particles can change the other, even if they are very far away from each other. Particles, and even living atoms, seem to share information this way. It is thought that quantum effects might be how plants, trees and bacteria photosynthesize. Plants may trap light and turn it into energy this way.

The new science of quantum biology suggests quantum effects might be implicated more generally within biological systems. The way we smell, for example, has always been a mystery. Our olfactory system is highly sensitive despite having just hundreds of receptors. A growing evidence base suggests we might smell through quantum entanglement. The quantum world might even interact with the molecules of life, our DNA. Quantum phenomena might enable our cells to catalyze enzymes at speed. It has been proposed that general anesthetic switches off consciousness through quantum means, leading to fascinating work exploring whether quantum entanglement plays a role in a lot of the brain activity—how neurotransmitters work and communicate, how antidepressants work—that researchers don't yet understand. In one 2018 study, quantum effects were found to affect the mothering behavior of rats. "This seems extraordinary, that changing something as small as the spin of a nucleus might result in macroscopic changes on the level of something as complex as the mothering instinct or, indeed, consciousness itself," write physicists at the University of KwaZulu-Natal in South Africa.[1]

As the field develops, quantum biology might offer us new ways of seeing and thinking about life on Earth and human consciousness. It suggests there is a lot we don't yet know. It suggests that the barriers between particles at the smallest level are not so firm. Transfer, coupling and entanglement might be more integral parts of life than we think.

Getting a microscope has upended the "classical" wisdom I was taught about molecular biology, with its discrete individuals and adamantine borders. The more time I spend watching tiny critters, the more I can imagine and understand that I am a holobiont: made up of more nonhuman cells than human cells, so much more porous than I had realized. How much of my behavior, my emotional life and my actions might be directed by my symbionts, that use me as a niche? How mistaken have we been to think humans are so separate from the rest of life, and can act accordingly?

The tardigrade bumbles about, exploring the amoebas and rotifers and worms on the slide, sniffing about the specks of soil and moss, bumbling around like a cartoon character, like its thousands, if not millions, of cousin tardigrades are doing right outside the window.

O

Even into the second year of motherhood, my sense of self was ruptured. Shaky, up for grabs. Like a caterpillar in its chrysalis, my imaginal discs were still suspended in goo, yet to turn into a new form, but I began to recombobulate.

The sense of dissolution that I experienced was, in part, easy to explain.

Looking after a new human necessarily requires self-sacrifice which, inevitably, limits and shrinks one's sense of self. She needed my full attention. So I put myself to one side. As she grew into an older baby, and then a toddler, she required different and more constant relational engagement. I learned new ways of caring, new ways of thinking, new depths of empathy.

In *Mysteries of Small Houses,* the poet Alice Notley described the obliteration of the self and the identity crisis many new mothers experience: "He is born and I am undone . . . for two years there's no me here."[2]

But this disorientation could not be entirely accounted for by the biological and social impacts of pregnancy, birth and new motherhood. It wasn't until I came across a third school of thought, influenced by existential philosophy, that I could clearly see the situation I was in.

As I tried to reorient myself, I realized how much of my angst had emanated from an existential crisis. Not in the clichéd sense that I couldn't find meaning in my life; rather, that the weight of my choices and responsibilities, combined with a new, sustained confrontation with mortality, was bamboozling. This was a world tilted.

The existential psychotherapist Claire Arnold-Baker is at the forefront of this new approach to understanding matrescence. In 2020, she authored and compiled the first textbook about the existential crisis of motherhood.[3] In her research and her studies of new mothers, she found that in all the four dimensions of existence—physical, social, personal and spiritual—women were facing huge changes.

"Some people think of an existential crisis as a literal threat to existence, and in some sense it is," she explained, when we talked. "Mortality is very much there for women. But I also talk about it using crisis from the Greek crisis (κρίσις), to choose or to decide. Everything has to be chosen again. What is important to them? How are they going to mother? How are they going to incorporate this identity of mother into themselves?"

Through the lens of existential thought, it seems inevitable that many women should find the transition to motherhood challenging, even madness-invoking. "The burden of responsibility" is at the heart of existentialism: Sartre argued that we are "condemned" to individual freedom because, "once thrown into the world," we are responsible for everything we do. Keeping a baby alive, making decisions for another person, is surely the ultimate fraught pinnacle of responsibility.

Caring for a child is a uniquely weighty and serious pursuit. Even with the desire to parent equally, the fact remains that mothers are still the primary caregivers, especially at the beginning of life. I was responsible for the literal survival of an actual human person. The dissonance between what I felt in myself—that this was a big deal—and what I felt society and culture were telling me—that this was not valuable work (although you have to get it totally right)—was bewildering.

"It's the most important job in the world, with no manual, no instructions, and you have to keep this baby alive. You don't know how to change a nappy, how to feed them, and yet you have this huge responsibility," said Arnold-Baker. Acknowledging this burden is useful for the women she works with. "All those choices are so loaded."

It made me think of Kierkegaard's spider and the void of the future in front of it:

> What is to come? What does the future hold? I don't know, I have no idea. When from a fixed point a spider plunges down as is its nature, it sees always before it an empty space in which it cannot find a footing however much it flounders.[4]

When there is so much conflicting baby-care advice, mothers are left with no obvious path, no clear footing. We have to take a step into the unknown, into that empty space. Will it damage the baby psychologically if she cries for a while on a car journey? Will our attachment be damaged if I can't breastfeed exclusively? Will her sense of security and stability be affected if she goes to childcare? "Terrible, unendurable," Kierkegaard called this lack of knowing—and sometimes I felt this about the heaviness of potential harm.

Learning about the existential approach to motherhood was consoling. It helped me make sense of what happened and why I found it so disconcerting. It helped me to feel less ashamed.

For Arnold-Baker, as for so many others, the solution is trying to normalize it: to "acknowledge the enormity of what actually happens to women and help them to understand how they have changed in all of these ways and what that struggle means and that the response they are having is normal to that experience."

I needed mental health care after giving birth, and I'm glad I was treated quickly, and responded to medication and therapy. But I wonder whether understanding the existential crisis that pregnancy and birth could precipitate might have helped me avoid some of the shame and self-loathing.

Existential theorists and therapists have noted that a new sense of temporality is an essential facet of becoming a mother. One of the stranger experiences I had was a sense that time was speeding up as my daughter grew. I looked at the clock and the second hand seemed to be moving faster. When she started nursery, with the year separated into six half terms, the months vanished as quickly as biscuits in a packet.

One night I had a vivid dream, which was rare. It was summer, a bright and hot day. I ran outside and saw that all the leaves had turned red, yellow, orange. No longer green. The leaves were autumn leaves but it was only the beginning of the summer. It is too early, I panicked. I was appalled. What is happening?

Becoming a mother had also forced me to face an inconvenient truth: that my time on Earth was limited, and my time with my baby, and then with my children, had an end point.

O

Academics and historians have long pointed out the absence of meaningful rituals in WEIRD countries. In other cultures, rituals acknowledge times of existential transition, role change, new responsibilities and the need for social support. New mothers in many if not most cultures across the world—including China, Japan, India, South America—follow similar traditional confinement practices after giving birth. These often involve some combination of nutrient-rich meals, massages, drinks, herbal baths and recipes prepared by close female relatives, women in the community, or hired postnatal assistants who will care for the mother and baby for around forty days. The mother is expected to rest and be looked after, while feeding and bonding with her baby. In Vietnam, the period is called *namo*, meaning "lying in a nest," where the new mother will be given special tonics and soups.[5] In Nigeria, *omugwo* is the name of the Igbo cultural practice of care given to the new mother, usually by their own mother or a close relative, for a period of time.[6] In India, special massages with herbal-infused oils are called *abhyanga*. Wrapping the belly is common in Indo-Malay traditions and in Mexico, where a "closing of the bones" ceremony helps to emotionally and physically close the woman's body after the extreme opening of birth.[7] In the Tundra Nenets nomadic community, women and girls gather *Sphagnum* moss to make diapers and post-birth pads for the new mother, who is given a new name after the birth of her first child.[8] In The Gambia, traditional social singing by Kanyelang groups supports maternal and baby health.[9] These rites recognize the psychological and emotional transition of becoming a mother, as well as what a body goes through in pregnancy and childbirth.

But in Western societies, the mother is mostly left to her own devices after birth, her own privacy and autonomy. While being told to stay inside for forty days does sound quite intense, our approach means we don't honor or acknowledge what a woman has done, or have a sufficient cultural way of marking the passage into a new stage of existence.

"The individual mother is left to grapple with the fact that she is not only the source of life but also of potential death for her child," writes Rozsika Parker.[10]

I met with my father—an Anglican priest—to speak about rituals around motherhood. I wondered if my ancestors would've taken part in any that had died out. He mentioned the Christian custom of the "churching of women." It originally began as a purification rite. Women would receive a blessing on around the fortieth day after birth. Later, I found more details in the Book of Common Prayer:

> *The Woman, at the usual time after her delivery, shall come into the Church decently apparelled, and there shall kneel down in some convenient place, as hath been accustomed, or as the Ordinary shall direct: And then the Priest shall say unto her, FORASMUCH as it hath pleased Almighty God of his goodness to give you safe deliverance, and hath preserved you in the great danger of child-birth: You shall therefore give hearty thanks unto God.*

After more prayers, the priest gives thanks:

> *O* ALMIGHTY *God, we give thee humble thanks for that thou hast vouchsafed to deliver this woman thy servant from the great pain and peril of child-birth.*[11]

Churching also happened in the Roman Catholic Church, Methodism and several Eastern Churches. The ritual was mostly discontinued in the mid-twentieth century. Some women felt ostracized by the rite, as it suggested that they were defiled and unclean to the point of not being able to touch anything or go anywhere. Baptism of a child became more important. Childbirth became safer. Society became secular.

Despite my complicated relationship with the Christian church, this ritual—any ritual—sounds appealing. To have the "pain and peril" of childbirth recognized and not erased or swept under the carpet. To have the momentous occasion of childbirth acknowledged. For a community to give thanks and join in relief that the dangers of birth had been endured. To not be forgotten after birth.

Instead, women "are left to overcome this traumatic life crisis, and work things out for themselves, with little or no support," writes Arnold-Baker.

Are the care and maternal mental health crises also, in part, a spiritual crisis?

It is interesting that both the Qur'an and the Bible contain a much stronger sense of the physical and psychological experience of matrescence than our dominant secular discourse. As the scholar Irene Oh shows, the Qur'an tells Muslims to revere their mothers because of the "hardship" they go through to give birth and wean children. Oh argues that the Bible also shows a deeper acknowledgment of the "suffering" of motherhood: "And alas for those who are with child and those who give suck in those days!"[12]

As time passed after my daughter was born, I realized I was searching for, and trying to create my own, matrescent rituals—rituals that went beyond popping an SSRI every morning along with many thousands of other mothers. These were: weekly Rhymetime at the library, honest chats in WhatsApp groups with friends who had babies the same age, receiving clothes and books from neighbors and passing on our own, watching *Better Things*, a comedy show about a single mother of three girls, my Evil Witches subscription, starting a "listening time" with another mother, looking for pockets of resistance and community, going to my pelvic floor physio appointments, and spending time with friends who were a little older, and much wiser, than me. These social connections became a lifeline and gave me strength and resilience.

I also found relief in the woods: witnessing ecological processes, cycles of growth and decay. Here were the hazards, mortality, symbiosis, relationality, possibilities and new ways of seeing that matrescence had rocketed me into.

The woods were a blank slate; there was no judgment. I could imagine a new future, a new self. In the woods, I could be neither woman nor man, neither mother nor child, neither my father nor my mother. Among the trees, I could shed my social tethers. Become animal. Feel that bone-closeness, that sap-closeness, that matrescence had brought me to.

Academics are starting to consider the positive possibilities for change that matrescence may bring. Writing in *Philosophical Inquiries into Pregnancy, Childbirth, and Mothering Maternal Subjects*, the philosopher Brooke Schueneman describes becoming a mother as a time of "substantial imagination and self-exploration" that has been neglected and obscured. She argues that according to the Socratic, Platonist and Hellenistic assertion of philosophy as a way of learning how to die in order to live more fully, mothers are in a "prime position to embrace this ancient, but relevant, exercise."

"Many women report their experiences as paradigm shifts from being self-centred to collective, or just the opposite, from other-centred to self-centred; from being free to burdened; as lacking to fulfilled," she writes.[13]

After I had children, for the first time in my life, I found that I had the confidence and gumption to get actively involved in the democratic process. Through my twenties I would sometimes have panic attacks when speaking in public or in meetings. I never talked in class at school or university unless forced. But over matrescence, I found I could stand up in front of hundreds of people at a council meeting and talk about air pollution and children's health and barely bat an eyelid.

O

There are signs of progress being made. Grassroots community groups are attempting to resist the widespread isolation and loneliness that new mothers experience. Informal meetings that bring new mothers together are growing in number across Britain, both face-to-face and online. You could even call these groups modern matrescent rituals. Unlike the NCT courses, which focus on the baby—planning for a positive birth, feeding—these groups center on maternal mental health. The first of its kind in the UK—Mothers Talking—run by the esteemed psychotherapist and best-selling author Naomi Stadlen, has been running for over thirty-one years in north London, in the tradition of consciousness-raising feminist groups that began in the 1960s and 1970s. Other groups operate in areas across the country, including the Motherhood Group, a community based in London for Black mothers. In the US, Postpartum Support International offers online support groups, local groups and phone calls with perinatal mental health practitioners. "You are not alone and you are not to blame. Help is available. You will get better," says its tagline.

Mothers Uncovered, in Brighton, has run for over a decade. Its founder, Maggie Gordon-Walker, attended Mothers Talking in London and was inspired to set up her own group. We talked over Zoom. Her hair was glossy red and she was funny and forthright. She told me about her experience of matrescence.

"I cried every day for six months. What's happened? My life's over. There's no one I can talk to about this, I'm really miserable. I loved my baby. But it was entirely awful, the whole thing. Where are all the actual people I can talk to about this?"

She found Mothers Talking helpful and applied for funding to set up Mothers Uncovered for her registered charity Livestock. She has a background in performing arts, so the group has a creative angle and each session is loosely based around a theme or exercise. One week might involve listening to a new mother telling their birth story which, said Maggie, is "hugely, hugely important."

"It's giving it the formality. This space is here to listen to you tell this tale."

Another might begin with writing on a piece of paper what their day entailed until the start of the meeting, which is normally at 11:00 a.m. "We say, write down what you were doing at midnight, 1:00 a.m., 2:00 a.m. The day does not start like most people's does at 7:00 a.m. Then, there's a whole sheet of how much they've done up until that point and then they're like, oh, no wonder I'm tired."

The objective is to allow new mothers to assess their role, to see the importance of what they do, to take pride in it and share it with each other.

"It's bigger than all the practical things—you've changed this many nappies, they've had this much sleep, this much food. It's actually the process of bringing them into the world and bringing them up, the mothers don't really realize that."

She mentioned three new mothers in a recent group with babies under six months. "They say, I'm a bit tired, and then they list this whole litany of crap they've been through that they don't acknowledge. The focus is all on the baby, but what about you?"

Unlike a more formal group run in a healthcare setting, where the practitioner might not have direct experience of new motherhood, all the women running these sessions do.

"People don't need to be talked down to, or managed, they need to be reassured and invested in," she said.

Postnatal depression, she continues, is a diagnostic term and lots of the women who come to the group say they don't feel depressed. Others say that the group has pulled them back from the brink of developing mental illness.

Participants use art, writing, singing or mindfulness to explore their perspectives and experience. Creativity "helps build self-esteem and validate a woman's perspective. It also brings the often-hidden nature of motherhood into the open."

These groups are oases of resistance and community; they are the beginnings of a new mothering culture. When I was five years into matrescence, after the birth of my third child, I started attending Naomi Stadlen's Mothers Talking group and found listening to the struggles and delights and bewilderments of other mothers a relief. I joined an informal group online with other local mothers and it became an important support line. I listened to mothers talking on podcasts about parenting for highly sensitive and neurodiverse people; about reparenting and battling sensory overload and mindful self-compassion and navigating meltdowns. I planted seeds furiously and watched the green leaves peeking through. I swam in ice-cold rivers to soothe my nervous system. My attachment to local places, to the woods and the trees and the rivers, became profoundly important; they hushed my anxiety, and made me feel secure.

I had the renewed sense that my body didn't feel capable of the level of (mostly) solo care I was giving. I craved community and people. Sometimes, my body would send up a warning flare via various symptoms, such as chronic eczema, a stomach ulcer, fatigue. I felt a growing anger and resentment towards our broken society and the conditions it imposes on caregivers. One evening, at the Mothers Talking group, I surprised myself by bursting out in frustration: "So at the time women are most likely to suffer from mental illness we isolate them inside, expect them to match unrealistic human ideals, judge their every move, demand they get their body back after the violence of birth, silence their lived experience, and expect them to survive on inadequate sleep?" I had always repressed my anger. It felt strange and new to express it.

Hold on to that anger, said Stadlen. That is good anger.

O

Experiencing matrescence has helped me see how badly we need new, informal ecologies of care—how we need to repair our sense of community and connectedness across society.

After I gave birth to our first son, in 2019, any delusions of self-reliance and independence were truly shattered.

Mothering alone felt increasingly unsustainable. I would take my eyes off the baby and he'd topple over. The toddler would need soothing. The baby would be screaming for milk. I'd need the loo. The baby would need changing. The toddler would need a drink. The baby would need to be soothed to sleep. I'd need sleep. The toddler would need fresh air. I'd need to make lunch. The baby would need to be held. The toddler would need to be held and soothed. The baby would need to show me his new treasures. The toddler would want my full attention. Everyone would cry. I'd ricochet frantically. I couldn't meet my basic needs when I was alone with them.

For a while, I felt unable to leave the house and keep them safe. Both infants seemed to need someone tending to them more or less the whole time.

One day, when my son was a few weeks old, and curled up embryonic in the sling, our then-two-year-old daughter ran, suddenly, very fast through the back gate. I was surprised by how fast she was moving. I yelled, expecting her to stop. At that point, she had never run away from me. I shouted again, but she was still moving, across the back field and down an alley which meets a busy road with various intersections, parked vehicles, and cars that people are often driving too fast. I started to run but I was terrified that by moving my body this way I could crush the delicate bones and ribs of my baby and damage his neck and spine. I tried to form a protective shield with my hands over his body and ran with my arms stiff and constricted, shouting for her to stop. She was out of sight around the corner. In my imagination, she was being hit by a car. In my imagination, he was being shaken to death. I reached her just as she got to the side of the road, and yanked her towards me. I was wide-eyed with fear and fury. I crouched on the pavement and dragged her close, and tried to conceal how much I was shaking, trying to get my breath back, drenched in cortisol, pursing my lips, checking the baby was alive.

When their father was here, in the evenings after work and at the weekends, or we were with close family members, the experience of mothering was very different. It felt safer, less frightening, less fraught. I was able to panic less. Get a drink. Go to the loo.

It was safer to care for the baby and toddler at home, but it was also driving everyone—including me—mad with boredom. One day, I woke feeling confident enough to take the children in the car to a local garden center. I had an idea to buy some autumn bulbs.

Leaving the house felt risky. Tantrums, meltdowns, screaming fits in public, parking, getting everyone out safely, using my best powers of persuasion to direct behaviors on little sleep could, yes, get on top of me.

But I had a sliver of gumption that day. I was trying to get everyone out in the morning after reading that light therapy could help perinatal depression, which I was being treated for again. Women with perinatal depression had been found to have altered circadian rhythms. There was some evidence that outdoor exposure to sunlight could help relieve symptoms of depression by resetting the body clock. I wanted to counteract the hours we spent indoors, to use the sun and its health benefits to try and lift my mood.

In the car park of the garden center, alert to the danger of heavy vehicles and my children's small bodies, I folded the baby into the sling using the reflection from the car window. The toddler wanted to be carried, like the baby, into the store, but I persuaded her to walk with the promise of choosing flower bulbs to buy. It worked for a few seconds but, once inside, she lay on the cold cement floor howling. I picked her up on one side of my body and slotted her between my hip and rib cage. I could just about carry both. I watched in case the baby was being poked and walked through the store.

Excuse me.

A woman in her sixties or seventies appeared in front of us.

Your shoelaces are undone.

I peered down around the toddler's blonde curls and the baby's spherical head. It was true. My shoelaces were loose.

You could slip.

I couldn't put the toddler down and risk another screaming fit, and I couldn't tie up my shoelaces anyway with the baby in a sling. What did she want me to do?

She disappeared from view. I felt my shoes tighten and realized that she was kneeling on the floor, tying up my shoelaces.

I stood, looking at the rows of paint and bathroom fixtures and shelving units, bathed in her kindness, and my tension and agitation loosened its grip.

Sea squirts

Sea squirts are small, tubelike creatures that live in all types of marine environments. They suck plankton in through a siphon, squirting waste through another opening. Some species glow, producing their own bioluminescence. Others have colorful, gilded edges or spots in highlighter yellow, cornflower blue, burnt umber. Some live alone, others live in groups, stuck to reefs, shipwrecks and rocks.

Sea squirts begin life as completely different creatures: tadpole larvae. They have brains, a nerve cord, a heart, the classic wriggly tail that moves them around, and a vertebrate-like body, the kind that all vertebrates, including humans, evolved from. This existence may last for a few hours to a few days. Once ready to morph, a tadpole larva swims to the floor of the ocean, sticks its head to a surface and digests its tail, brain and nerve cord. It gobbles up the stuff it doesn't need. It won't swim again, but remains sessile.

So which one is the main event? Is the tadpole larva an individual life-form in itself? Or is it just the rehearsal?

12.

Care work and creativity in late-stage capitalism

They call it love, we call it unpaid labour.

Silvia Federici, *Wages Against Housework*

What do we lose as a culture when we make the tacit assumption that mothers will stop dreaming?

Rachel Yoder

Somehow all of the baggage that I had accumulated as a person about what was valuable just fell away. I could not only be me—whatever that was—but somebody actually needed me to be that . . . If you listen to [your children], somehow you are able to free yourself from baggage and vanity and all sorts of things, and deliver a better self, one that you like. The person that was in me that I liked best was the one my children seemed to want.

Toni Morrison

REGISTRY OF MATRESCENCE GIFTS

Pomegranate bath salts from Florence
Steak
Jojoba shower gel
A book of poetry
Silk hairband
Pineapples
Tisanes
Plant oils
Calendula seeds
Cashmere socks
Necklace of individually chosen beads for birth including tortoise, dog, moonstone
Fenugreek
Drawings
A rowan tree
Lavender bath oil
Lentil soup
Marmalade
Pajamas
Tartiflette
Lucozade
Sweets

It was half past three in the afternoon and I had spent hours trying to focus my mind. It was a workday, and I had so far been unable to make progress. Since our son had turned nine months old, my statutory maternity pay (£156 a week) had stopped, so I needed to return to paid work. My husband had taken the day off to care for the children. And yet, I couldn't help but feel that the work I really ought to be doing was happening downstairs.

The baby had been asleep for a while and I was settling down to write. From my desk, in our bedroom, I looked on to a new housing estate, telephone pylons and roofs. To the right was the old Eli Lilly factory, which made Prozac for years, now luxury flats. A steady stream of cars drove down the road. A red kite soared above. On my bookshelf, *The Myth of Motherhood, The Mask of Motherhood, How Mothers Love, Little Labours, The Argonauts, Torn in Two, From Here to Maternity, Operating Instructions, Guidebook to Relative Strangers, Three Poems, Songs for the Unborn Second Baby, The Republic of Motherhood, Silences.* I should be washing his clothes. I should be preparing his food.

I listened out keenly and heard the baby's awakening mews. My concentration spooled out even more.

Motherhood is an occupation in all senses of the word. Those who have occupied me are now living both outside and inside me. By which I mean, sometimes there is no membrane between us, despite appearances. They have annexed my consciousness.

Each yelp and giggle pulled my attention away from an attempt to write up my research into work and early motherhood. I felt his sounds in my body. Each vocalization was another sheet of colored cellophane paper over my tasks.

I broke off, stopped fighting the urge to go to him. I pulled him towards me, kissed his marzipan cheeks and syrup neck, felt the soft spring of his animal body alongside mine. I squeezed his thighs and we searched for ways of making him laugh, fixing, like addicts, on the pull of his lips and mouth sideways and up.

Instead of returning to work I decided to collect our daughter from childcare, hoping movement and a change of scene would help me focus. I arrived at the nursery and waited. She ran into my arms and my heart leapt. We talked about what she did: playing with cars, singing happy birthday, blue lollipop, banana, apple, tangerine, candles for a birthday cake. Back at home, I ate lunch quickly (fish, to try and boost my attention; coffee, ditto), while feeding the baby mashed-up broccoli, apple and yogurt.

Upstairs, the fish and coffee failed me. I was still skating on the surface, unable to let myself fall into the writing and reading, unable to quash the guilt.

At this point, neither child was even asking for me. I usually worked outside the house, in the library or a coffee shop, knowing that I couldn't focus when the children were around. That day, though, I had a heavy cold, and the library had been so loud the day before.

I tried to explain to my husband why I couldn't concentrate but it was difficult to articulate. A part of me feels like it should be with the children, so I can't fully give myself to work. I am entangled. When I work, there is most often a low-level hum of discomfort, unless they are asleep, unconscious. How much of that is a result of my new brain—their zombie cells inside me, or peptides, perhaps—and how much is my internalization of the requirements of the Institution of Intensive Motherhood, is hard to say.

In matrescence my paid work suddenly became a moral issue. How much of myself should I give to my children, and how much to my career? Was it right to continue pursuing my professional dreams outside of economic need? Should I work evenings and weekends, just enough to pay for half of our house and food and living?

Society is still ambivalent about whether and how much a mother should work in the early years of her child's life. As Shari L. Thurer puts it, people's ideas about mothers and work are unprocessed. Most women I know work part-time after having children, putting themselves at an economic disadvantage and limiting their pensions, financial autonomy and career progression. Those who work full-time are often stressed. A major study found that eleven indicators of stress were 40 percent higher for women working full-time while bringing up two children than among women working full-time with no children.[1] Parents of young children are at particular risk of work–family conflict. The organization of work and the division of labor hasn't changed nearly enough, and women pay the price.

In most families, both partners work. If one partner does stay at home, the other may have to work every hour God sends, and then rarely see his or her children. Women usually work a "second shift" at home on top of their paid work, taking on much of the care of children and housework.[2] Then there's the "third shift," which builds on Arlie Hochschild's metaphor, and has been used to refer to the work of maintaining harmony in the marriage, learning about child development and assuming the psychological burden of the family's emotional well-being.

Back in our bedroom, I continued to write notes, anxious about the time I was wasting and an impending deadline. Accidentally, I dozed off—there had been multiple wakings the night before. On stirring, the guilt about not being with my children, and the magnetic pull of their bodies, was too much, so I headed downstairs to spend time with my daughter on the sofa. We made towers out of cars and read books. I drew my fingernail around her palm and sang "round and round the garden."

After a while, I said that I would need to get back to work for a bit.

No Mummy, no work. Mummy, NO work. Please, please don't work.

I know, but it's only for a while. Daddy is going to do art with you, and that will be fun!

She was distracted so I slipped off, back upstairs. Finally, I started writing and then—

A knock at the door.

Mummy, I need you! Please don't work. Please don't work, Mummy. Mummy, Mummy, Mummy, open the door! Mummy! Pleeeease.

I'm taffy, streeeeeeetched until it breaks.

And so, I am writing here now with a small elbow resting on my arm and a little leg curled under my thigh and she's watching a cartoon on my phone aWE32 and the sky outside is turning lavender and rust and the baby ASC∂ßΩeftw43e

O

For the decade before matrescence, which began when I had lived for thirty years, my central daily purpose had been, above all, to earn money through work.

Before that, from the time my conscious memories formed, my purpose was, I understood, to learn, to pass exams with the highest possible marks, to excel, to achieve so that I could one day get a good job and salary. I needed to prove I wasn't stupid; I needed not to fail. My achievements were valuable: the exams I passed, the job I got, the paycheck I earned, the conventions I conformed to, the items I could acquire. I was encouraged towards a creative life in childhood, but the cultural messaging around me was limiting and loud. I was a child when the prime minister was Margaret Thatcher, whose work pattern included surviving on four hours' sleep a night. There was no such thing as society and greed was good. I was schooled in competition and the pressure to win and improve and optimize. By the time I entered the workplace my industrial psyche had been formed. Work happened from Monday to Friday, often for twelve hours a day. My body became machinelike, trained in the rhythms of the working week. I had to earn money, and aim to earn more and more. What do you do? I would ask the people I met, by which I meant, what do you do for work?

When I wasn't earning, my focus was on relationships: maintaining friendships and romantic attachments, spending time and money building social connections, learning to be kind and agreeable in order, ultimately, to find a mate, to make myself attractive to others, mostly men. And when I wasn't working or studying or socializing, I could seek pleasure and reward: watching Almodóvar and Lynch at the cinema; lying in the sun and traveling to Paris and Berlin and Marrakech; eating kebabs and macaroons and drinking whiskey and wine; swimming in the sea in Turkey and Greece; putting this color with that color, this texture with that texture; looking at Kandinskys and Hogarths; reading Tartt and Easton Ellis; boarding trains and cars and airplanes to Helsinki, Montreal, Austin.

It was strange, then, when I fell through the portal of motherhood, to feel that these central drives—to work, to earn, to self-actualize—were now, as soon as the baby left my womb, out of place and even immoral. Why, then, was I sent to school and university? Why was I told "You Can Do Anything"? For a game of dress-up? Why the pretense that I could live my life like a man? Or that being a woman counted for something other than maternal duties once you had a baby? Something snapped shut. I was trapped and bound, suddenly, by new bars of restrictive and prescriptive gender norms. This newfound "traditional" code of intensive motherhood clashed with the capitalistic culture I had been instructed in: to be, first and foremost, a worker, an earner and a consumer.

In matrescence, I felt a strange but strong pressure to pretend that I a) wasn't really working much, b) didn't want to work, and c) only worked because our household financial needs required it, not because I found fulfillment outside of motherhood, as I had for my previous decades of existence. It was this desire for fulfillment elsewhere that seemed abhorrent and stigmatized in my new context. The world I had grown up in, been formed by, the person I had become, was at odds with my present. It was time now to be satisfied by constant, total, isolated caregiving. The aspirations, desires and pleasures of the past were in direct conflict with my new life. The more I shrank my self, I sensed, the better mother I would be. You career girls struggle to adapt to motherhood, I'd hear. But, at the same time—I know, I know, it sounds contradictory and, believe me, the conflicting expectations are uniquely maddening—I also felt intense pressure to hold on to my place in the professional world.

The unsustainable, machinelike exertions the institution of motherhood required were similar to the demands of my job at a newspaper in my twenties. A shift pattern which sometimes saw my working day finish at 9:00 p.m., to get home at 10:00 p.m., followed by waking up at 4:30 a.m. the next morning to be at my desk at 6:00 a.m. led, in part, to the high levels of stress that contributed to substance and alcohol addiction. At the time, I thought I was simply weak, for there was no mention that these shift patterns could be damaging. Now, looking back, I see them as the harmful, distorting symptoms of an economic system based entirely on growth. Then, the capitalist system required my body to be a machine of earning and accumulation. Now, the capitalist system required my body to be a machine to raise the labor market.

But there was a paradox: This uber-devotional, self-denying maternal care was so important that if I messed up it was the worst catastrophe a person could commit. But it was also the drudge job of society; the glorification was hollow. A subordinate role under patriarchy. Low-grade work. "Just" a stay-at-home mum. Of little real significance or value. Too basic and boring to even mention. The messages I had internalized about motherhood were deeply oxymoronic, schizophrenic, even.

Casting care work as easy work that anyone can do alone is a way of justifying the undervaluation, and underpayment, of carers. By naturalizing the work of caregiving and raising children, society can obscure and mystify what it actually is: the infrastructure propping up capitalism. Without workers, there is no work. The largest section of our economies is actually unpaid labor. In 2016, the Office for National Statistics (ONS) found that the value of unpaid childcare—mothering, fathering, parenting—was £351.7 billion. Overall, unpaid household service work was equivalent to 63.1 percent of gross domestic product (GDP).[3]

The way GDP is calculated obscures reality and penalizes caregivers. In our society, wages, benefits and access to resources are all tied to economic output—unless it is the caregiving kind. (The problems with GDP are multiple. The measure doesn't include the costs of degradation of human habitats worldwide, environmental degradation or the harm inflicted on people across the world in terrible working conditions.)

Framing unpaid care work as a source of individual personal satisfaction conceals the fact that it is also a public good with immense social benefits. Children grow up to pay taxes, work for public services, support the older generation, repay public debt, keep society going.

It is easy to see why there has been a reluctance to recognize the immense challenges and demands of maternal work. It makes it easy to pay less for it, or nothing. It makes it possible for men and employers to "free ride on voluntary contributions to the production and maintenance of human and social capital," as the American economist Nancy Folbre puts it.[4]

As she writes, "The true cost of inequality is obscured by national income accounts that treat care for others and investments in human capabilities as just another form of consumption, rather than a fundamentally important investment in human and social capital."

In fact, the work of motherhood was much harder than the paid work I had done previously (which, admittedly, wasn't saving lives). There were no breaks and I often worked for sixteen or more hours a day.

O

Good morning, I sing softly and brightly as I walk into his room. I leave the door open, so the light in the hall illuminates my way. I pick him up and hold him to my body. I feel his forehead to check his temperature. I look at his face to see how he is feeling. I feel his back to check if it is wet. I kiss his face and neck and hold his fat cheeks against mine. I make chattering, cooing noises. I read and scrutinize his facial expressions. I lay him down on the table and undress him. Looking into his eyes and making funny faces, I hold his chest with one hand and clean him with the other. I apply diaper cream, then a diaper. His clothing is damp so I remove his onesie and pajamas. I put on a dry outfit: undershirt, top, trousers, socks, a tiny sweater, making noises and explaining what I'm doing to distract him from crawling away. The two-year-old is up now. I stroke her head with one hand. I placate her cries by talking about pancakes for breakfast and what would you like to have on them? Maple syrup? Jam? I carry the baby down the stairs. The toddler stops at the top and wants to be carried down, too. I put the baby in the middle of the room, checking for nearby marbles or small pieces of plastic, and run back up. I kiss and cuddle her and carry her downstairs. To give me time to feed the baby, I suggest making a castle out of blocks. I put the sterilized bottle's parts together and press the button on the machine. I put the kettle on and pour milk into another bottle. The baby is whining so I pick him up, making a clicking noise with my tongue, his favorite at the moment. It doesn't work. I make a "k k" sound then an "x x" sound. I open the powdered milk with one hand

and spoon in one, two, three, four, five—concentrate, I sometimes lose count—six, seven. I press the next button. I put a slug of hot water into the milk bottle for my older child. I screw on the lid. I put on a bib, cooing as I do it, as he hates clothes around his head. I feed the baby. The toddler is wanting to be fed. I think back to what she had for supper last night, how she slept, her fettle yesterday. She wants to sit on my lap. I ask her to wait a minute. I watch her face to see how she is accepting my request. I watch the baby as he feeds to make sure it's going down OK. He coughs and splutters. I sit him up and put him slightly over my shoulder. I grab a tissue and help the toddler blow her nose with the baby-free hand. I tell a story to distract her from her irritation at my feeding the baby first. I put my arms around her and twist my wrist so I can hold the bottle into the baby's mouth with one hand. I use my foot and toe to move a book towards us and turn the pages with the hand that is around her waist. I ask questions about what she can see in the book. What color is the ship? Where is the spider? Can you see a plate of spaghetti? She tries to pull the bottle away and I explain that I have to feed the baby first and then I will play. I have been awake for eight minutes.

O

I couldn't find a language or vocabulary to describe the subtle intricacies of mother work. But I was determined to study "maternal thinking," as Sara Ruddick puts it, even if it had been suppressed.

In the feminist tradition with which I was raised, motherhood and caregiving had been divested of value, belittled and disparaged in order to let some women become free. Motherhood was embarrassing, uncool servitude. We'd have to do it at some point, but the work would be beneath us.

It took a while for me to truly see the value and complexity of caregiving: how to watch and listen, to regulate emotions, to know when to go in and when to hold back.

What was all this watching and listening and attending and

comforting and soothing and holding and containing doing? I was using my body and my brain to allow our baby's body and brain to survive. Increasingly, scientists argue for the importance of "allostasis" in human health and well-being. Homeostasis might be more familiar from science lessons at school. That's the steady maintenance and regulation of a system or organism to a set point, such as the control of body temperature. Allostasis is broader and more intricate. It means the ongoing and dynamic process of reacting to complex environments and predicting change in order, ultimately, to achieve stability.[5] So, when an infant cries and a caregiver picks them up and cuddles and kisses them, they are communicating that human touch is a means of achieving allostasis, a way of being a human in the world.

O

Care work is hardcore. It is life-and-death work. It is fevers and risk and birth and illness and screaming and love and transference. It is transformation and hope. It is quick thinking and deep patience. It is resentment and anger. It is sacrifice and gift. In these years of caring, our vulnerability becomes so stark. I thought mothering would just be changing diapers and cuddling a baby.

Instead it took me to the edge of what it means to be human. It tested my empathy to the limit, it challenged me intellectually, it required me to answer and ask questions constantly, to consider metaphysics and the origins of matter. I learned how to talk to preverbal humans. How to listen and respond with sounds and noises and breath. The language was tone of voice, skin color, pace of movement, facial expression, heat, clinginess, small bodily movements like rubbing eyes or ears or a faraway stare. The language grew and altered daily. I learned how to subtly reel in and out a presence when the baby was learning something new: delicately using my hands and fingers and arms to support climbing at an inch remove without their knowing that my hands and arms were right there. I became a kind of doctor and a nurse, learning essential pediatric health and medicine: what rashes are what, the healthy temperature of skin, signs of infection or the hatching of it. I had to learn a new language for each child. I learned how to be a shock absorber or airbag between my young children with their underdeveloped prefrontal cortexes and inner wildness, their appetites for destruction and the rest of the world. I learned what it's like to feel two conflicting things at the same time: to want to see my friends and have time away, but also never to want to leave for very long. I was both vulnerable and newly strengthened. My reflexes had never been quicker. Sometimes the baby might fall off a chair and I would have been watching her in my peripheral vision, my hands just there to catch her without any conscious thought. I could see how that woman lifted a car off her child in the 1980s, and why Marvel creator Jack Kirby came up with the character of the Hulk after seeing another mother lifting a car to save her baby.[6]

It didn't surprise me to read that researchers at the University of Massachusetts found, in a synthesis of literature on working mothers, that matrescence was associated with enhanced knowledge, skills and capacity. They found evidence that it "strengthened women's mindset, willpower, and overall emotional intelligence."[7]

Nothing that I had previously read, heard or watched about motherhood suggested that it would be an intellectually stimulating, creative time.

O

The creativity started to effervesce when my daughter turned three. I was inspired by her directness, her imaginative urges unsullied by social anxieties or cultural expectations or self-consciousness. I wanted what she had. The house filled with pencils and paints and stickers and impressions and pompoms and clay and chalk. It was catching. I picked up a paintbrush again. Played music for the first time in years. She needed me to make up stories, so I had to learn. I wrote short stories one sentence long. I wrote with my left hand to see what happened. I was ravenous for the world. She needed me to answer questions about space and time, rocks and minerals, evolution and death. Our house filled with encyclopedias from the library. What made space? Why do birds sing at dusk and dawn? Why don't boys wear skirts? What would I be like if I was a book? In times of good health, my brain felt at its most absorbent and flexible.

She was my new boss, and she knew exactly how to get me to do the work she required. She taught me how to slow down and pay attention, for a start. This first boss, poor thing, had her work cut out: she had to teach us how to do the job, and sometimes it was frustrating for her.

Of all the bosses I had worked for, these baby bosses had the most neural activity and connections. You should have seen their whirring, changing, growing brains! Thirty thousand synapses per square centimeter of brain cortex forming per second! A quarter of a million nerve cells every minute!

They made hypotheses about the world and updated their understanding as new evidence rolled in. They used probability, logic and reason, as well as statistical patterns. It was remarkable to witness the exuberant expansion of their consciousness and their delight in learning and exploring—their delight in being alive. In the morning, they would stand in their cots and smiles would erupt. Laughter and joy and wonder were right under the surface for these babies. They seemed to have a spring of delight and excitement within them, and a spring of love. We adopted their malapropisms and emphases. They changed the way we saw the world.

Sarah Blaffer Hrdy suggests that our capacities for empathy, cooperation and altruism—our so-called human capacities—have come about because of the extended period of caregiving human children require. "Mothers would have been among the earliest intellectuals," she writes. "Enlisting natural history, myth, and ritual to explain anomalies, justify their actions, and reconcile necessity with emotions."[8] How could I have thought this was not important and interesting work?

Babies and young children look at us with full eye contact, and none of the self-consciousness and shame that comes with adulthood. They "are the R&D department of the human species, the blue-sky guys, while we adults are production and marketing," as Alison Gopnik, professor of psychology at the University of California, Berkeley, says.[9] No snark, no cynicism, no sarcasm, no sniping. I wanted to be a blue-sky guy. My children were leading me back to the world of childhood.

They demanded new ways of being. Silliness. Cuddles. Repetition. Echoes. Some of it was painful and boring, some of it was magical. Spontaneity and surprise were key attributes of these babies' employees. They had no time for self-doubt. They were *exactly* who they wanted to be. They wanted to move! They wanted to dance! To touch. To laugh! They needed me to be in the present and give them a stream of immediate experiences, and so I fell in love with the world again.

Have you seen the shape of water as it is being poured?
Have you let a bumblebee's spun-sugar legs walk across your palm?
Have you tried to say two words at the same time?
Have you seen the opalescence of a bubble?
Have you watched a slug slither?

Have you tried to feel the planet moving?

I was paid with kisses and heavenly bodies, with gallons of dopamine and canisters of oxytocin, with kōans and drawings and beauty. I live, now, with Marilyn Monroe and James Dean. I was paid with the signature sound of their laughter and rat-a-tat giggles. They showed me how life could encompass play. I had lost touch with how it felt to be in a body, to horse around, to live through the senses. My creativity-for-the-sake-of-it had gone underground but they unearthed it. They taught me how to glory in the simple pleasures of being a sensuous creature alive on Earth.

Children live in the moment, outside the marketplace. Their days are a constant remaking and creating and shedding and imagining. I live with a tiny Edward Lear, in a world of smumpy juice, bikstap, shax, hangangy, gookgooks, bafe. They invent words and questions and ideas I couldn't dream of. I live with a small artist who draws made-up creatures every day. Their minds overflow with ideas and possibilities. They cherish the world; they cherish being alive.

The tension between this work and my earning work was high. I realized I had been molded into a loyal, obedient earner, addicted to acquisition and the external metrics of success. Increasingly, though, I was trying to find a path towards a new way of caring, a radical way, an authentic way, beyond the martyred maternal ideal. I wanted to start recovering from my indoctrination in hyper-consumerism and turbo-capitalism, from the Enlightenment values of conquest and mastery and domination that I feel—and resent—in my cellular being, and step out of the value system that placed capital and goods accumulation way too high.

O

When the Covid-19 pandemic hit, my husband was made redundant and stopped working long days full-time away from home. Our first son was ten or so months old and our daughter was three and a half. Suddenly, we were parenting side by side, in the egalitarian way we had planned, but never succeeded in doing. For a few months we were supported by government grants, because I was self-employed, which meant we could focus on caring for the children. I felt less daily stress, fear and burnout than ever before in matrescence. It showed me what it could be like to have more equality at home and gave us a glimpse of what a care wage for reproductive labor might look like, or what it would be like to look after children alongside another adult. In this way, it was a utopian time. We spent much of it in the woods.

This made room for more questions. Beyond affording basic living expenses, what was work for? What was its value? What was a good life? What if we didn't have to work so hard? How much do we need? No, how much do we *actually* need? What am I entitled to? What is my time worth? Who am I serving? Who is benefiting?

Two years into the pandemic, during which time our third child, a son, was born, we both attempted to work part-time and care for the children part-time and, to do that, only earn for the basic essentials. We were able to live on the earnings of part-time work for a while. But, as the world emerged from Covid-19, it didn't last. Part-time work was too insecure and unpredictable.

O

I know I am fortunate to be able to work from home while the children are young, though I worry about how freelance precariousness will affect our long-term economic security. I am also aware that, although I, as an introvert, am predisposed to be happy working from home, office culture and colleagues provide a huge amount of social capital and health and well-being benefits for the majority of people. Indeed, working outside the home is essential for many women's well-being.

But for the majority of mothers, working conditions are in direct conflict with family life. Working culture hasn't caught up with women needing and wanting to work, nor allowed fathers adequate opportunities to take up caring responsibilities and equalize the division of labor. Men aren't yet shouldering their fair share of obligations and women still drive the economy through reproductive work. This is, as Silvia Federici and other feminists have put it, the "capitalist organization of the reproduction of the workforce."

The way we approach reproductive labor—the way we treat mothering bodies and minds—is similar to the way we destroy the living world, habitats, human life, and health and well-being, in the fetish for growth at any cost. We do it all in the service of an extractivist capitalism which uses and exploits "public goods"—human and nonhuman life, in other words—in order to confer advantages and power to those at the top.

There's a photograph on Reddit captioned "reproduction under late-stage capitalism." A woman is leaning back in an armchair with a baby feeding from her breast. In front of her is a computer and notes on a pad of paper. She has fallen asleep.

What else does reproduction in the Capitalocene look like?

It's going back to work two weeks after you've given birth, worrying that your Cesarean scar is going to split open and your organs fall out (a quarter of American mothers are back to work within a fortnight of giving birth).[10]

It's living on credit so you can afford to take time out of work to look after children. It's two weeks of paternity leave, if that. It's lying about why you have to leave work early to conceal the fact that you have children at home who need you. It's rising living costs, including high rent and mortgage payments, that require two parents to work full-time. It's financially penalizing care workers who take time out of full-time work through unfair pension and taxation systems. It's air pollution. It's inequality of access to restorative natural areas, with children rarely playing in wild places.

It's thousands of mothers wanting to incorporate work into their lives, but not being able to. It's not having children because governments are failing to take the climate crisis seriously, or because wages have fallen, or because you won't get any paid leave. It's 4.3 million children in the UK living in poverty.[11] It's almost half of children in lone-parent families living in poverty. It's almost half of children in Black or minority ethnic families living in poverty. It's the widening and deepening of health inequalities under neoliberalism, as poor women have to work more while caring for their families with winnowing social support and infrastructure.

It's television screens in prenatal clinics playing adverts for an electric baby nail file—with two speed controls and a left and right option for £29.99, the safest choice for you and your baby free shipping included—instead of messaging about maternal health.

It's promoting breastfeeding because it's "free" when it can be a full-time job. It's mothers being offered lower salaries than men or women without children. It's mothers being less likely to be hired than men or women without children. It's fathers taking on extra jobs in the evenings, to make up for the loss of a second income. It's the privatization of childcare for under-threes and lack of a proper national childcare strategy. It's demotions instead of promotions for women of "childbearing age" (40 percent of employers in the UK avoid hiring women of a certain age).[12] It's benefits cuts that penalize single mothers.

It doesn't have to be this way. Some countries in the Global North do value caregiving. In Berlin, there are family centers in every neighborhood. In Sweden, parents can stay home with a sick child for up to 120 days a year until children turn twelve. In Finland, both mothers and fathers receive nearly seven months of paid leave. In Romania, mothers are given two years of paid leave. In Norway, use-it-or-lose-it periods of paid leave dispel the stigma fathers experience if they want to take time off work to care for their families. In Denmark, and some other countries, childcare in the early years is state-subsidized (while the UK has the second-most-expensive childcare in the world).[13] These policies place value on nurturing and rearing children—and they make citizens happier. Finland, Sweden, Norway and Denmark consistently top the charts of the happiest countries in the UN's World Happiness Report.

But in most affluent nations in the West, relationships of nurture are not seen as contributing to the public good, so it is convenient if they can be kept invisible, with mothers engaged in unpaid, private, solitary labor, raising the future citizens who, we hope, will be kind when they wipe our butts in the nursing home.

Moon

The moon has a new story. It is so similar to the Earth, in chemical composition, that scientists now believe it may have been formed inside the Earth, when Earth was in synestia.

A synestia is a state that lasts a couple of hundred years. A collision of planet-sized objects spins rapidly in huge pressures at extremely high temperatures, with part of the body in orbit around itself.

The moon, researchers think, was produced in the aftermath of a giant impact from chunks of molten rock.

The moon, then, was an unpredictable by-product, and a good one.

13.

Matroreform

we are each other's
harvest:
we are each other's
business:
we are each other's
magnitude and bond.

Gwendolyn Brooks, "Paul Robeson"

NASA's working definition of life is that it is a self-sustained system capable of undergoing evolution and I have a real problem with the word self-sustained, because life isn't self-sustained, it's sustained by the environment and what tends to be forgotten is this continuous chemical reaction that is going on.

Nick Lane

Society has waited a long time for an understanding of the critical importance of mental health, and of the earliest years of our lives, to our wellbeing and our future. Women, babies and families have already waited too long for us to do something with this powerful knowledge.

Alain Gregoire

People change. I've seen it. Once the growing pains of matrescence began to ease, I saw that that process was a hallmark of life.

When I was an embryo, twenty-one days old in my mother's womb, I had vestigial gills left over from our marine past, from our great-great-great-great-great-great-great-great-grandmother fish. I had a vestigial tail, for a while. So did you. We shed them. They turned into something else: my jawbones, my tailbone. We didn't need them.

The collective stories of metamorphosis tell us that Gregor Samsa turns into a beetle, a human turns into a monster, a frog turns into a prince. But this storytelling isn't quite right. We are never fixed in our new state. A butterfly isn't the end point. Earth is a system of "exquisite disequilibrium," as James Lovelock says.

"You are not the same person from one moment to the next," I read in an issue of *New Scientist*.[1]

O

In these intimate relationships with my children, the way I relate to people and to myself has been newly revealed to me.

The past returns: the scrape of armbands removed from an arm, the lemon-pine smell of hedgerow leaves and shrubs at adult knee height, the dried-out film of a dead snail, the bright white sap in a dandelion stalk, the warm smell of swimming pools, the scent of my mother's navy mohair cardigan.

Maybe this could be the beginning of a do-over, an edit, a new version. Maybe I can meet myself as a child or teenager and be kinder, less critical, less afraid of painful emotions. Maybe, through caring for my children, through the deep satisfaction of making, with their father, a harbor of love, I can find a healthier and more compassionate relationship to myself, and change how I imagine the world.

Times of transformation, whatever they might be, are opportunities to find new connectedness; to choose and consolidate the things that matter; to bring repressed selves out of the shadows into the light; to forgive; to grow layers of nacre, of resilience, of acceptance.

My dismay at realizing that I will fail in many ways at the work of mothering is starting to fade into acceptance. I have railed against the lack of control, been confronted with mortality, and made furious by the fact that I cannot ultimately keep my babies safe. "Defeat is rarely pleasant," writes Lisa Marchiano. "But such experiences help us grow roots into an embodied sense of meaning and purpose."[2]

Carl Jung has become one of my wayfinders; his work a map as I orient myself in this transformation. He believed that individuation—the process of becoming a whole person, of maturing—happened throughout a person's life rather than just in adolescence. I have found this framing a useful and empowering way of thinking about matrescence.

Even if it is painful, lonely and frightening, writes Marchiano, mothering is one of life's great opportunities. She describes it as a crucible in which the dross can be burned off and the wilder, more authentic self remains. "Mothering can be like being thrown down a deep well," she says.[3] At the bottom, I realized how puny my understanding of the world was—I don't know anything at all! I have no idea who I am!—and that was, eventually, liberating. I could construct my life again.

"We all reach adulthood having sustained some injury to our developing sense of self," writes Marchiano. "These wounds will surface in new ways when we become parents, creating unique challenges for us but also offering us new opportunities to heal them."[4]

Early motherhood—when infants are pure animal, pure bodily desire, pure instinct and want—can be particularly challenging for parents who weren't allowed to be wild in their own childhood, who had to split off parts of their personality. Jung would say, though, that instead of unconsciously rejecting that which we find irritating (because it was found irritating within us), integration with "the shadow self" is possible: "If there is anything that we wish to change in the child, we should first examine it and see whether it is not something that could better be changed in ourselves."[5]

Until matrescence, I held fast to the idea that I was self-reliant, felt uncomfortable being dependent on others. I didn't want to be a burden or an imposition. But that illusion has been shattered and I am coming to terms with it.

In my conversations with friends grappling with matrescence, I have found an absence of self-compassion, and that absence can make change harder. It made sense when I read a study by psychologists in Portugal that found that, for women at risk of postnatal depression, practicing self-compassion could increase emotional health and improve overall health outcomes.[6]

I am learning to reject what society expects of me and define what "mother" means on my own terms.

But I am in a privileged position. Maternal power depends on many factors: on housing, education, job security, familial and social support. A single mother who has to work in a factory all night and sleep while her child is at school may not have the time or energy to fight patriarchal gender norms. Neither may a mother with insecure housing and the need to use food banks, a mother worn down by racism and fears for her children, a mother with insecure employment stricken with guilt because of her inflexible working hours, a mother with incontinence who isn't able to leave the house.

O

Crucially, motherhood can itself be a vehicle of social change, as well as a sphere of individual transformation. Mothers are overlooked in history but, as the writer Anna Malaika Tubbs shows in her book *Three Mothers*, about the mothers of James Baldwin, Martin Luther King and Malcolm X, mothers are the first teachers, the first leaders, the first caretakers. As the writer Angela Garbes argues in her book *Essential Labor*, motherhood can be a kind of creative rebellion. There is power in parenting that teaches children to challenge the harms of the status quo.

Scholars of motherhood are starting to approach it as a site of potential empowerment, rather than inevitable oppression. Gina Wong-Wylie coined the word "matroreform" to refer to the "act, desire and process of claiming motherhood power, a progressive movement to mothering that attempts to instate new mothering rules and practices." Other academics write about "matricentric feminism" or "feminist mothering." Andrea O'Reilly believes that patriarchy resists empowered mothering "precisely because it understands its real power to bring about a true and enduring cultural revolution."[7]

In the anthology *Revolutionary Mothering*, a group of mothers and academics posed the question: "How do we get from a conservative definition of mothering as a biological destiny to mothering as a liberating practice that can thwart runaway capitalism?"[8] In the United States, the Marshall Plan for Moms is a national movement to "center mothers in our economic recovery from the pandemic and value their labor" by calling for affordable childcare, paid family leave and equal pay.[9]

Concurrently, the "reparenting" or "intergenerational trauma healing" movement is rising within different cultures. Leslie Priscilla Arreola-Hillenbrand, a first-generation non-Black Chicana mother in the US, founded the Latinx parenting movement, which works to end "Chancla culture." *La Chancla* refers to a flip-flop or sandal which has been used by Latina mothers to discipline children, either by use or by threat.

Yolanda Williams runs Parenting Decolonized, a collective, podcast and online platform, featuring "life lessons and reflections on the art of decolonizing your parenting to raise liberated Black children." It has the added objective of working to dismantle white supremacy, patriarchy and capitalism. Williams believes that everyone, no matter their skin color, needs to "decolonize their parenting," and her pages are followed by thousands of people.

Iris Chen is an American-born Chinese mother who runs a platform centered around "untigering," which she defines as the process of detoxing from being "tiger-parented," and from being a tiger parent. "Tiger mom" was a term coined by the author and lawyer Amy Chua in her 2011 memoir *Battle Hymn of the Tiger Mother.* Chen started her collective after realizing that her authoritarian practices in early motherhood were traumatizing her son. She began learning about gentle, peaceful parenting and now offers workshops, coaching and Untigering Circles for people to meet online and support each other.

What all these platforms of resistance have in common is a desire to liberate parents and children from the dynamics of control, abuse, hierarchy and oppression institutionalized by the dominant culture. They all embrace a quietly radical idea: that recognizing suffering and truly repairing it is a creative, generative act. It creates opportunities for healing, both one-to-one and across wider social ecosystems. This is a novel movement, a new way of raising children. It will be fascinating to see what happens next.

O

The first step for any transformative movement is raising consciousness. We have to see the structures we've inherited in order to tear them down. So many women believe their struggles with matrescence are the result of their own weakness and moral failing. This is a lie and it inhibits honest talk and social change. The difficulties of modern matrescence in neoliberal Western societies are structural and systematic. Seeing the oppressive nature of the institution of motherhood for what it is, and acknowledging the failure of society to support care work, allows us to think critically. Talking makes the structures of discrimination more visible. It allows us to identify what must change.

From pregnancy, women need health professionals who will give them full and accurate information without ideology or misinformation. We want the facts about birth and postnatal recovery, about breastfeeding, about what happens to the brain and our psychological lives. We need to improve maternal mental healthcare by introducing screening for issues in pregnancy and far more investment so mothers can get specialist treatment quickly. We need a meaningful focus on tackling systemic inequalities in maternal health outcomes. We need new birth rituals that acknowledge the gravity of childbirth without obscuring the reality and risks.

The government must urgently invest in midwives, mental health practitioners and wider postpartum care to fix the maternity crisis. Not investing in maternal health is a political decision. In England, over half of maternity wards are now judged unsafe, for the first time since records began.[10] We need to prioritize equality of care for the most disadvantaged groups in society. (In the UK, Black women are 13 percent more likely than other ethnic groups to suffer from postnatal depression and anxiety.[11]) We need midwives to be trained in perineal clinics. We need investment in improved care for women suffering pregnancy loss, who often have to sit in the same room as pregnant women because of the way hospitals are structured. As well as their babies, mothers need six-week checks for their own mental health. We need more beds in hospitals for latent labor which can go on for days. A 2022 report commissioned by the Maternal Mental Health Alliance sets out the economic case for expanding access to treatment and care for women with common mental health problems during the perinatal period.[12] Following their suggestions for creating a new workforce is a no-brainer.

We need to ditch the sexist lexicon. Lactation failure. Hostile uterus. Incompetent cervix. We need new words and phrases. Our understanding of matrescence is limited by the lack of language to describe it. "We have become the first civilization which lacks a discourse on the complexity of motherhood," says Kristeva.[13] We urgently need that language.

The art historian Griselda Pollock is right when she says that the maternal-feminine could be a "thinking apparatus for human subjectivity that goes way beyond the utilitarian process of generating little humans."[14] This potential is currently dammed up by the cultural neutering of motherhood as a site of unthinking drudgery, "natural" fulfillment and staid social norms that belie its wildness, passion, universality and queerness.

While reductionism and essentialism are violent harms that we must be alert to, we all miss out by keeping maternal subjectivity trapped in the nursery.

As Pollock writes, it can be a "matrix for other logics, for ethics, for aesthetics, for poetics, and even for social relations." I would push this into ecology (matroecology) and suggest that the experience—one we have all had—of being part of another has much to teach us about our relations with the earth, the psychic and corporeal reality of our interdependence and interconnectedness with other species.

We have all experienced this becoming-within-another who is both known and unknown, an "otherness-in-proximity." "Since the gift is primordial and open to every human it created, it does not need childbearing to realize its potential in human sociality or creativity," as Pollock writes.

What kind of world could we imagine and create if, instead of pretending we were thrown into existence, as though by magic, we truly considered our vulnerable, intimate, tactile, entangled, animal origins?

We need much more scientific research into matrescence: how the hormonal and brain changes affect health and well-being in the postnatal period, how social care and intervention can mediate mental illness, how diseases that affect fertility such as endometriosis can be cured. We need more research on how "mothering" and patrescence affects the male brain, the caregiver brain, the grandparent brain. There is a galling paucity of research and data into postnatal depression, its risk factors and evidence-based treatments, let alone other mental health issues common to matrescence.

We need new social support programs for mothers. Thankfully, we already have a social model for this. The Netherlands has a program called Kraamzorg, which gives new mothers a certain number of hours of postnatal maternity assistance from a maternity nurse at home. Normally women are given forty-nine hours of help over eight days with jobs such as helping with feeding (whichever method the woman chooses), cleaning the bathroom and bedroom, light household duties, and support with physical and emotional health.[15] The rate of postnatal depression in the Netherlands has been found to be 8 percent, while in England, a country without such social support, it is 10–15 percent. Financially, it makes good sense: providing proper care and support for women before and during the most vulnerable time for psychiatric illness avoids interventions down the line for both children and mothers.

We need to reorganize the working world. This would mean ending the "motherhood penalty," the phrase used by sociologists to describe the systemic disadvantages to women in the workplace when they have a child. These include disparities in pay, benefits, promotions and perceived competence (which makes up 80 percent of the gender pay gap), as well as pension inequality and pension penalties for part-time employment.[16] We need to end discrimination against pregnant women and women returning from maternity leave. We need truly flexible working for fathers and mothers. We need top-down policies and incentives that allow men to parent more while working, including part-time contracts and flexible hours. Crucially, we need much more investment in quality early-years childcare. We need to ask: Why do one in ten nursery workers live in poverty?[17] We need to pay caregivers according to their actual value, rather than the bogus and distorted market value that erodes the worth of care and love. We need benefits for carers such as carers' leave for anyone in a caregiving role. We need longer paternity leave and, while we're at it, we need to stop calling it "leave": it's not a holiday—it's work. We need to look at shorter working weeks, shorter working days, a national living wage or care income. We need to weaken the pressure on men to be "ideal workers" in cultures of presenteeism. We must acknowledge reproductive labor by including care work in GDP.

It is taking time for social norms to change—and they may even be regressing. A 2022 UN study of twenty countries found that attitudes to gender roles had deteriorated over the Covid-19 pandemic.[18] Acceptance of domestic violence had increased and young men in particular had regressive attitudes to gender. Even in the late 2010s when my daughter was young, the vast majority of culture—television shows, films, books—had male characters as protagonists. Sometimes there might be a female character, but often they would be token, a stereotype. Even though I tried to skew her cultural diet towards stories that weren't all about boys, and changed the pronouns in her books, soon I noticed she would imitate the mainstream gender bias in her own stories and play. We must challenge sexist ideology so men can take a fairer part in caregiving. We need to question the pervasive denigration of care work and mother work so that it is more appealing and culturally expected of men, as well as women, which would benefit society in many different and intersecting ways. We need to continue deconstructing taboos around female bodies and the myth of perfect motherhood. We sorely need a cultural recognition of the radical metamorphosis of matrescence.

Shall we get down to the bones? We need to create a new society, an economic system based on well-being, health, equality, life and staying within planetary boundaries rather than profit. Perhaps we need a new Commons: urban gardening, time banks, community centers, childcare groups, clothing and appliance exchanges, meal-sharing, shared living areas and spaces.

Good change—big and small—has happened already. On London buses there are new stickers showing pregnant women and women holding young children, to remind people of their need for seats. "We're hitting a moment," Jodi Pawluski told me, about the science of the maternal brain. "There's a matriarchy of women and a few men who have come together to move things forward." There are signs that postnatal pelvic health and mental health may be starting to be given the gravity, attention and investment they require. In the early 2020s, pelvic health clinics providing accessible treatment for the many women who suffer childbirth-related injuries were opening in fourteen areas across England.[19] Maternal mental health clinics that offer therapies for birth trauma and baby loss are also starting to open in regions of the UK.[20]

The old ways will be hard to dismantle, but the Earth can teach us possibilities. For the wider world is more symbiosis, interconnectedness and metamorphosis than it is isolation, extractivism and fantasy. It is more kinship, beauty and wonder than it is capital, domination and self-reliance. More multifarious than binary. More abundance than scarcity. More wholes than parts. More creative than destructive. And, always, it is more change and flux than it is static and unbending.

Epilogue

I am holding my two-year-old son's hand after collecting him from nursery, and acting in a way that probably looks strange.

I am peering through willows and berries and lichen into the playground of my daughter's school next door. She has recently started. I look through the twigs for her and listen out for her cadence. I know it might appear deviant, peering through the fence at children, but I can't help it.

It's almost exactly six years since I became pregnant with my first child, and this story began, and I am a different creature to what I was before. A scientific paper has been published, the first of its kind, which shows that pregnancy-induced brain changes remain for at least six years after giving birth.[1] Researchers could identify whether or not a woman had been pregnant by looking at scans of their brains six years on, with 91.67 percent accuracy. A study published soon after found that mothers had larger areas of gray matter in their brains for decades. My brain hasn't returned to the way it was before, and neither will I. It is possible, say the researchers, that the changes are permanent. I am settling in. Matrescence continues.

My three children moved through my body at different times. The weather patterns have changed over the last six years. When we first moved to this house, with its apple, plum and cherry trees, the blossom appeared in the middle of May. Now it appears in April. Our first child was born when carbon dioxide in the atmosphere was 404.4 parts per million. Our third child was born, five years later, when it was at 417.3. The field close to the station where we heard a cuckoo a few years ago is now a building site for a new housing development.

I am no longer dangerously sleep-deprived, nor is my sympathetic nervous system activated to an intolerable level every day. I am adapting to the responsibility, to the alteration of temporality, to the presence of mortality and risk, to the theme park of emotions, intense but fickle, to the constant buzz of potential horror, albeit lower now, to the truth of human vulnerability. I have had to throw out all my old shoes because my feet are a size bigger. My period is completely different: I bleed more, and my body ovulates aggressively, as if a starting gun has gone off. I am softer, and harder. The birth of my first child, after the maelstrom passed, was a deliverance. It brought me closer to my real self. I have learned how to surrender when I need to. I am learning to live in the rhythm of other lives; I have learned to share my life. I am trying to learn how to rest, so I can show my children it is important to rest, be, exist, not just to do. I am trying to accept help when it is offered. I can't work myself to the bone anymore, or play fast and loose with my health, because I must look after them. A consequence: I must look after me. I seek wonder and awe in the woods, in the transcendent ordinary of moss and lichen on brick walls, through planting seeds in our garden, with friends I can talk honestly to, in a community project with neighbors to restore a small patch of amenity grass to a biodiverse wildflower meadow, in local community groups, in micro-awe. I have been learning how to sink my body into the world. I rub soil on my hands, stroke dying bumblebees. I scour my urban locale for signs of flux: mushrooms popping up overnight, sporophytes glowing, the moon waxing. I track slime mold plasmodium and study sticks and twigs to find their fruiting bodies.

It takes five years or so for a human being to turn from a child into an adult. It has taken me over five years to adapt to this stage of early motherhood, to emerge from matrescent angst, from its existential shattering, and to find ways to live with the fragility of our babies. At times I think my matrescence is over, but perhaps it never will be.

I spy my daughter standing to one side of the school building. I can't take my eyes away. She looks fine; smiles, calls out to friends, runs across the playground. I feel a deep sense of satisfaction on seeing her happy without me, with her peers, on the other side of the fence, a separate being. Still, there is a shadow, a shudder of growing redundancy, a reminder of the paradox that my job is to make it possible for her to leave me, to walk away from our present intimacy and form her own life. My children are the main actors, and I am the audience. I will always be in thrall to them, but they won't always be in thrall to me. And I won't always be able to watch over them, to keep them safe in my protection. This intimacy has a shelf life. Already, it hurts. I feel a premonition as I watch them grow before my eyes. This is life, and it is hard, and it is right.

As I walk back, hand in hand with my little son, the baby at home with his father, seeds break through pods around us; buds break open with the leaves they have been holding folded, grown by the sunlight of the previous summer; green beads flecking the hedgerows break open; red beads in the maple trees above break open. The moon is up, and it pulls the ocean back and forth: a spring tide, the biggest tide, transforming the coasts of this island, breaking apart shell and stone, fish and bone. Beneath us, the trees are talking, making plans, breaking through soil and sediment. Above us, stars are being born and others are dying. We walk through the cemetery where organisms are being born and others are dying and creatures are being eaten and others are eating. The continent we are on is moving (at the speed of a fingernail growing), and the round rock we are on is moving (tilted on its axis, spinning). Farther below, plates are crushing and stretching, magma is cooling and heating and leaking, rock is forming and changing. The ebb and flow, the ebb and the glow. The lilting earth, and we lilting, too, in our one flicker of consciousness in this incessant motion. We sit underneath the canopy of a beech tree, a mother tree, and rake the earth, the soft brown soil, and the broken beech mast casings, and the hard brown seeds, and the chunks of soft white chalk made from the skeletons of ancient creatures from the sea, lit by a tender light, and we breathe.

Notes

1. Francesca E. Duncan et al., "The zinc spark is an inorganic signature of human egg activation," *Scientific Reports* 6, 24737, 2016; <https://www.nature.com/articles/srep24737>

Prologue

1. Barry Webb Images, "Slime moulds (Myxomycetes)"; <https://www.barrywebbimages.co.uk/Images/Macro/Slime-Moulds-Myxomycetes/>
2. T. Nakagaki et al., "Maze-solving by an amoeboid organism," *Nature* 407 (470), 2000; <https://www.nature.com/articles/35035159>
3. J. Barone, "Slime molds show surprising degree of intelligence," *Discover* magazine, 9 December 2008.
4. NASA, "Slime mold simulations used to map dark matter holding universe together"; <https://www.nasa.gov/feature/goddard/2020/slime-mold-simulations-used-to-map-dark-matter-holding-universe-together/>
5. "The 'blob': zoo showcases slime mould with 720 sexes that can heal itself in minutes," *Guardian*, 17 October 2019; <https://www.theguardian.com/world/2019/oct/17/the-blob-zoo- unveils-baffling-new-organism-with-720-sexes>

Introduction

1. Adrienne Rich, *Of Woman Born: Motherhood as Experience and Institution* (Virago, 1977).
2. Ibid., p. 223.
3. Ibid., p. 22.
4. R. Thorpe, "Mother, writer, monster, maid," *Vela* magazine, 2016; <http://velamag.com/mother-writer-monster-maid/>
5. L. Wylie et al., "The enigma of post-natal depression: An update," *Journal of Psychiatric and Mental Health Nursing* 18 (1), 2010, pp. 48–58.
6. A. Sacks, "The birth of a mother," *The New York Times*, 8 May 2017; <https://www.nytimes.com/2017/05/08/well/family/the-birth-of-a-mother.html>

7. Dana Raphael (ed.), *Being Female: Reproduction, Power and Change* (Mouton & Co., 1975), p. 65.
8. Ibid., p. 66.
9. WHO, "Maternal mortality," 2019; <https://www.who.int/news-room/fact-sheets/detail/maternal-mortality>
10. NHS, "Funding boost for new mums' mental health," February 2018; <https://www.england.nhs.uk/2018/02/funding-boost-for-new-mums- mental-health/>
11. Z. Wang et al. "Mapping global prevalence of depression among postpartum women," *Translational Psychiatry* 11 (543), 2021; <https://www.nature.com/articles/s41398-021-01663-6>
12. H. Watson et al., "A systematic review of ethnic minority women's experiences of perinatal mental health conditions and services in Europe," *PLOS One* 14 (1), 2019; <https://journals.plos.org/plosone/article?id=10.1371/journal.pone.0210587>
13. L. Ban et al., "Impact of socioeconomic deprivation on maternal perinatal mental illnesses presenting to UK general practice," *British Journal of General Practice* 62 (603) 2012; <https://bjgp.org/content/62/603/e671>
14. M. Knight et al., "Saving Lives, Improving Mothers' Care," November 2021; <https://www.npeu.ox.ac.uk/assets/downloads/mbrrace-uk/reports/maternal-report-2021/MBRRACE-UK_Maternal_Report_2021_-_FINAL_-_WEB_VERSION.pdf>
15. A. Tubb, "Suicide remains the leading cause of direct maternal death in first postnatal year," *Maternal Mental Health Alliance*, 11 November 2021; <https://maternalmentalhealthalliance.org/news/mbrrace-suicide-leading-cause-maternal-death/>
16. NCT, "The hidden half," 2019; <https://www.nct.org.uk/sites/default/files/2019-04/NCT%20The%20Hidden%20Half_0.pdf>
17. Sandra Igwe, *My Black Motherhood: Mental Health, Stigma, Racism and the System* (Jessica Kingsley Publishers, 2022).
18. Personal interview with Dr. Alain Gregoire, 10 April 2017.
19. S. C. Davies, Annual Report of the Chief Medical Officer, 2014, "The Health of the 51%: Women," London: Department of Health, 2015.
20. "How are you really feeling?," *Motherdom* (Spring 2019), p. 5.
21. Susan Maushart, *The Mask of Motherhood* (Penguin, 1999), p. 9.
22. B. M. Melnyk and P. Lusk, "Pandemic parenting: Examining the epidemic of working parental burnout and strategies to help," *National Association of Pediatric Nurse Practitioners and Springer Publishing Company*, 2022; <https://wellness.osu.edu/sites/default/files/documents/2022/05/OCWO_ParentalBurnout_3674200_Report_FINAL.pdf>
23. Personal interview with Dr. Alexandra Sacks, 5 September 2018.

PART I

1. All-day sickness

1. NHS, "What can I do during pregnancy to make birth easier?"; <https://www.youtube.com/watch?v=8KJJD6Accsg&t=81s>
2. Sandra Steingraber, *Having Faith: An Ecologist's Journey to Motherhood* (Perseus Publishing, 2001).
3. S. M. Flaxman and P. W. Sherman, "Morning sickness: A mechanism for protecting mother and embryo," *Quarterly Review of Biology* 75 (2), 2000, 113–48; <https://pubmed.ncbi.nlm.nih.gov/10858967/>
4. NICE, "How common is it?"; <https://cks.nice.org.uk/topics/nausea-vomiting-in-pregnancy/background-information/prevalence/>
5. Sandra Steingraber, *Having Faith: An Ecologist's Journey to Motherhood* (Perseus Publishing, 2001), p. 24.
6. Ibid., p. 19.
7. Simone de Beauvoir, *The Second Sex* (Johnathan Cape, 1953), p. 479.
8. Britannica, "Maternal imagination"; <https://www.britannica.com/science/maternal-imagination>
9. T. Kapsalis, "Hysteria, witches, and the wandering uterus: A Brief History," *LitHub*, 5 April 2017; <https://lithub.com/hysteria-witches-and- the-wandering-uterus-a-brief-history/>
10. R. Gadsby et al., "Nausea and vomiting in pregnancy is not just 'morning sickness': Data from a prospective cohort study in the UK," *British Journal of General Practice* 70 (697), 2020.
11. NHS, "Vomiting and morning sickness"; <https://www.nhs.uk/pregnancy/related-conditions/common-symptoms/vomiting-and-morning-sickness/>
12. Kings College London, "Women driven to terminate wanted pregnancies due to hyperemesis gravidarum," 20 October 2021; <https://www.kcl.ac.uk/news/women-terminate-wanted-pregnancies-due-to-hyperemesis-gravidarum>
13. NHS, "Foods to avoid in pregnancy"; <https://www.nhs.uk/pregnancy/keeping-well/foods-to-avoid/#:~:text=If%20you%20eat%20too%20much,harmful%20to%20your%20unborn%20baby.>
14. Sandra Steingraber, *Having Faith: An Ecologist's Journey to Motherhood* (Perseus Publishing, 2001), p. 121.
15. T. Y. Adamou et al., "Blood mercury and plasma polychlorinated biphenyls concentrations in pregnant Inuit women from Nunavik: Temporal trends, 1992–2017" *Sci. Total Environ.*, 2020; <v\https://pubmed.ncbi.nlm.nih.gov/32758811/>
16. G. Muckle et al., "Prenatal methylmercury, postnatal lead exposure, and evidence of Attention Deficit/Hyperactivity Disorder among Inuit children in Arctic Québec," *Environmental Health Perspectives* 120 (10), 2012; <https://ehp.niehs.nih.gov/doi/10.1289/ehp.1204976>

17. Sandra Steingraber, *Having Faith: An Ecologist's Journey to Motherhood* (Perseus Publishing, 2001), p. 105.
18. Ibid., p. 107.
19. D. Carrington, "Microplastics revealed in the placentas of unborn babies," *Guardian*, 22 December 2020.
20. D. Carrington, "Small increases in air pollution linked to rise in depression, finds study," *Guardian*, 24 October 2020.
21. J. Hamzelou, "High levels of air pollution seem to be linked to early miscarriages," *New Scientist*, 14 October 2019.
22. R. Kukla, "The ethics and cultural politics of reproductive risk warnings: A case study of California's Proposition 65," *Health, Risk & Society* 12 (4), 2010, pp. 323–34.
23. J. Jardine et al., "Adverse pregnancy outcomes attributable to socioeconomic and ethnic inequalities in England: A national cohort study," *Lancet* 398 (10314), 2021, pp. 1905–12.

Imaginal discs

1. D. J. Blackiston et al., "Retention of memory through metamorphosis: Can a moth remember what it learned as a caterpillar?" *PLOS One*, 3 (3), 2008.

2. The emotional placenta

1. "I don't even know if we know all the hormones." Personal interview with Dr. Liisa Galea, 3 February 2021.
2. B. Clegg, "What is the human body made of?," *Science Focus*, August 2020; <https://www.sciencefocus.com/the-human-body/what-is-the-human-body-made-of/>
3. Simone de Beauvoir, *The Second Sex* (Johnathan Cape, 1953), pp.476–7.
4. R. Balsam, "The vanished pregnant body in psychoanalytic female developmental theory," *J. Am. Psychoanal. Assoc.*, 2003; <https://journals.sagepub.com/doi/abs/10.1177/00030651030510040201>
5. R. Balsam, "Freud, the birthing body, and modern life," *J. Am. Psychoanal. Assoc.*, 2017; <https://journals.sagepub.com/doi/abs/10.1177/0003065116686793?journalCode=apaa>
6. Adrienne Rich, *Of Woman Born: Motherhood as Experience and Institution* (Virago, 1977), p. 189.
7. Julia Kristeva, *Powers of Horror: An Essay on Abjection* (Columbia University Press; Reprint edition, 1984), p. 3.
8. Joan Raphael-Leff, *Psychological Process of Childbearing* (Chapman and Hall, 1991), p. 48.
9. Joan Raphael-Leff, *Pregnancy: The Inside Story* (Routledge, 2001), p. 36.

10. Ibid., p. 47.
11. Joan Raphael-Leff, *Psychological Process of Childbearing* (Chapman and Hall, 1991), p. 47.
12. Ibid., p. 124.
13. L. M. Glynn et al., "When stress happens matters: Effects of earthquake timing on stress responsivity in pregnancy," *Am. J. Obstet. Gynecol.* 184 (637–42), 2001; <https://cds.psych.ucla.edu/wp-content/uploads/sites/48/2020/11/2001-Glynn-et-al-When-stress-happens.pdf>
14. L. Geddes, "Pregnant women develop emotion-reading superpowers," *New Scientist*, 9 December 2009.
15. R. M. Pearson et al., "Emotional sensitivity for motherhood: Late pregnancy is associated with enhanced accuracy to encode emotional faces," *Hormones and Behavior* 56 (5), 2009, pp. 557–63.
16. Britannica, "Womb envy"; <https://www.britannica.com/science/womb-envy>
17. Reddit, "I'm a guy and I wish I could be pregnant"; <https://www.reddit.com/r/unpopularopinion/comments/cwnndk/im_a_guy_and_i_wish_i_could_be_pregnant/>
18. Siri Hustvedt, *Mothers, Fathers and Others* (Sceptre, 2021), p. 228.
19. Ibid., p. 243.
20. Ibid., p. 228.
21. The Summa Theologiæ of St. Thomas Aquinas; <https://www.newadvent.org/summa/1092.htm>

3. *Zombie cells*

1. D. W. Bianchi et al., "Male fetal progenitor cells persist in maternal blood for as long as 27 years postpartum," *Proc. Nat. Acad. Sci.* USA 93 (2), 1996, pp. 705–8.
2. W. F. Chan et al., "Male microchimerism in the human female brain," *PLOS One*, 7(9), 2012; < https://doi.org/10.1371/journal.pone.0045592>
3. A. Boddy et al., "Fetal microchimerism and maternal health: A review and evolutionary analysis of cooperation and conflict beyond the womb," *BioEssays*, 37 (10), 2015; <https://pubmed.ncbi.nlm.nih.gov/26316378/>
4. D. W. Bianchi et al., "Male fetal progenitor cells persist in maternal blood for as long as 27 years postpartum," *Proc. Nat. Acad. Sci.* USA, 93 (2), 1996, pp. 705–8.
5. J. Benson and A. Wolf, "Where did I go? The invisible postpartum mother," in Sheila Lintott and Maureen Sander-Staudt (eds), *Philosophical Inquiries into Pregnancy, Childbirth and Mothering* (Routledge, 2012); p. 34.
6. Ibid., p. 38. Quoting Bartky (1990, 31).
7. M. C. Logsdon et al., "Do new mothers understand the risk factors for maternal mortality?," MCN *Am. J. Matern. Child Nurs.* 43(4), 2018, pp. 201–5.

PART II

4. Birth

1. NCT, "Labour pain relief: Epidurals and combined spinal epidurals"; <https://www.nct.org.uk/labour-birth/your-pain-relief-options/labour-pain-relief-epidurals-and-combined-spinal-epidurals>
2. J. Drife, "The start of life: A history of obstetrics," *Postgraduate Medical Journal* 78, 2002, pp. 311–15; <https://pmj.bmj.com/content/78/919/311>
3. Jean Donnison, *Midwives and Medical Men: A History of the Struggle for the Control of Childbirth* (Taylor & Francis, 2023, originally published 1977).
4. J. Drife, "The start of life: A history of obstetrics," *Postgraduate Medical Journal* 78, 2002, p. 314; <https://pmj.bmj.com/content/78/919/311>
5. Ibid., p. 313.
6. L. Helmuth, "The disturbing, shameful history of childbirth deaths," *Slate*, 10 September 2013.
7. Jean Donnison, *Midwives and Medical Men: A History of the Struggle for the Control of Childbirth* (Taylor & Francis, 2023, originally published 1977).
8. J. Drife, "The start of life: A history of obstetrics," *Postgraduate Medical Journal* 78, 2002, p. 314; <https://pmj.bmj.com/content/78/919/311>
9. Ibid., p. 313.
10. S. Laskow, "In 1914, feminists fought for the right to forget childbirth," *Atlas Obscura*, 23 February 2017.
11. Ibid.
12. C. L. Todd, "Analgesia in Childbirth: Early writer on Twilight Sleep defends the practice," *The New York Times*, 30 May 1936.
13. Wellcome Collection, "National birthday trust fund"; <https://wellcomecollection.org/works/qsg4wv74>
14. J. Drife, "The start of life: A history of obstetrics," *Postgraduate Medical Journal* 78, 2002, p. 313; <https://pmj.bmj.com/content/78/919/311>
15. M. F. Mason, "Favoring Twilight Sleep: More mothers protest against strand of certain physicians," *The New York Times*, 21 May 1936.
16. Pope Pius XII, "Text of address by Pope Pius XII on the science and morality of painless childbirth," *Linacre Quarterly* 23 (2) 1956; <https://epublications.marquette.edu/cgi/viewcontent.cgi?article=3786&context=lnq>
17. E. Glaser, "The cult of natural childbirth has gone too far," *Guardian*, 5 March 2015.
18. D. Campbell, "It's good for women to suffer the pain of a natural birth, says medical chief," *Guardian*, 12 July 2009.
19. "Sheila Kitzinger 19 facing the pain of labour," *The Face of Birth*, YouTube, 2012; <https://www.youtube.com/watch?v=Pcje8TMIzkU>
20. Grantly Dick-Read, *Revelation of Childbirth* (William Heinemann Medical Books Ltd, 1948), p. ix.

21. NCT, "History," <https://www.nct.org.uk/about-us/history>
22. D. Caton, "Who said childbirth is natural?: The medical mission of Grantly Dick-Read," *Anesthesiology* 84, April 1996, pp. 955–64.
23. Grantly Dick-Read, *Childbirth Without Fear* (William Heinemann Medical Books, 1942).
24. Grantly Dick-Read, *Revelation of Childbirth* (William Heinemann Medical Books, 1948), p. 5.
25. Ibid.
26. Ibid., p. 9.
27. D. Caton, "Who said childbirth is natural?: The medical mission of Grantly Dick-Read," *Anesthesiology* 84, April 1996, pp. 955–64.
28. Grantly Dick-Read, *Childbirth Without Fear* (William Heinemann Medical Books, 1942), p. xii.
29. D. Caton, "Who said childbirth is natural?: The medical mission of Grantly Dick-Read," *Anesthesiology* 84, April 1996, pp. 955–64.
30. Ibid.
31. R. A. Sanders and K. Lamb, "Non-pharmacological pain management strategies for labour: Maintaining a physiological outlook," *BMJ* 25 (2), 2 February 2017.
32. Grantly Dick-Read, *Revelation of Childbirth* (William Heinemann Medical Books, 1948), p. 165.
33. C. A. Smith et al., "Relaxation techniques for pain management in labour," *Cochrane Database of Systematic Reviews*, 28 March 2018.
34. L. A. Smith et al., "Parenteral opioids for maternal pain management in labour," *Cochrane Database of Systematic Reviews*, 5 June 2018.
35. C. Caron, "Marie Mongan, 86, who developed hypnotherapy for childbirth, dies," *The New York Times*, 16 March 2021.
36. K. Madden et al., "Hypnosis for pain management during labour and childbirth," *Cochrane Database of Systematic Reviews*, 19 May 2016.
37. S. Boseley, "Health secretary to investigate allegations of women denied epidurals," *Guardian*, 26 January 2020.
38. G. Baptie et al., "Birth trauma: The mediating effects of perceived support," *BMJ* 28 (10), October 2020.
39. C. T. Beck et al., "Traumatic childbirth and its aftermath: Is there anything positive?," *J. Perinat. Educ.* 27 (3), June 2018, pp. 175–84.
40. Personal interview with Katie Vigos, 14 December 2017.
41. G. Sandeman, "Midwives to end campaign to promote 'normal births,'" *Guardian*, 12 August 2017.
42. Gov.uk, "Ockenden review: Summary of findings, conclusions and essential actions," 20 March 2022; <https://www.gov.uk/government/publications/final-report-of-the-ockenden-review/ockenden-review-summary-of-findings-conclusions-and-essential-actions>
43. S. Lintern, "Top midwife says sorry for lives lost to 'normal birth' drive," *The Sunday Times*, 6 March 2022.

44. Juju Sundin, *Birth Skills* (Vermillion, 2008).
45. RCOG, "Third- and fourth-degree tears (OASI)"; <https://www.rcog.org.uk/for-the-public/perineal-tears-and-episiotomies-in-childbirth/third-and-fourth-degree-tears-oasi/>
46. I. E. K. Nilsson et al., "Symptoms of fecal incontinence two decades after no, one, or two obstetrical anal sphincter injuries," *Original Research Gynecology* 224 (3), August 21, 2020, p. 276.
47. Personal interview with Ranee Thakar, 17 December 2021.
48. RCM, "RCM calls for investment in maternity services as midwife numbers fall in every English region," August 2022; <https://www.rcm.org.uk/media-releases/2022/august/rcm-calls-for-investment-in-maternity-services-as-midwife-numbers-fall-in-every-english-region/#:~:text=England%20has%20seen%20midwife%20numbers,has%20affected%20every%20English%20region.>

PART III

5. Feeding

1. NHS, "Breastfeeding: The gentle art of caring"; <https://www.dorsethealthcare.nhs.uk/download_file/view_inline/2198>
2. La Leche League, "Importance of breastfeeding"; <https://www.llli.org/breastfeeding-info/benefits/>
3. Emily Oster, *Cribsheet: A Data-Driven Guide to Better, More Relaxed Parenting, from Birth to Preschool* (Souvenir Press, 2019), p. 87.
4. UNICEF, "The Baby Friendly Initative"; <https://www.unicef.org.uk/babyfriendly/>
5. K. Russell, "Maternal mental health—women's voices," RCOG, February 2017; <https://www.rcog.org.uk/media/3ijbpfvi/maternal-mental-health-womens-voices.pdf>
6. C. Borra et al., "New evidence on breastfeeding and postpartum depression: The importance of understanding women's intentions," *Maternal and Child Health Journal* 19, 2015, pp. 897–907.
7. V. M. Fallon et al., "The impact of the UK Baby Friendly Initiative on maternal and infant health outcomes: A mixed-methods systematic review," *Maternal & Child Nutrition* 15 (3), July 2019.
8. Personal interview with Dr. Alain Gregoire, 10 April 2017.
9. UNICEF, "Breastfeeding in the UK"; <https://www.unicef.org.uk/babyfriendly/about/breastfeeding-in-the-uk/>
10. L. Santhanam, "Infant Feeding," the GP Infant Feeding Network (UK); <https://gpifn.org.uk/infant-feeding/>
11. E. E. Stevens et al., "A History of Infant Feeding," *J. Perinat. Educ.* 18 (2), 2009, pp. 32–9.

12. Personal interview with Dr. Leila Frodsham, 23 March 2017.
13. V. Schmied and D. Lupton, "Blurring the boundaries: Breastfeeding and maternal subjectivity," *Sociology of Health & Illness* 23 (2), 23 December 2001, pp. 234–50.
14. Camille T. Dungy, *Guidebook to Relative Strangers: Journeys into Race, Motherhood, and History* (W. W. Norton, 2017).
15. Diane Wiessinger and Diana West, *The Womanly Art of Breastfeeding* (Pinter & Martin Ltd, 2010), p. 57.
16. Ibid., p. 39.
17. K. Bonyata, "I'm not pumping enough milk. What can I do?," *KellyMom*; <https://kellymom.com/hot-topics/pumping_decrease/#:~:text=Try%20cluster%20pumping%2C%20instead%20of,super%20charge%E2%80%9D%20their%20milk%20supply.>
18. Public Health England, "New survey of mums reveals perceived barriers to breastfeeding," March 2017; <https://www.gov.uk/government/news/new-survey-of-mums-reveals-perceived-barriers-to-breastfeeding>
19. Public Health England, "New mothers are anxious about breastfeeding in public," November 2015; <https://www.gov.uk/government/news/new-mothers-are-anxious-about-breastfeeding-in-public>
20. S. Young, "Author sparks outrage after comparing public breastfeeding to urinating in the street," *Independent,* 23 August 2018.
21. L. H. Amir, "Breastfeeding in public: 'You can do it?,'" *Int. Breastfeed J.* 9 (187), 20 December 2014.
22. Margaret R. Miles, *A Complex Delight: The Secularization of the Breast, 1350–1750* (University of California Press, 2009).
23. O. Petter, "One in six mothers have received unwanted sexual attention while breastfeeding in public," *Independent,* 2 August 2020.
24. ITV, "New law to protect breastfeeding mothers from being photographed," 28 June 2022; <https://www.itv.com/news/granada/2022-06-28/up-to-two-years-in-prison-for-people-caught-photographing-breastfeeding-mums>
25. The sexualization of breasts has been shown to cause complications for mothers in a number of ways. A study of adolescent mothers from socioeconomically deprived areas of the UK suggests that in some demographics negative judgment is more likely to be directed at breastfeeding rather than formula-feeding. One of the mothers said, "I just don't think it's that natural, I know it is natural so that sounds silly, but to me . . . I think the public eye nowadays has made boobs a sexual object, well men have haven't they in magazines and page three and everything else? And I see them, I know they're not there for men, but I think that is how today's society, that boobs are there for men to look at whereas that isn't actually what they're there for but that is what I saw it as. I thought I don't want my child sucking on my boob, that sounds really silly, but that was my feeling."
26. Aviation Pros, "Mamava announces active fleet of 182 lactation pods across 76 airports in anticipation of busy holiday travel season," 25 October 2022; <https://www.aviationpros.com/airports/press-release/21285013/mamava-mamava-announces-active-fleet

-of-182-lactation-pods-across-76-airports-in-anticipation-of-busy-holiday-travel-season>

27. Personal interview with Dr. Dawn Leeming, 8 February 2021.
28. Personal interview with Dr. Alain Gregoire, 10 April 2017.
29. S. Rinkunas, "The scary breast-feeding disorder people aren't talking about," the *Cut*, 28 July 2016.
30. Lucy A. Hutner et al. (eds), *Textbook of Women's Reproductive Mental Health* (APA, 2022).
31. B. Schaal and L. Marlier, "Maternal and paternal perception of individual odor signatures in human amniotic fluid—potential role in early bonding?," *Biol. Neonate* 74(4), 1998, pp. 266–73.

Othermothers

1. I. Razik et al., "Non-kin adoption in the common vampire bat," *Royal Society Open Science* 8 (2), 2021; <https://royalsocietypublishing.org/doi/10.1098/rsos.201927>

6. The maternal brain

1. H. Spencer, "Psychology of the sexes," *Popular Science Monthly* 4, November 1873.
2. J. L. Pawluski, "Memory and motherhood: Is it better than what we think?," *Journal of Women's Health* 31 (8), 2022, pp. 1067–68.
3. E. R. Orchard et al., "Evidence of subjective, but not objective, cognitive deficit in new mothers at 1-year postpartum," *Journal of Women's Health* 31 (8), 2022, pp. 1087–96.
4. B. Callaghan et al., "Evidence for cognitive plasticity during pregnancy via enhanced learning and memory," *Memory* 30(5), 2022, pp.519–36.
5. E. R. Orchard et al., "The maternal brain is more flexible and responsive at rest: Effective connectivity of the parental caregiving network in postpartum mothers," *bioRxiv*, 2022; <https://dx.doi.org/10.1101/2022.09.26.509524>
6. E. R. Orchard et al., "Matrescence: Lifetime impact of motherhood on cognition and the brain," *Trends in Cognitive Sciences,* January 2023; <https://doi.org/10.1016/j.tics.2022.12.002>
7. C. McCormack, B. L. Callaghan, J. L. Pawluski, "It's Time to Rebrand 'Mommy Brain,'" *JAMA Neurol.* 80(4), 2023.
8. E. Hoekzema, E. Barba-Müller, C. Pozzobon et al., "Pregnancy leads to long-lasting changes in human brain structure," *Nat. Neurosci.* 20, 2017, pp. 287–96.
9. Personal interview with Elseline Hoekzema, by email, November 2021.
10. E. Hoekzema et al., "Becoming a mother entails anatomical changes in the ventral striatum of the human brain that facilitate its responsiveness to offspring cues," *Psychoneuroendocrinology* 112, 2020.

11. K. M. Seip et al, "Incentive salience of cocaine across the postpartum period of the female rat," *Psychopharmacology (Berl).* 199 (1), 2008.
12. E. Barba-Müller, S. Craddock, S. Carmona et al., "Brain plasticity in pregnancy and the postpartum period: Links to maternal caregiving and mental health," *Arch. Womens Ment. Health* 22, 2019, pp. 289–99.
13. S. Carmona et al., "Pregnancy and adolescence entail similar neuroanatomical adaptations: A comparative analysis of cerebral morphometric changes," *Hum. Brain Map* 40 (7), 2019, pp. 2143–52.
14. E. Hoekzema, H. van Steenbergen, M. Straathof et al., "Mapping the effects of pregnancy on resting state brain activity, white matter microstructure, neural metabolite concentrations and grey matter architecture," *Nat. Commun.* 13 (6931), 2022.
15. C. Dreifus, "Catherine Dulac Finds Brain Circuitry Behind Sex-Specific Behaviors," *Quanta Magazine*, December 14, 2020.
16. M. Paternina-Die et al., "The paternal transition entails neuroanatomic adaptations that are associated with the father's brain response to his infant cues," *Cereb. Cortex Commun.* 1 (1), 2020; <10.1093/texcom/tgaa082>
17. E. Norton, "Parenting rewires the male brain," *Science*, 27 May 2014.
18. J. Welsh, "Fatherhood lowers testosterone, keeps dads at home," *Scientific American*, 12 September 2011.
19. E. Abraham and R. Feldman, "The neurobiology of human allomaternal care; implications for fathering, coparenting, and children's social development," *Physiology & Behavior* 193, September 2018, pp. 25–34.
20. V. Leong et al., "Speaker gaze increases information coupling between infant and adult brains," *PNAS* 114 (50), 2017.
21. W. Hollway, "Rereading Winnicott's 'Primary Maternal Preoccupation,'" *Feminism & Psychology* 22(1), 2012, pp. 20–40.
22. A. S. Fleming, "Plasticity in the maternal neural circuit: Experience, dopamine, and mothering," *Neurobiology of the Parental Brain,* 2008, pp. 516–35.
23. P. Kim, "How stress can influence brain adaptations to motherhood," *Front Neuroendocrinol.* 60, 2020.
24. Ibid.
25. A. G. de Lange et al., "Population-based neuroimaging reveals traces of childbirth in the maternal brain, *PNAS* 166 (44), 2019, pp. 22341–46.
26. P. Kim, "How stress can influence brain adaptations to motherhood," *Front Neuroendocrinol.* 60, 2020.
27. Michigan Medicine, "Mom Power"; <https://medicine.umich.edu/dept/psychiatry/programs/zero-thrive/clinical-service/mom-power>
28. P. Churchland, "Deliver us from evil: How biology, not religion, made humans moral," *New Scientist*, 25 September 2019.
29. Roland Barthes, *A Lover's Discourse: Fragments* (Vintage, 2002), p. 16.
30. P. Churchland, "Deliver us from evil: How biology, not religion, made humans moral," *New Scientist*, 25 September 2019.

31. J. P. Burkett et al., "Oxytocin-dependent consolation behavior in rodents," *Science* 351 (6271), 2016, pp. 375–78.
32. Susan Maushart, *The Mask of Motherhood* (Penguin, 1999), p. 27.
33. Sarah Blaffer Hrdy, *Mother Nature: Maternal Instincts and How They Shape the Human Species* (Ballantine Press, 1999), p. 177.
34. Ibid., p. 101.
35. Ibid., p. 494.
36. NCT, "How much crying is normal for a baby?"; <https://www.nct.org.uk/baby-toddler/crying/how-much-crying-normal-for-baby>
37. S. J. Sheinkopf, "Atypical cry acoustics in 6-month-old infants at risk for Autism Spectrum Disorder," *Autism Research* 5 (5), 2012, pp. 331–9.
38. Otto Rank, *The Trauma of Birth* (Ravenio Books, 1929).
39. Sarah Blaffer Hrdy, *Mother Nature: Maternal Instincts and How They Shape the Human Species* (Ballantine Press, 1999), p. 461.
40. Ibid., p. 388.

7. Motherhood and sociality

1. J. Hyland, " 'Winter adventures with my man': Elyse Knowles flaunts her trim post-baby body at the beach with her five-month-old son Sunny," *Daily Mail*, 29 July 2021.
2. S. Suri, "Emily Ratajkowski flaunts her VERY slender midsection just two months after welcoming her child as she is seen in NYC with husband Sebastian and their dog Colombo," *Daily Mail*, 18 May 2021.
3. A. Wynne, "New mum Danielle Lloyd flaunts her post-baby body and incredibly toned abs in a sports bra and tight jeans a month after giving birth," *Daily Mail*, 17 December 2021.
4. A. Klein, "It really is difficult to get fit after giving birth, study reveals," *New Scientist*, 24 August 2021.
5. K. Morton, "New Government figures reveal true scale of children's centre closures," *Nursery World*, 31 January 2020.
6. M. Duras, "Motherhood makes you obscene," *Paris Review*, 1 October 2019.
7. M. M. Kroll, "Prolonged social isolation and loneliness are equivalent to smoking 15 cigarettes a day," *University of New Hampshire*, 2 May 2022.
8. J. Kent-Marvick, S. Simonsen, R. Pentecost et al. "Loneliness in pregnant and postpartum people and parents of children aged 5 years or younger: A scoping review," *Syst. Rev.* 11, 196, 2022.
9. B. L. Taylor et al., "Mums alone: Exploring the role of isolation and loneliness in the narratives of women diagnosed with perinatal depression," *Journal of Clinical Medicine* 10 (11), 2271, 2021.
10. Ibid.

11. J. Kent-Marvick, S. Simonsen, R. Pentecost et al. "Loneliness in pregnant and postpartum people and parents of children aged 5 years or younger: A scoping review," *Syst. Rev.* 11, 196, 2022.
12. R. Sear, "The male breadwinner nuclear family is not the 'traditional' human family, and promotion of this myth may have adverse health consequences," *Phil. Trans. R. Soc. B* 376, May 2021.
13. Adrienne Rich, *Of Woman Born: Motherhood as Experience and Institution* (Virago, 1977).
14. B. L. Taylor et al., "Mums alone: Exploring the role of isolation and loneliness in the narratives of women diagnosed with perinatal depression," *Journal of Clinical Medicine* 10 (11), 2271, 2021.
15. Ibid.
16. "Motherhood, shame and society: An interview with Brené Brown, Ph.D., author of 'Women & Shame,'" *Mothers Movement*; <http://www.mothersmovement.org/features/bbrown_int/bbrown_int_1.htm>
17. Megan Hebdon et al., "Stress and supportive care needs of millennial caregivers: A qualitative analysis," *Journal of Pain and Symptom Management* 63 (6), June 2022, pp. 1113–4.
18. Orna Donath, *Regretting Motherhood: A Study* (North Atlantic Books, 2017).

8. Sertraline and sleep deprivation

1. Maggie Nelson, *The Argonauts* (Melville House UK, 2016).
2. Sam Hart, "Mother's Little Helpers," *Druglink*, July/August 2004; <https://www.drugwise.org.uk/wp-content/uploads/Mothers-little-helpers.pdf>
3. J. Salisbury, "'You felt your life was ending': Inside *Shattered*—the televised sleep deprivation experiment," *New Statesman*, 13 August 2018.
4. S. Keating, "The boy who stayed awake for 11 days," BBC Future, 18 January 2018; <https://www.bbc.com/future/article/20180118-the-boy-who-stayed-awake-for-11-days>
5. E. Pilkington, "UN torture report condemns sleep deprivation among US detainees," *Guardian*, 28 November 2014.
6. Matthew Walker, *Why We Sleep* (Penguin, 2018), p. 150.
7. Ibid., p. 305.
8. British Library, "Ann Oakley discusses motherhood and depression"; <https://www.bl.uk/collection-items/ann-oakley-motherhood-and- depression>
9. Sandra Igwe, *My Black Motherhood: Mental Health, Stigma, Racism and the System* (Jessica Kingsley Publishers, 2022), p. 22.
10. Personal interview with Dr. Liisa Galea, 3 February 2021.
11. MGH Center for Women's Mental Health, "Brexanolone for postpartum depression: More data, but still some questions," 26 September 2018; <https://womensmentalhealth.org/posts/brexanolone-for-postpartum-depression>

12. A. Mullard, "FDA approves first oral drug for postpartum depression, but rejects it for major depressive disorder," *Nature,* 11 August 2023; <https://www.nature.com/articles/d41573-023-00134-5#:~:text=The%20FDA%20has%20approved%20Sage,)%2C%20a%20potentially%20bigger%20market>
13. Y. Dowlati, A. V. Ravindran, Z. V. Segal and Jeffrey H. Meyer, "Selective dietary supplementation in early postpartum is associated with high resilience against depressed mood," *PNAS* 114 (13), 13 March, 2017; <https://www.pnas.org/doi/full/10.1073/pnas.1611965114>
14. E. A. Spry, "Preventing postnatal depression: A causal mediation analysis of a 20-year preconception cohort," *Royal Society*, 2021; <https://royalsocietypublishing.org/doi/10.1098/rstb.2020.0028>
15. V. Lindahl, J. L. Pearson and L. Colpe, "Prevalence of suicidality during pregnancy and the postpartum," *Arch. Women's Ment. Health* 8(2), pp. 77–7.

PART IV

9. Maternal ambivalence

1. Rozsika Parker, *Torn in Two: The Experience of Maternal Ambivalence* (Virago, 1995), p. 220.
2. S. Freud, "The Ego and the Id," *The Standard Edition of the Complete Psychological Works of Sigmund Freud,"* XIX (Hogarth Press and Institute of PsychoAnalysis, 1923), p. 43; <https://www.sas.upenn.edu/~cavitch/pdf-library/Freud_SE_Ego_Id_complete.pdf>
3. Reddit; <https://www.reddit.com/r/Jokes/comments/thh6b6/youre_offered_50000_but_if_you_accept_it_the/>
4. The School of Life, "Melanie Klein"; <https://www.theschooloflife.com/article/the-great-psychoanalysts-melanie-klein/>
5. Melanie Klein, *Love, Guilt and Reparation and Other Works* (The Free Press, 1975), p. 311; <https://www.sas.upenn.edu/~cavitch/pdf-library/Klein%20Love%20Guilt.pdf>
6. Rozsika Parker, *Torn in Two: The Experience of Maternal Ambivalence* (Virago, 1995).
7. Siri Hustvedt, *Mothers, Fathers and Others* (Sceptre, 2021).
8. J. Steiner, "The equilibrium between the paranoid-schizoid and the depressive positions," *Clinical Lectures on Klein and Bion* (Tavistock/Routledge, 1992), pp. 46–58.
9. Julia Kristeva, "Stabat Mater," *Poetics Today* 6 (1–2), 1985. (1985), p. 133.
10. Rozsika Parker, *Torn in Two: The Experience of Maternal Ambivalence* (Virago, 1995), p. 100.
11. Sarah Blaffer Hrdy, *Mother Nature: Maternal Instincts and How They Shape the Human Species* (Ballantine Press, 1999), p. 391.
12. S. A. Silverio et al., "When a mother's love is not enough: A cross-cultural critical review of anxiety, attachment, maternal ambivalence, abandonment, and infanticide,"

in C. H. Mayer & E. Vanderheiden (eds), *International Handbook of Love* (Springer); <https://doi.org/10.1007/978-3-030-45996-3_16>

13. R. Parker, "The production and purposes of maternal ambivalence," in B. Featherstone and W. Holloway (eds), *Mothering and Ambivalence* (Routledge, 1997), p. 20.
14. Melanie Klein, "The Early Development of Conscience in the Child," in *Love, Guilt and Reparation and Other Works 1921–1945: The Writings of Melanie Klein, Volume I* (The Free Press, 1975) p. 257.
15. Rozsika Parker, *Torn in Two: The Experience of Maternal Ambivalence* (Virago, 1995), p. 206.
16. Rachel Cusk, *A Life's Work: On Becoming a Mother* (Picador, 2001).
17. R. Cusk, "I was only being honest," *Guardian*, 21 March 2008; <https://www.theguardian.com/books/2008/mar/21/biography.women>
18. "Rachel Cusk. Autopsy of a marriage," CCCB, YouTube; <https://www.youtube.com/watch?v=907QJ-OzFeg>
19. Claire Zulkey, "Evil Witches the newsletter"; <https://evilwitches.substack.com/about>
20. Personal interview with Claire Zulkey, 9 May 2022.
21. H. Seligson, "This is the TV ad the Oscars didn't allow on air," *The New York Times*, 19 February 2020; <https://www.nytimes.com/2020/02/19/us/postpartum-ad-oscars-frida.html>

10. Intensive motherhood

1. Lynn O'Brien Hallstein, Andrea O'Reilly and Melinda Vandenbeld Giles, *The Routledge Companion to Motherhood* (Routledge, 2020), p. 24.
2. Caitlin Collins, *Making Motherhood Work* (Princeton University Press, 2019), p. 263.
3. Rachel Fuchs, *Abandoned Children: Foundlings and Child Welfare in Nineteenth-Century France* (Suny Press, 1984).
4. Adrienne Rich, *Of Woman Born: Motherhood as Experience and Institution* (Virago, 1977), p. 48.
5. Rozsika Parker, *Torn in Two: The Experience of Maternal Ambivalence* (Virago, 1995), p. 173.
6. Adrienne Rich, *Of Woman Born: Motherhood as Experience and Institution* (Virago, 1977), 52.
7. Ibid., p. 53.
8. Siri Hustvedt, *Mothers, Fathers and Others* (Sceptre, 2021), p. 23.
9. Sarah Knott, *Mother: An Unconventional History* (Penguin, 2020), p. 157.
10. Michael Underwood, *A Treatise on the Diseases of Children, with Directions for the Management of Infants from the Birth; Especially Such as Are Brought Up by Hand* (1784), p. 217; <https://wellcomecollection.org/works/qypvrrw5/items?canvas=229>
11. Luther Emmett Holt, *The Care and Feeding of Children: A Catechism for the Use of Mothers and Children's Nurses* (D. Appleton and Company, 1907).

12. Shari L. Thurer, *The Myths of Motherhood* (Penguin, 1994), p. xvii.
13. Ibid.
14. Ibid., p. 275.
15. John Bowlby, *A Secure Base* (Brunner-Routledge, 1988), pp. 26–7.
16. Mary D. Salter Ainsworth, *Infancy in Uganda: Infant Care and the Growth of Love* (Johns Hopkins University Press, 1967).
17. M. Ainsworth and S. M. Bell, "Attachment, exploration, and separation: Illustrated by the behavior of one-year-olds in a strange situation," *Child Dev.,* 1 March 1970.
18. Ibid.
19. H. Keller, "Universality claim of attachment theory: Children's socioemotional development across cultures," *PNAS* 115 (45), 2018, pp. 11414–19.
20. A. E. Page et al., "Children are important too: Juvenile playgroups and maternal childcare in a foraging population, the Agta," *Phil. Trans. R. Soc. B* 376, 1827, 2021.
21. J. Bowlby, "Caring for Children," 1980; <https://www.increaseproject.eu/images/DOWNLOADS/IO2/HU/CURR_M4-A13_Bowlby_(EN-only)_20170920_HU_final.pdf>
22. Jean Liedloff, *The Continuum Concept* (Addison-Wesley, 1975).
23. Ibid., p. 6.
24. Ibid., p. 109.
25. P. Buskens, "The impossibility of 'natural parenting' for modern mothers: On social structure and the formation habit," in A. O'Reilly (ed.), *Mother Matters: Motherhood as Discourse and Practice* (Toronto: Association for Research on Mothering, 2004), pp. 98–110.
26. Ibid.
27. Silvia Federici, *Wages Against Housework* (The Power of Women Collective and the Fading Wall Press, 1975), p. 6.
28. A. O'Reilly, "Matricentric feminism: A feminism for mothers," *Journal of the Motherhood Initiative* 10, 1–2, 2019.
29. "Parents now spend twice as much time with their children as 50 years ago," *Economist*; 27 November 2017; <https://www.economist.com/graphic-detail/2017/11/27/parents-now-spend-twice-as-much-time-with-their-children-as-50-years-ago>
30. C. E. Kirkpatrick and S. Lee, "Comparisons to picture-perfect motherhood: How Instagram's idealized portrayals of motherhood affect new mothers' well-being," *Computers in Human Behavior* 137, December 2022.
31. Shari L. Thurer, *The Myths of Motherhood* (Penguin, 1994), p. 269.
32. S. Orgad, "The parenting happiness gap," *LSE,* October 2019; <https://blogs.lse.ac.uk/parenting4digitalfuture/2019/10/09/the-parenting-happiness-gap/>
33. A. Bauer, M. Parsonage, M. Knapp, V. Iemmi and B. Adelaja, "The costs of perinatal mental health problems: Report summary," *LSE;* <https://www.centreformentalhealth.org.uk/sites/default/files/2018-09/costsofperinatalsummary.pdf>
34. C. Verniers, V. Bonnot and Y. Assilaméhou-Kunz, "Intensive mothering and the perpetuation of gender inequality: Evidence from a mixed methods research," *Acta Psychologica,* 2022.

35. Gov.uk, "Parental rights and responsibilities"; <https://www.gov.uk/parental-rights-responsibilities>
36. Lisa Marchiano, *Motherhood: Facing and Finding Yourself* (Sounds True, 2021), p. 15.
37. NHS, "Adverse childhood experiences (ACEs) and attachment"; <https://mft.nhs.uk/rmch/services/camhs/young-people/adverse-childhood-experiences-aces-and-attachment/>
38. N. Racine, C. Devereaux, J. E. Cooke et al., "Adverse childhood experiences and maternal anxiety and depression: A meta-analysis," BMC *Psychiatry* 21, 28, 2021.
39. Orna Donath, *Regretting Motherhood: A Study* (North Atlantic Books, 2017), p. 106.
40. Maggie Nelson, *On Freedom: Four Songs of Care and Constraint* (Jonathan Cape, 2021), p. 69.
41. Philippa Perry, *The Book You Wish Your Parents Had Read (and Your Children Will Be Glad That You Did)* (Penguin Life, 2019), p. 21.
42. Glenn Boozan, *There Are Moms Way Worse Than You: Irrefutable Proof That You Are Indeed a Fantastic Parent* (Workman Publishing, 2022).

PART V

11. Recombobulation

1. B. Adams and F. Petruccione, "Do quantum effects play a role in consciousness?," *Physics World*, 26 January 2021; <https://physicsworld.com/a/do-quantum-effects-play-a-role-in-consciousness/>
2. Alice Notley, *Mysteries of Small Houses* (Penguin Poets, 1998), p. 39.
3. Claire Arnold-Baker, *The Existential Crisis of Motherhood* (Palgrave Macmillan, 2020).
4. Søren Kierkegaard, *Either/Or: A Fragment of Life* (Princeton University Press; Reprint edition, 1944), p. 19.
5. Kimberly Ann Johnson, *The Fourth Trimester* (Shambhala, 2017), p. 29.
6. BBC, "Omugwo: Igbo's postpartum cultural practice," *Focus on Africa*; <https://www.bbc.co.uk/sounds/play/p08onpbh>
7. Naoli Vinaver, "Mexican Postpartum Ritual—Closing of the body"; <https://www.youtube.com/watch?v=scE5WvOxAqA>
8. Z. V. Ravna, "'Catching a Child': Giving birth under nomadic conditions. The methods of pre- and postnatal care of the Nenets mothers and babies," *International Journal of Circumpolar Health* 78, 1, 2019.
9. L. Stewart et al., "Social singing, culture and health: Interdisciplinary insights from the CHIME project for perinatal mental health in The Gambia," *Health Promotion International* 37, 1 May 2022, pp. 18–25.
10. Rozsika Parker, *Torn in Two: The Experience of Maternal Ambivalence* (Virago, 1995), p. 12.

11. The Church of England, "The Thanksgiving of Woman after Child-Birth Commonly Called The Churching of Woman"; <https://www.churchofengland.org/prayer-and-worship/worship-texts-and-resources/book-common-prayer/churching-women>
12. I. Oh, "The performativity of motherhood: Embodying theology and political agency," *Journal of the Society of Christian Ethics* 29, 2, 2009, pp. 3–17.
13. Sheila Lintott and Maureen Sander-Staudt (eds), *Philosophical Inquiries into Pregnancy, Childbirth, and Mothering Maternal Subjects* (Routledge, 2015).

12. Care work and creativity in late-stage capitalism

1. J. Doward, "Working mothers 'up to 40% more stressed,'" *Observer,* 27 January 2019.
2. Arlie Russell Hochschild and Anne Machung, *The Second Shift: Working Families and the Revolution at Home* (Viking Penguin, 1989).
3. C. S. Payne and G. Vassilev, "Household satellite account, UK: 2015 and 2016," ONS; <https://www.ons.gov.uk/economy/nationalaccounts/satelliteaccounts/articles/householdsatelliteaccounts/2015and2016estimates>
4. Nancy Folbre, *The Rise and Decline of Patriarchal Systems: An Intersectional Political Economy* (Verso, 2020).
5. S. Atzil and L. F. Barrett, "Social regulation of allostasis: Commentary on 'Mentalizing homeostasis: The social origins of interoceptive inference' by Fotopoulou and Tsakiris," *Neuropsychoanalysis* 19 (1), 2017, pp. 29–33.
6. G. Groth, "Jack Kirby interview," *Comics Journal*, May 23, 2011; <https://www.tcj.com/jack-kirby-interview/6/>
7. E. Ma et al., "On the bright side of motherhood—A mixed method enquiry," *Annals of Tourism Research* 92, 2022.
8. Sarah Blaffer Hrdy, *Mother Nature: Maternal Instincts and How They Shape the Human Species* (Ballantine Press, 1999), p. 417.
9. Alison Gopnik, "What do babies think?," TED; <https://www.ted.com/talks/alison_gopnik_what_do_babies_think?language=en>
10. M. Bryant, "'I was risking my life': Why one in four US women return to work two weeks after childbirth," *Guardian,* 27 January 2020.
11. Joseph Rowntree Foundation, "Overall UK Poverty rates"; <https://www.jrf.org.uk/data/overall-uk-poverty-rates#:~:text=More%20than%20one%20in%20five,and%202.1%20million%20are%20pensioners.>
12. Press Association, "40% of managers avoid hiring younger women to get around maternity leave," *Guardian*, 12 August 2014.
13. WEF, "These countries have the most expensive childcare," 23 April 2019; <https://www.weforum.org/agenda/2019/04/these-countries-have-the-most-expensive-childcare/>

13. Matroreform

1. T. O'Callaghan, "You are not one person: Why your sense of self must be an illusion," *New Scientist*, 9 December 2020.

2. Lisa Marchiano, *Motherhood: Facing and Finding Yourself* (Sounds True, 2021), p. 147.
3. Ibid., p. 1.
4. Ibid., p. 15.
5. Carl Jung, *Vom Werden der Persönlichkeit*, 1932; <https://www.oxfordreference.com/display/10.1093/acref/9780191826719.001.0001/q-oro-ed4-00006107;jsessionid=8234A72B4A4F97D60B62B7E0D25A2E15>
6. C. Carona et al., "Self-compassion and complete perinatal mental health in women at high risk for postpartum depression: The mediating role of emotion regulation difficulties," *Psychology and Psychotherapy: Theory, Research and Practice* 95 (2), 2022, pp. 561–74.
7. Lynn O'Brien Hallstein, Andrea O'Reilly and Melinda Vandenbeld Giles (eds), *The Routledge Companion to Motherhood* (Routledge, 2020), p. 39.
8. Alexis Pauline Gumbs, China Martens and Mai'a Williams, *Revolutionary Mothering: Love on the Front Lines* (PM Press, 2016).
9. Marshall Plan for Moms; <https://marshallplanformoms.com/>
10. E. Hayward, "More than half of maternity units now judged unsafe," *The Times* 21 October 2022; <https://www.thetimes.co.uk/article/more-than-half-of-maternity-units-now-judged-unsafe-d6rpc9pkt>
11. H. Watson et al., "A systematic review of ethnic minority women's experiences of perinatal mental health conditions and services in Europe," *PLOS One* 14(1), 2019; <https://journals.plos.org/plosone/article?id=10.1371/journal.pone.0210587>
12. A. Bauer, M. Tinelli and M. Knapp, "The economic case for increasing access to treatment for women with common mental health problems during the perinatal period is a publication," *Care Policy and Evaluation Centre, London School of Economics and Political Science*, 2022.
13. J. Kristeva, "Motherhood Today," 2005; <http://www.kristeva.fr/motherhood.html>
14. G. F. S. Pollock, "Mother trouble: The maternal-feminine in phallic and feminist theory in relation to Bratta Ettinger's Elaboration of Matrixial Ethics," *Studies in the Maternal* 1 (1), 2009, pp. 1–31.
15. "Kraamzorg (postnatal maternity care) in the Netherlands," ACCESS; <https://access-nl.org/healthcare-netherlands/having-a-baby/kraamzorg-postnatal-care/what-is-kraamzorg/>
16. K. Whiting, "The motherhood penalty: How childcare and paternity leave can reduce the gender pay gap," WEF, 19 May 2022; <https://www.weforum.org/agenda/2022/05/reduce-motherhood-penalty- gender-pay-gap/>
17. H. Crown, "Childcare practitioners 'living in poverty'—exclusive survey," *Nursery World*, 12 September 2019.
18. <https://www.unwomen.org/en/news-stories/press-release/2022/06/un-women-reveals-concerning-regression-in-attitudes-towards-gender-roles-during-pandemic-in-new-study>
19. NHS England, "NHS pelvic health clinics to help tens of thousands of women across the country," 13 June 2021; <https://www.england.nhs.uk/2021/06/nhs-pelvic-health-clinics-to-help-tens-of-thousands-women-across-the-country/>

20. NHS England, "New dedicated mental health services for new expectant and bereaved mums," 6 April 2021; <https://www.england.nhs.uk/2021/04/dedicated-mh-services/>

Epilogue

1. M. Martínez-García et al., "Do pregnancy-induced brain changes reverse? The brain of a mother six years after parturition," *Brain Sci.* 11 (2), 168, 2021.

Bibliography

Agarwal, Pragya, *(M)otherhood: On the Choices of Being a Woman* (Canongate, 2021)

Arnold-Baker, Claire, *The Existential Crisis of Motherhood* (Palgrave Macmillan, 2020)

Badinter, Elisabeth, *The Conflict: How Modern Motherhood Undermines the Status of Women* (Metropolitan Books, 2010)

Barthes, Roland, *A Lover's Discourse: Fragments* (Vintage, 2002)

Benjamin, Jessica, *The Bonds of Love* (Pantheon, 1988)

Berry, Liz, *The Republic of Motherhood* (Chatto & Windus, 2018)

Boozan, Glenn, *There Are Moms Way Worse Than You: Irrefutable Proof That You Are Indeed a Fantastic Parent* (Workman Publishing, 2022)

Bowlby, John, *A Secure Base* (Brunner-Routledge, 1988)

Brathwaite, Candice, *I Am Not Your Baby Mother* (Quercus, 2021)

Carson, Anne, *Plainwater* (Vintage, 2000)

Cho, Catherine, *Inferno* (Bloomsbury Circus, 2020)

Colette, *My Mother's House and Sido* (Modern Library, 1995)

Collins, Caitlin, *Making Motherhood Work* (Princeton University Press, 2019)

Cusk, Rachel, *A Life's Work: On Becoming a Mother* (Picador, 2001)

de Beauvoir, Simone, *The Second Sex* (Johnathan Cape, 1953)

Dick-Read, Grantly, *Childbirth Without Fear* (William Heinemann Medical Books, 1942)

Dick-Read, Grantly, *Revelation of Childbirth* (William Heinemann Medical Books, 1948)

Donath, Orna, *Regretting Motherhood: A Study* (North Atlantic Books, 2017)

Donnison, Jean, *Midwives and Medical Men: A History of the Struggle for the Control of Childbirth* (Taylor & Francis, 2023, originally published 1977)

Dungy, Camille T., *Guidebook to Relative Strangers: Journeys into Race, Motherhood, and History* (W.W. Norton, 2017)

Federici, Silvia, *Beyond the Periphery of the Skin* (PM Press, 2020)

Federici, Silvia, *Caliban and the Witch* (Penguin Classics, 2021)

Federici, Silvia, *Wages Against Housework* (The Power of Women Collective and the Fading Wall Press, 1975)

Ferrante, Elena, *Frantumaglia* (Europa Editions, 2017)

Firestone, Shulamith, *The Dialectic of Sex: The Case for Feminist Revolution* (Bantam Books, 1970)

Folbre, Nancy, *The Rise and Decline of Patriarchal Systems: An Intersectional Political Economy* (Verso, 2020)

Fuchs, Rachel, *Abandoned Children: Foundlings and Child Welfare in Nineteenth-Century France* (Suny Press, 1984)

Ginzberg, Natalia, *The Little Virtues* (Daunt Books Publishing, 2018)

Glaser, Eliane, *Motherhood* (Fourth Estate, 2021)

Goldin, Claudia, *Career and Family: Women's Century-Long Journey Toward Equity* (Princeton University Press, 2021)

Gumbs, Alexis Pauline, China Martens and Mai'a Williams, *Revolutionary Mothering: Love on the Front Lines* (PM Press, 2016)

Hochschild, Arlie Russell, *The Commercialization of Intimate Life* (University of California Press, 2003)

Hochschild, Arlie Russell and Anne Machung, *The Second Shift: Working Families and the Revolution at Home* (Viking Penguin, 1989)

Holt, Luther Emmett, *The Care and Feeding of Children: A Catechism for the Use of Mothers and Children's Nurses* (D. Appleton and Company, 1907)

hooks, bell, *Feminist Theory: From Margin to Center* (Pluto Press, 2000)

Hrdy, Sarah Blaffer, *Mother Nature: Maternal Instincts and How They Shape the Human Species* (Ballantine Press, 1999)

Hustvedt, Siri, *Mothers, Fathers and Others* (Sceptre, 2021)

Igwe, Sandra, *My Black Motherhood: Mental Health, Stigma, Racism and the System* (Jessica Kingsley Publishers, 2022)

Johnson, Kimberly Ann, *The Fourth Trimester* (Shambhala, 2017)

Jung, Carl, *Vom Werden der Persönlichkeit*, 1932

Kafka, Frank, *The Metamorphosis* (Kurt Wolff Verlag, 1915)

Kierkegaard, Søren, *Either/Or: A Fragment of Life* (Princeton University Press; Reprint edition, 1944)

Kimmerer, Robin Wall, *Braiding Sweetgrass: Indigenous Wisdom, Scientific Knowledge and the Teachings of Plants* (Milkweed Editions, 2013)

Klein, Melanie, *Love, Guilt and Reparation and Other Works* (The Free Press, 1975)

Knott, Sarah, *Mother: An Unconventional History* (Viking Penguin, 2019)

Kristeva, Julia, *Powers of Horror: An Essay on Abjection* (Columbia University Press; Reprint edition, 1984)

Lancy, David, *Raising Children* (Cambridge University Press, 2017)

Lazarre, Jane, *The Mother Knot* (Virago, 1987)

Levinovitz, Alan, *Natural* (Profile Books, 2020)

Liedloff, Jean, *The Continuum Concept* (Addison-Wesley, 1975)

Lintott, Sheila and Maureen Sander-Staudt (eds), *Philosophical Inquiries into Pregnancy, Childbirth, and Mothering Maternal Subjects* (Routledge, 2015)

Marchiano, Lisa, *Motherhood: Facing and Finding Yourself* (Sounds True, 2021)

Margulis, Lynn, *Symbiotic Planet* (Basic Books, 1999)

Maushart, Susan, *The Mask of Motherhood* (Penguin, 1999)

McNish, Hollie, *Nobody Told Me* (Fleet, 2020)

Nelson, Maggie, *The Argonauts* (Melville House UK, 2016)

Nelson, Maggie, *On Freedom: Four Songs of Care and Constraint* (Jonathan Cape, 2021)

Notley, Alice, *Mysteries of Small Houses* (Penguin Poets, 1998)
Notley, Alice, *Songs for the Unborn Second Baby* (United Artists, 1979)
Oakley, Ann, *From Here to Maternity* (Pelican, 1981)
O'Brien Hallstein, Lynn, Andrea O'Reilly and Melinda Vandenbeld Giles (eds), *The Routledge Companion to Motherhood* (Routledge, 2020)
Olsen, Tillie, *Silences* (Delacorte, 1978)
Oster, Emily, *Cribsheet: A Data-Driven Guide to Better, More Relaxed Parenting, from Birth to Preschool* (Souvenir Press, 2019)
Ostriker, Alicia, *The Mother/Child Papers* (University of Pittsburgh Press, 2009)
Parker, Rozsika, *Torn in Two: The Experience of Maternal Ambivalence* (Virago, 1995)
Perry, Philippa, *The Book You Wish Your Parents Had Read (and Your Children Will Be Glad That You Did)* (Penguin Life, 2019)
Putnam, Robert B., *Bowling Alone* (Simon & Schuster, 2000)
Rank, Otto, *The Trauma of Birth* (Ravenio Books, 1929)
Raphael, Dana (ed), *Being Female: Reproduction, Power and Change* (Mouton & Co, 1975)
Raphael-Leff, Joan, *The Dark Side of the Womb: Pregnancy, Parenting, and Persecutory Anxieties* (The Anna Freud Centre, 2015)
Raphael-Leff, Joan, *Pregnancy: The Inside Story* (Routledge, 2001)
Raphael-Leff, Joan, *Psychological Process of Childbearing* (Chapman and Hall, 1991)
Rich, Adrienne, *Of Woman Born: Motherhood as Experience and Institution* (Virago, 1977)
Rose, Jacqueline, *Mothers: An Essay on Love and Cruelty* (Faber & Faber, 2018)
Ruddick, Sara, *Maternal Thinking: Toward a Politic of Peace* (Beacon Press, 1995)
Shafak, Elif, *Black Milk* (Viking Penguin, 2011)
Sloterdijk, Peter, *Bubbles: Spheres Volume I: Microspherology* (MIT Press, 2011)
Spretnak, Charlene, *Relational Reality* (Green Horizon Books, 2011)
Stadlen, Naomi, *How Mothers Love* (Piatkus, 2015)
Stadlen, Naomi, *What Mothers Do* (Piatkus, 2005)
Stadlen, Naomi, *What Mothers Learn* (Piatkus, 2020)
Steingraber, Sandra, *Having Faith: An Ecologist's Journey to Motherhood* (Perseus Publishing, 2001)
Thurer, Shari L., *The Myths of Motherhood* (Penguin, 1994)
Walker, Matthew, *Why We Sleep* (Penguin, 2018)

Acknowledgments

I would like to acknowledge the writers whose work fortified me to break the "feeling rules" (Arlie Hochschild) in the "psychological police state" of motherhood (Susan Douglas and Meredith Michaels), and simply write it as it was: Rachel Cusk, Elena Ferrante, Elif Shafak, Camille T. Dungy, Jane Lazarre, Rozsika Parker, Liz Berry, Deborah Levy, Sarah Blaffer Hrdy, Adrienne Rich, Julia Kristeva, Griselda Pollock, Sara Ruddick, Ann Oakley, Shari L. Thurer, Sharon Hays, Alice Notley, Naomi Stadlen, Maggie Nelson, Anne Lamott, Arlie Hochschild, Natalia Ginzburg.

I'd like to acknowledge the work of scientists, writers, activists and academics working in this area, and thank those who gave me their time: Jodi Pawluski, Elseline Hoekzema, Susanna Carmona, Amy Boddy, Liisa Galea, Andrea O'Reilly, Margie Profet, Rosemary Balsam, Joan Raphael-Leff, Ranee Thakar, Dawn Leeming, Emily Oster, Claire Zulkey, Claire Arnold-Baker, Maggie Gordon-Walker, Nancy Folbre, Sandra Igwe, Alison Fleming, Pilyoung Kim, Catherine Dulac. There are, of course, many more, and it is exciting that this field is finally expanding. I thank Alexandra Sacks, for introducing me to the word "matrescence," and to the late Dana Raphael, who coined the word and concept in the 1970s.

Suze Olbrich commissioned and published early essays on new motherhood for Somesuch Stories and I thank her for her encouragement and friendship.

At Penguin Press in the UK, I would like to thank Alba Ziegler-Bailey, Ceylan Stafford-Bloor, Karin Barry, Ronnie Hanna, Francisca Monteiro, Imogen Scott, Anna Wilson, Corina Romonti, Julie Woon, Stuart Simpson and Desiree Adams; and thank you to Thea

Tuck for early reading and astute comments on the text. My wonderful UK editor, Chloe Currens, edited this book with such intelligence, grace and care.

My agent, Jessica Woollard, believed in this idea from the beginning and has inspired, shepherded and nurtured the work and the vision in so many ways. Thank you.

I am so fortunate to be published in the United States by Pantheon Books, and I thank and tip my hat to the acuity, wisdom and legendary brilliance of Victoria Wilson, whom I am so glad to call my editor. Thank you hugely to Michiko Clark, a publicist extraordinaire. I'm also thankful to Belinda Yong and to the wider team at Pantheon: marketing manager Sarah Pannenberg, production editor Nicole Pedersen, text designer Maggie Hinders, jacket designer Jenny Carrow, and managing editor Altie Karper.

I am thankful to people I corresponded with: the microbial ecologist Jake Robinson; the translator of Marguerite Duras, Emma Ramadan; the mothers who responded to my survey.

I couldn't have written this book without the love and support of my family and friends: my brother and sister-in-law, my parents-in-law (whose kindness, generosity and huge support with our children I am especially grateful for), my grandmothers, my aunts, my cousin Heather, and friends who provided conversations and bolster: Lucy Lorraine, Lucy Houghton, Antonia Peck, Alexandra Jacoumis, Jane Berry, Ellie Bramley, Lexi Powner, Panda Gavin, Rupert van den Broek, Sophie Mason, Georgie Spavins, Georgina Blanc, Nassim Hatam Bancroft Cooke, Yeun san Naylor-Lui, Brooke Laing, Jenny Stevens, Celia Glass, the late Tim Cole, and the RG21 village I found in my early matrescence: Lottie Aird, May Curtis-Broadhurst, Chloe Scott-Moncrieff and Naomi Escott, in particular.

My husband has supported the writing of this book in endless ways. And, well, our children made it possible—and impossible, at times—more than anyone. Except, perhaps, my father, and, of course, my mother. Thank you; I love you.

Index